# Macromedia® Flash® 8 For Dummies

## Common Keyboard Shortcuts

### File Menu Commands

| Command | Windows | Mac |
|---|---|---|
| New | Ctrl+N | ⌘+N |
| Open | Ctrl+O | ⌘+O |
| Import to Stage | Ctrl+R | ⌘+R |
| Import to Library | Ctrl+Shift+O | |
| Close | Ctrl+W | ⌘+W |

| Command | Windows | Mac |
|---|---|---|
| Save | Ctrl+S | ⌘+S |
| Publish Settings | Ctrl+Shift+F12 | Option+Shift+F12 |
| Publish | Shift+F12 | Shift+F12 |
| Quit | Ctrl+Q | ⌘+Q |

## Tools Panel

Selection — Subselection
Free Transform — Fill Transform
Line — Lasso
Pen — Text
Oval — Rectangle
Pencil — Brush
Ink Bottle — Paint Bucket
Eyedropper — Eraser

Hand (pan) — Zoom

Stroke color
Fill color
Black and white — Swap colors
No color
Object Drawing mode — Lock fill
— Brush mode

Brush size
Brush shape
Use Pressure — Use Tilt

## Edit Menu Commands

| Command | Windows | Mac |
|---|---|---|
| Undo | Ctrl+Z | ⌘+Z |
| Redo | Ctrl+Y | ⌘+Y |
| Cut | Ctrl+X | ⌘+X |
| Copy | Ctrl+C | ⌘+C |
| Paste in Center | Ctrl+V | ⌘+V |
| Paste in Place | Ctrl+Shift+V | ⌘+Shift+V |
| Clear | Delete/Backspace | Delete/Clear |
| Duplicate | Ctrl+D | ⌘+D |
| Select All | Ctrl+A | ⌘+A |
| Deselect All | Ctrl+Shift+A | ⌘+Shift+A |
| Copy Frames | Ctrl+Alt+C | ⌘+Option+C |
| Paste Frames | Ctrl+Alt+V | ⌘+Option+V |

## View Menu Commands

| Command | Windows | Mac |
|---|---|---|
| Magnification 100% | Ctrl+1 | ⌘+1 |
| Magnification: Show All | Ctrl+3 | ⌘+3 |
| Snap to Objects | Ctrl+Shift+/ | ⌘+Shift+/ |
| Work Area | Ctrl+Shift+W | ⌘+Shift+W |

### For Dummies: Bestselling Book Series for Beginners

# Macromedia® Flash® 8 For Dummies®

Cheat Sheet

## Insert Menu Commands

| Command | Windows | Mac |
|---|---|---|
| New Symbol | Ctrl+F8 | ⌘+F8 |
| Frame | F5 | F5 |
| Keyframe | F6 | F6 |
| Blank Keyframe | F7 | F7 |

## Modify Menu Commands

| Command | Windows | Mac |
|---|---|---|
| Document | Ctrl+J | ⌘+J |
| Convert to Symbol | F8 | F8 |
| Break Apart | Ctrl+B | ⌘+B |
| Add Shape Hint | Ctrl+Alt+H | ⌘+Option+H |
| Distribute to Layers | Ctrl+Shift+D | ⌘+Shift+D |
| Group | Ctrl+G | ⌘+G |
| Ungroup | Ctrl+Shift+G | ⌘+Shift+G |

## Control Menu Commands

| Command | Windows | Mac |
|---|---|---|
| Play | Enter | Return |
| Rewind | Ctrl+Alt+R | ⌘+Option+R |
| Step Forward | . (period) | . (period) |
| Step Backward | , (comma) | , (comma) |
| Test Movie | Ctrl+Enter | ⌘+Return |
| Enable Simple Buttons | Ctrl+Alt+B | ⌘+Option+B |

## Window Menu Commands

| Command | Windows | Mac | Command | Windows | Mac |
|---|---|---|---|---|---|
| Properties | Ctrl+F3 | ⌘+F3 | Info | Ctrl+I | ⌘+I |
| Timeline | Ctrl+Alt+T | ⌘+Option+T | Transform | Ctrl+T | ⌘+T |
| Tools | Ctrl+F2 | ⌘+F2 | Actions | F9 | Option+F9 |
| Library | Ctrl+L/F11 | ⌘+L | Behaviors | Shift+F3 | Shift+F3 |
| Align | Ctrl+K | ⌘+K | History | Alt+F10 | ⌘+F10 |
| Color Mixer | Shift+F9 | | Movie Explorer | F3 | Option+F3 |
| Color Swatches | Ctrl+F9 | ⌘+F9 | Hide Panels | F4 | F4 |

*For Dummies: Bestselling Book Series for Beginners*

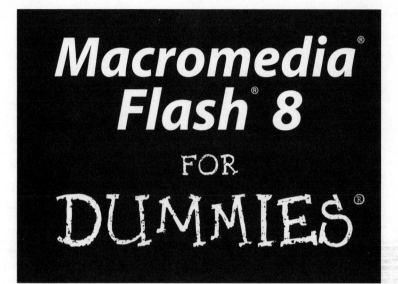

# Macromedia® Flash® 8 FOR DUMMIES®

**Ellen Finkelstein and Gurdy Leete**

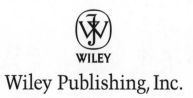

Wiley Publishing, Inc.

**Macromedia® Flash® 8 For Dummies®**

Published by
**Wiley Publishing, Inc.**
111 River Street
Hoboken, NJ 07030-5774

www.wiley.com

For general information on our other products and services, please contact our Customer Care Department within the U.S. at 800-762-2974, outside the U.S. at 317-572-3993, or fax 317-572-4002.

For technical support, please visit www.wiley.com/techsupport.

Wiley also publishes its books in a variety of electronic formats. Some content that appears in print may not be available in electronic books.

Library of Congress Control Number: 2005932587

ISBN-13: 978-0-7645-9691-9

ISBN-10: 0-7645-9691-8

Manufactured in the United States of America

10  9  8  7  6  5  4  3  2

1B/SW/RQ/QV/IN

WILEY

# About the Authors

**Ellen Finkelstein** has written numerous bestselling computer books on AutoCAD, PowerPoint, and Flash. She also writes articles on these programs for Web sites, e-zines, and magazines. The five editions of her *AutoCad Bible* have sold more than 80,000 copies in the United States and abroad. As an Adjunct Instructor of Management, she teaches eBusiness and Human Resource Management courses. Her latest book is *Syndicating Web Sites with RSS Feeds For Dummies.* She writes at home so that she can take the bread out of the oven on time.

**Gurdy Leete** has been working as a computer animator, computer animation software engineer, and teacher of computer animation since 1981. He has been teaching Flash and other computer animation programs for 14 years at Maharishi University of Management, where he is an Assistant Professor of Digital Media. You can see his art on the Web at www.infinityeverywhere.net.

# Dedication

To MMY, for explaining that life is meant to be lived in happiness and teaching us how to realize that reality in daily life.

# Authors' Acknowledgments

This book was very much a group effort. First, I'd like to thank my coauthor, Gurdy Leete, without whom I could not have completed this book nor even thought of writing it. Gurdy was always a pleasure to work with, always in a good mood, and helpful. He's a brilliant artist and something of a programmer, too, while I am neither. I've been quite impressed.

At Wiley, I'd like to thank Steve Hayes, our acquisitions editor, for trusting us with this book. Great kudos go to Kim Darosett, our project editor, for doing such a tremendous job.

Personally, I'd like to thank my husband, Evan, and my kids, Yeshayah and Eliyah, who helped out and managed without me as I wrote every day, evening, and weekend. I love you all.

Thanks to Macromedia, for creating Flash and supporting Flash authors during the beta period while we were learning all the new features of Flash 8, testing Flash, and writing, all at the same time.

Finally, I'd like to thank the Flash community and specifically all the Flash designers who contributed Flash movies to make this book and its companion Web site more valuable. Most computer books use dummy files, and we made up a few of our own to illustrate the point, but the real-world files we received for this book will help open up new vistas for our readers. And now, a few comments from Gurdy:

I'd like to echo all of Ellen's words and thank her for being such a great collaborator. She has such a talent for explaining things with the simplicity, precision, and humor that are so characteristic of the deeper workings of the cosmos. I'd also like to thank my brilliant students Alek Lisefski (www.bluesheepstudios.com) and Benek Lisefski (www.exhibit52.com), and my intrepid research assistants, Nutthawut Chandhaketh, of Thailand; Radim Schreiber, of the Czech Republic; Burcu Cenberci, of Turkey; and Praveen Mishra, of Nepal, whose research activities on the Internet were so helpful in the writing of this book. Thanks to my omnitalented M.A. in Animation student Mike Zak, for the wonderful collection of clip art drawings he created in Flash for the companion Web site. And thanks to my adorable wife, Mary, and my children, Porter and Jackie, for being so supportive during the many hours I spent working on this book.

## Publisher's Acknowledgments

We're proud of this book; please send us your comments through our online registration form located at www.dummies.com/register/.

Some of the people who helped bring this book to market include the following:

*Acquisitions, Editorial, and Media Development*

**Project Editor:** Kim Darosett

**Senior Acquisitions Editor:** Steven Hayes

**Copy Editor:** Virginia Sanders

**Technical Editor:** Sally Cruikshank

**Editorial Manager:** Leah Cameron

**Media Development Manager:** Laura VanWinkle

**Media Development Supervisor:** Richard Graves

**Editorial Assistant:** Amanda Foxworth

**Cartoons:** Rich Tennant (www.the5thwave.com)

*Composition Services*

**Project Coordinator:** Adrienne Martinez

**Layout and Graphics:** Carl Byers, Andrea Dahl, Barry Offringa

**Proofreaders:** Leeann Harney, Jessica Kramer, TECHBOOKS Production Services

**Indexer:** TECHBOOKS Production Services

---

**Publishing and Editorial for Technology Dummies**

  **Richard Swadley,** Vice President and Executive Group Publisher

  **Andy Cummings,** Vice President and Publisher

  **Mary Bednarek,** Executive Acquisitions Director

  **Mary C. Corder,** Editorial Director

**Publishing for Consumer Dummies**

  **Diane Graves Steele,** Vice President and Publisher

  **Joyce Pepple,** Acquisitions Director

**Composition Services**

  **Gerry Fahey,** Vice President of Production Services

  **Debbie Stailey,** Director of Composition Services

# Contents at a Glance

# Table of Contents

# Introduction

*W*elcome to *Macromedia Flash 8 For Dummies,* your friendly Web-
animation companion. In this book, we explain in plain English how to
make the most of Flash to create stunning Web site animations. *Macromedia
Flash 8 For Dummies* aims to give you all the information you need to start
using Flash right away — with no hassle.

## About This Book

As though you hadn't guessed, *Macromedia Flash 8 For Dummies* covers the
powerful animation product Flash 8, from Macromedia. (The preceding version was Flash MX 2004.) Flash 8 is the latest version of the popular software
used on some of the coolest Web sites on the Internet.

Flash comes in two versions: Flash 8 Basic and Flash 8 Professional (Pro). In
addition to including all the features of Flash 8 Basic, the Pro version of Flash
has powerful features for programmers and production teams, such as project file management, version control of Flash files, and the ability to connect
Flash to live external data sources and Web services. In addition, Flash 8 Pro
offers special graphics effects, custom animation controls, better handling of
bitmap scaling, and improvements in the way video content is handled. In
this book, we focus on the features of Flash 8 Basic rather than Flash 8 Pro
because they're much more useful to people who are new to Flash. However,
we do sometimes describe the Flash 8 Pro features. We comprehensively
explain the Flash features, including

- ✔ Working with the Flash screen, toolbars, and menus
- ✔ Creating graphics and text in Flash
- ✔ Adding sound and video
- ✔ Using layers to organize your animation
- ✔ Creating *symbols,* which are objects that you save for repeated use
- ✔ Animating graphics (the key to Flash)
- ✔ Creating interactive Web sites
- ✔ Publishing Flash movies to your Web site

# How to Use This Book

You don't have to read this book from cover to cover. We provide just the information you need, when you need it. Start with the first three chapters. Then play around with graphics until you create what you need for your Web site. You might want to check out Chapter 6, on layers, to help you organize it all, and Chapter 7, which covers symbols. Then feel free to jump right to Chapter 9, on animation, to create your first real Flash movie. Chapter 13 tells you how to get your movie on your Web site. Then fire up your browser, sit back, and marvel.

Of course, you'll want to check out other chapters when you need them so that you can create text and buttons, add sound and video, and create an interactive Web site. Chapter 12 provides some ideas for putting all the Flash features together for your best Web site ever.

Keep *Macromedia Flash 8 For Dummies* by your computer while you work. You'll find it to be a loyal helper.

# Foolish Assumptions

We assume that you're not already a master Flash developer. If you want to use Flash to create high-quality Web sites and you're not an expert animator already, you'll find this book to be a great reference. *Macromedia Flash 8 For Dummies* is ideal for beginners who are just starting to use Flash or for current Flash users who want to further hone their skills.

Because people usually add Flash movies to Web sites, we also assume that you know some of the basics of Web site creation. You should know what HyperText Markup Language (HTML) is and understand the process of creating and structuring HTML pages as well as uploading them to a Web site.

If you want some help on the topic of Web sites, you might want to take a look at *Web Design For Dummies,* by Lisa Lopuck (Wiley Publishing, Inc.).

# Conventions Used in This Book

Sometimes it helps to know why some text is bold and other is italic so that you can figure out what we're talking about. (A typographic convention is *not* a convention of typographers meeting to discuss the latest typography techniques.)

New terms are in *italics* to let you know that they're new. When we suggest that you type something, we show you we want you to type in **bold.** Messages and other text that come from Flash, including programming code, are in a `special typeface, like this.`

When we say something like "Choose File⇨Save As," it means to click the File menu at the top of your screen and then choose Save As from the menu that opens. When we want you to use a toolbar or toolbox button (or tool), we tell you to click it.

# How This Book Is Organized

We start by presenting an overview of the Flash universe and then continue in the general order that you would use to create a Flash animation. More basic material is at the beginning of the book, and more advanced material (but not too advanced!) comes later on. You might never use all the material in this book in one Flash movie.

To be more specific, this book is divided into seven parts (to represent the seven states of consciousness — okay, we don't have to get too cosmic here). Each part contains two or more chapters that relate to that part. Each chapter thoroughly covers one topic so that you don't have to go searching all over creation to get the information you need.

## Part 1: A Blast of Flash

Part I contains important introductory information about Flash. In Chapter 1, we tell you what Flash is all about, show you what the Flash screen looks like, and explain how to get help when you need it most. You can also find instructions for starting Flash, starting a new movie, and opening an existing movie, and we give you a short list of steps for creating your first animation. Chapter 2 explains in more detail the steps for creating a Flash movie. We also explain some basic concepts that all Flash users need to know.

## Part II: 1,000 Pictures and 1,000 Words

Part II explains all the tools available for creating graphics in Flash. Chapter 3 explains the unique drawing tools included in Flash. Of course, we also explain how to import graphics if you don't feel like creating your own. Chapter 4 shows you how to edit and manipulate graphic objects, and Chapter 5 is all about creating text. Chapter 6 explains *layers,* which help you organize your graphics so that they don't interfere with each other.

## Part III: Getting Symbolic

*Symbols* are graphical objects that you save to use again and again. Whenever you want to place an object on a Web page more than once, you can save the object as a symbol. You can also group together many individual objects, making them useful when you want to manipulate, edit, or animate them all at one time. Chapter 7 explains creating and editing symbols. Chapter 8 describes how to create buttons — not the kind that you sew, but rather the kind that you click with your mouse. *Buttons* are a kind of symbol, but on a Web page they execute an action when clicked.

## Part IV: Total Flash-o-Rama

Part IV explains how to put all your graphics together and make them move. Chapter 9 covers animation in detail — from frame-by-frame animation to *tweening,* where Flash calculates the animation between your first and last frames. Tween movement to make your objects move or morph into new shapes. You can also tween color and transparency.

Chapter 10 shows how to create interactive Web sites that react to your viewers. For example, when a viewer clicks a button, Flash can jump to a different part of a movie or go to a different Web page entirely. To create interactivity, you use *ActionScript,* Flash's JavaScript-like programming language. We tell you how to put ActionScript to work.

Chapter 11 is about adding multimedia — sound, music, and video — to your Flash movies and buttons.

## Part V: The Movie and the Web

This part helps you put all your animated graphics and cool buttons together and publish your work on the Web. Chapter 12 outlines the various techniques that you can use to create a great Web site using only Flash.

Chapter 13 explains how to test your animation for speed and suitability for all browsers and systems. Then we cover all the details of publishing movies as well as the other available formats, such as HTML and GIF. You can also create *projectors* — movies that play themselves.

## Part VI: The Part of Tens

What's a *For Dummies* book without The Part of Tens? Chapter 14 answers some frequently asked questions about Flash and introduces some fun techniques, such as creating drag-and-drop objects and simulating 3-D effects. Chapter 15 provides you with the ten best resources for learning about Flash (besides this book, of course). Chapter 16 lists our winners for ten great Flash Web designers, although new ones emerge all the time.

## Part VII: Appendixes

Last, but not least, we come to the appendixes. They add some valuable information to the end of this book. Appendix A adds instructions on installing Flash as well as setting preferences and options, illustrations of all the tools and panels in Flash 8. In Appendix B, we show you what's what on the Property inspector and on the various panels.

Appendix C tells you what's on the companion Web site (www.dummies.com/go/flash8). We provide Flash movies that we illustrate in the book and others that you can just play with to see how they work. We also add our own library of graphics that you can add to your own movies. In addition, we provide a bonus chapter, which is a glossary of obscure terms.

# Icons Used in This Book

*Icons* help point out special information. For example, sometimes they tell you that you don't care about this information and can skip over it without fear.

This icon flags new features in Flash 8. If you have been using Flash MX 2004 or even an earlier version, you may want to skim through this book and look for this icon to help you quickly get up to speed in the new version.

Look for this icon to find all the goodies on the companion Web site, at www.dummies.com/go/flash8.

This icon alerts you to information that you need to keep in mind to avoid wasting time or falling on your face.

Flash has some advanced features you might want to know about — or skip over entirely. This icon lets you know when we throw the heavier stuff at you.

Tips help you finish your work more easily, quickly, or effectively. Don't miss out on these.

Uh-oh! "Watch out here!" is what this icon is telling you. If you skip these, you never know what might happen.

## *Where to Go from Here*

If you haven't already installed Flash, check out the complete instructions for installing Flash in Appendix A. Then open Flash, open this book, and plunge in.

We would love to hear your comments about this book. You can contact Gurdy Leete at gleete@mum.edu and Ellen Finkelstein at ellenfinkl@bigfoot.com. Please note that we can't provide technical support on Flash. (If you need technical support, check out the resources we list in Chapter 16.)

Enough of all this talk. It's time to move into the real part of this book and start creating cool movies! Enjoy!

# Part I
# A Blast of Flash

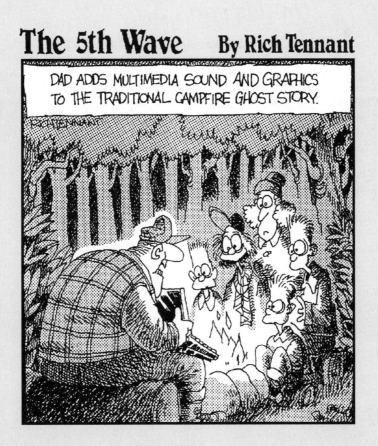

# In this part . . .

In this part, you discover what Flash can and can't do and start to make your way around the Flash world. In Chapter 1, we introduce you to Flash, show you what it looks like, and explain how to use its toolbars and menus. You find out about the Stage and the Timeline, two central Flash concepts. Play your way through your first animation to get firsthand experience in the power of Flash.

In Chapter 2, you get an overview of the entire process of creating a Flash animated movie, from developing your concept to publishing your movie in the format a browser can display. We explain how to set properties that affect your movie as a whole and how Flash works with various kinds of graphics. We close with the steps for printing your movie on paper. This part provides the foundation for future success.

# Chapter 1

# Getting Acquainted with Flash 8

*O*nce upon a time in a galaxy that seems far, far away by now, there was the Internet, which contained only plain, unformatted text. Then came the Web, and we gained text formatting and graphics. Then the Web grew up a little, and Web page graphics got fancier with things like small animations in banner ads. But people, being used to movies and TV, wanted an even more animated and interactive Web experience. Along came Flash.

*Flash,* from Macromedia, Inc., is the software that runs some of the coolest Web sites around. When you surf the Web and see sites that contain animation across the entire page or buttons that do spectacular stunts when you click them, you're probably seeing some Flash magic. If you create a Web site, you can use Flash to rev up the basics and actively respond to users' choices so that your viewers will say, "Wow!"

In this chapter, you find out what Flash is all about, what the Flash screen looks like, and how to use Help. Then you create your first, simple animation so that all the rest of this book makes sense.

# Discovering Flash

Flash offers a powerful system for creating animation for the Web. In a nutshell, here's an overview of how you use the system:

1. **Create a Flash movie by creating graphics and animating them over the duration of the movie.**

2. **Use the Publish command within Flash to publish the movie into a Flash Player file that a browser can display.**

   At the same time, Flash creates the appropriate HyperText Markup Language (HTML) code that you need for your Web page.

3. **Insert HTML code into your HTML document that references the Flash Player file.**

   It's similar to adding a graphic to a Web page. Or, you can use the HTML code alone as a new Web page for a fully Flashed page.

4. **Upload the new or edited HTML document and the Flash Player file to the location where you keep other files for your Web pages.**

5. **Open your browser, navigate to your Web page, and presto! — there's your cool animation on your Web page.**

You need the Flash Player to see the effects that Flash creates. These days, the Flash Player comes installed with most computer systems and browsers, so most people can view Flash-driven Web sites immediately without any special download or preparation. When you display a Web site that contains Flash effects, your system uses the Flash Player to play the animation. Users who don't have a Flash Player can download it for free from Macromedia at www.macromedia.com/go/getflash.

Web sites are getting more and more sophisticated. By using animation, special effects, and interactive techniques, you can distinguish your Web site from the also-rans. Creating animation isn't hard, and you don't have to be a professional graphic artist, either. Anyone can create simple animations to enhance a Web site; it just takes a little time.

To find the most up-to-date Web sites that use Flash, check out the Macromedia site at www.macromedia.com/software/flash/flashpro and click the Showcase button. Don't get discouraged by seeing some of the truly professional results at these sites. You can start with a simple, animated site and go from there. (Chapter 16 lists ten great Flash designers and where you can find their work.)

# *Understanding What You Can Create with Flash 8*

You can use Flash 8 to create simple animation to add to your Web page. Or, you can create an entire Web page or site using Flash and incorporate text, graphics, interactive buttons, and animation. You can even program applications in Flash.

This book helps you use Flash to create a simple or complex Web site. The following list describes some ways that you can manipulate text, graphics, and sound by using Flash 8:

- **Create still or animated text on your Web page.** You can choose to stop the animation after a few seconds or repeat it while your viewers view the page.

- **Use Flash tools to create your own graphics for your Web page or to import graphics.** You can lay out an entire Web page graphically or add graphics to only a part of a Web page.

- **Animate graphics and make objects appear and disappear by using the transparency feature.** Objects can move, get bigger or smaller, or rotate. Flash also lets you *morph* — that is, transform — shapes into new shapes.

- **Fill shapes and text with *gradients,* which are colors that gradually change into new colors.** You can even fill shapes and text with bitmap images that you import into Flash. For example, you could fill the letters of your name with dozens of flowers. (You aren't a flower child any more?)

- **Create Web page buttons that not only lead your viewers wherever you want them to go but also change shape or color at the same time.** You can make buttons change when you pass your mouse over them. People who view your page can click a button to display a movie (animation) or start a small application.

- **Add sound or video to your movie.** It's easy to add sound effects in Flash. You can control how long the sound or music plays and whether it loops to play continuously. You can play video files as well.

- **Create menus that viewers can use to navigate your site.** You can create navigation tools as well as forms, check boxes, and other interface elements that look a lot more stylish than plain HTML ones.

As you can see, you can go far with Flash if you want. And why not? It's great fun!

# Determining When Not to Use Flash 8

If Flash 8 is so wonderful, why doesn't every Web site designer use it? Why aren't most Web sites created completely with Flash?

Here's the other side of the story.

Although the vector graphics and animation of Flash load quickly, they don't load as quickly as plain text and simple graphics. Adding a movie to your Web page creates some overhead. There's no point in using Flash if you want simple pages consisting of mostly text and a few graphics that you want to stay put and not move.

You can create certain graphic effects more easily by using bitmap graphics. Painted brushstroke and textured effects are examples. Artists create these types of graphics by using graphics editing software, and the results are bitmaps. Similarly, to add photographs to your Web page, you need to scan the photographs as bitmaps. Flash creates *vector graphics* (defined mathematically), which are different from *bitmap graphics* (defined by lots of dots). You can find out more about bitmap and vector graphics in Chapter 2.

If you want simple animation, such as a few blinking dots or a marquee effect, animated *GIFs* (the animated bitmap graphics that you often see on the Web) might be smaller than Flash movies, so they load faster. You can create animated GIFs by using animated GIF editing software.

Some sites don't lend themselves to animation. Animation can distract from your content, and overdoing animation can make a serious site seem silly. Animation is great, but it has its place. Also, although Flash has some features that allow accessibility for people with disabilities, it still isn't as accessible as plain HTML. You need to determine whether animation is right for your Web site.

Flash provides little in the way of 3-D graphics or animation. For those, you need to go to more sophisticated software, such as Poser or 3D Studio Max. (See Chapter 14 for more 3-D possibilities in Flash.)

# Getting the Right Start

Well begun is half done, as the saying goes. The easiest way to begin using Flash 8 is with a shortcut or alias right on your desktop. Double-click the Flash icon, and you're on your way. (See Appendix A for information on installing Flash.)

# Starting Flash on a PC

Whether you installed Flash from the CD or by downloading it from the Macromedia Web site onto your PC, you might or might not have a shortcut on your desktop. To create one, choose Start⇨Programs⇨Macromedia⇨ Macromedia Flash 8. Right-click the Macromedia Flash 8 item and choose Create Shortcut from the pop-up menu that appears. The new shortcut appears on the menu. Drag that shortcut to your desktop.

To rename the shortcut, click the shortcut on your desktop. Then click the text beneath the icon. Type **Flash 8** (or whatever you want) and press Enter. Just double-click the icon to open Flash.

# Starting Flash on a Mac

You might find it handy to add the Flash 8 icon to your Dock for easy launching. To do this, click the Finder icon on the extreme left of the Dock to bring up a new Finder window. Navigate in the Finder window to the Applications folder, and in the Applications folder, double-click the Macromedia Flash 8 folder to open it. Click and drag the Flash 8 application icon to the Dock. A copy of the Flash 8 application icon appears on the Dock.

# Creating a new movie

Files that you create by using Flash are commonly called *movies*. When you start Flash, the startup screen appears (by default). In the Create New section, click Flash Document. If you have already opened a movie and have the menus available, choose File⇨New. In the New Document dialog box, select Flash Document on the General tab and then click OK. You usually start by creating or importing some graphics. (To find out more about working with graphics, see Chapter 3.)

# Opening an existing movie

If you want to work on a movie you've already created, when you first open Flash, choose the movie from the Open a Recent Item section or choose Open to find the file. If you've already opened a movie and have the menus available, press Ctrl+O (Windows) or ⌘+O (Mac) or choose File⇨Open; then double-click the movie to open it. The first frame appears on your screen, and you can edit the movie any way that you want.

When you open more than one movie, you see a tab at the top for each movie. You can click the tabs to move from movie to movie. The tabs appear in the order you created or opened the movies.

# Taking a Look Around

If you've never created animation, the Flash screen is different from the screens in other programs that you might be used to, so take the time to get to know it. You can also customize the Flash screen. Figure 1-1 shows one possible display.

If your screen opens with several rectangular panels strewn about the screen or docked on various sides, don't worry about them now. We explain how to open and use these panels throughout this book, but you don't need them for this chapter. If they drive you crazy, right-click (Windows) or Control+click (Mac) each panel's title bar and choose Close Panel Group from the menu that appears.

See Appendix B for a full layout of each panel and toolbar.

Tools panel            Timeline          Menu bar           More panels

**Figure 1-1:**
The Flash
screen.

Property inspector            Stage

# Tooling around the toolbars

Flash contains two toolbars in the Mac version: the Edit bar and the Controller. In Windows, Flash also offers the Main toolbar. To display or hide these toolbars, choose Window⇨Toolbars and click the toolbar that you want to display or hide. Here is a description of the toolbars:

- **Main toolbar (Windows only):** Contains commonly used commands. Many of these are familiar from the Standard toolbar in other Windows programs. By default, Flash does *not* display the Main toolbar.

- **Controller:** Lets you control the playback of movies. For more information, see Chapter 9.

- **Edit bar:** Helps you work with the Timeline and appears at the top of the Timeline. It includes a toggle to display and hide the Timeline, a button for editing scenes, and a zoom control. We discuss the Timeline briefly later in the chapter. For more information about the Timeline and scenes, see Chapter 9.

# Using panels

Panels give you access to the many Flash settings. You access the panels from the Window menu. We discuss the specific panels throughout this book. In this section, we explain how to keep control over your panels.

Most panels are *dockable,* which means that they can sit at the side or bottom of your Flash window without covering up your work. You can also stack them on top of each other. You control panels by doing the following:

- **To dock a panel:** Drag it to the side or bottom of your screen.

- **To undock a panel:** Drag it from its grabber, which is at the left edge of its title bar.

- **To open or close a panel:** Choose it from the Window menu.

- **To close an undocked panel:** Click its Close button.

- **To close a docked panel:** Right-click (Windows)/Control+click (Mac) its title bar and choose Close Panel.

You can stack panels just like you stack plastic containers in your refrigerator. Drag a panel (by its grabber) beneath another panel to stack it. You can also collapse or expand panels: A *collapsed* panel displays only its title bar, so it doesn't take up much space. Use the arrow on the left side of the title bar to collapse or expand a panel or click its title bar.

In Windows only, the Flash interface has new arrow buttons above panels that are docked at the bottom of your screen and to the left of panels docked at the right. Click an arrow to collapse the panels to just the tiny arrow button. Click the arrow again to expand the panels to their previous display.

The Tools panel contains all the tools that you need to draw and edit objects. At the bottom of the Tools panel are options that modify how the tools function. (See Chapters 3 and 4 for a complete description of the Tools panel.)

The Property inspector is another important panel. This panel displays information about selected objects, such as size, name, and location. You can modify objects in the Property inspector as well. It is *context-sensitive,* which means that its contents change according to what you're doing. For example, if you select a graphic object, the Property inspector provides settings relating to that object, and you can use the Property inspector to edit that object.

For the best in customization, you can save any layout of panels you like. Set up the panels and choose Window➪Workspace Layout➪Save Current. In the Save Workspace Layout dialog box that opens, give the layout a name and click OK. To restore that layout at any time, choose Window➪Workspace Layout and choose your very own layout.

## Discovering the Flash menus

Most drawing functions are available only in the Tools panel. Similarly, you often use the Timeline, as we discuss in the section "Following a timeline," later in this chapter, for creating animation. Almost every other function in Flash is on a menu somewhere. You just need to find it. In general, we discuss the specific menu functions where appropriate throughout this book. Table 1-1 offers a brief overview of the menus.

| Table 1-1 | Flash Menus |
|---|---|
| *Menu* | *What It Does* |
| Flash | (Mac only) Enables you to set preferences, create keyboard shortcuts, and quit Flash. |
| File | Enables you to open and close files; save files; import and export files; print; publish movies for the Web; send a movie as an e-mail attachment (Windows only); and quit Flash. |
| Edit | Provides commands that let you undo and redo actions; cut, copy, and paste to and from the Clipboard; delete, duplicate, select, and deselect objects; find and replace; copy and paste entire frames on the Timeline; edit symbols (see Chapter 7 for the whole story on symbols); set preferences (Windows only); and create keyboard shortcuts for commands (Windows only). |

| Menu | What It Does |
|------|--------------|
| View | Helps you get a better view by letting you zoom in and out; show or hide various parts of the screen; and view a grid for easy layout. |
| Insert | Enables you to insert symbols (Chapter 7 explains this topic); insert and delete Timeline features, such as frames and keyframes (see Chapter 9 for more); insert layers (check out Chapter 6); add Timeline effects (see Chapter 9); and add scenes (also in Chapter 9). |
| Modify | Helps you modify symbols, shapes, frames, Timeline effects, scenes, or the entire movie. Offers tools for transforming, aligning, grouping, and ungrouping objects, and breaking objects apart. |
| Text | Enables you to format text and check spelling. |
| Commands | Enables you to reuse and manage saved commands. A command is any action that you take in Flash, such as drawing or editing objects. You can save commands from the History panel. (See Chapter 4.) |
| Control | Provides options that let you control the playing of movies; test movies and scenes; engage certain interactive functions; and mute sounds. |
| Window | Enables you to open lots of things, including a new window; panels that help you control objects; the Library (more on the Library in Chapter 2); windows for creating interactive controls (which we explain in Chapter 10); and the Movie Explorer (to help manage your movie — see Chapter 12). |
| Help | Comes to the rescue when you need help. |

Many menu commands offer keyboard shortcuts. You can also create your own keyboard shortcuts. (See Appendix A for instructions.)

The shortcuts are displayed on the menus, next to the command name. Here are some of the most commonly used keyboard shortcuts (for more shortcuts, see the tear-out Cheat Sheet at the front of this book):

✔ **Ctrl+N (Windows) or ⌘+N (Mac):** Open the New Document dialog box so you can start a new movie.

✔ **Ctrl+O (Windows) or ⌘+O (Mac):** Open an existing movie.

✔ **Ctrl+S (Windows) or ⌘+S (Mac):** Save your movie. Use this shortcut often!

- **Ctrl+X (Windows) or ⌘+X (Mac):** Cut to the Clipboard. Chapter 4 explains more about using the Clipboard.

- **Ctrl+C (Windows) or ⌘+C (Mac):** Copy to the Clipboard.

- **Ctrl+V (Windows) or ⌘+V (Mac):** Paste from the Clipboard.

- **Ctrl+Z (Windows) or ⌘+Z (Mac):** Undo. Would you believe that by default Flash remembers your last 100 actions and can undo them? What a relief! And if you choose Window⇨Other Panels⇨History, the History panel lists each action, so you know what the next Undo will undo. Think of it as a journey into the long-forgotten past. (See Chapter 4 for more on the History panel, and see Appendix A for details on customizing the number of Undos that Flash remembers.)

- **Ctrl+Y (Windows) or ⌘+Y (Mac):** Redo. This redoes actions that you undid by using the Undo button. (Got that?) This button remembers just as many actions as the Undo button. If you undo more actions than you want, click Redo (or press Ctrl+Y/⌘+Y) until you're back where you want to be. Using the Undo and Redo buttons is like traveling through Flash time — and it gives you lots of slack while you're working.

- **Ctrl+Q (Windows) or ⌘+Q (Mac):** Exit Flash.

We mention other keyboard shortcuts throughout this book when we discuss their corresponding commands.

You should note, although it's not a shortcut, that you can find the Zoom Control box in the upper-right corner of your screen — if you open the Edit bar (choose Window⇨Toolbars⇨Edit Bar). Click the arrow and choose a zoom factor to zoom in and out. Zooming doesn't change the actual size of objects — it just makes them look bigger or smaller.

You aren't limited to the choices on the Zoom drop-down list. Type a number in the Zoom Control box and press Enter (Windows) or Return (Mac) to set your own zoom factor. For example, type **85** to set the zoom factor to 85 percent.

## Staging your movies

The white box in the center of your screen is the *Stage*. Think of the Stage as a movie screen where you place objects. You can place graphics and text there and then animate them. Flash also plays back movies on the Stage.

Around the edge of the Stage is a gray area called the *Pasteboard*. You can use the Pasteboard to store graphics that you plan to use soon but don't want on the Stage just yet. (For more permanent storage, use the Library, as we explain in Chapter 2.) You can also store data and other nongraphical content on the Pasteboard. Content that you put on the Pasteboard doesn't appear in your Flash movie.

# Following a timeline

The Timeline window divides your movie into *frames.* Each frame represents a tiny stretch of time, such as ½ of a second. Creating a movie is simply a matter of assembling frames, which are then quickly played in order.

Chapter 9 explains in detail how to make using the Timeline completely painless. For now, you should just understand the basics. See Figure 1-2 for the basic Timeline.

**Figure 1-2:**
The Timeline
is your key
to managing
animation.

On the left side of the Timeline is the layer list. When you open a new movie, you see only one layer, unimaginatively named Layer 1. A *layer* is like a sheet of transparent acetate on which you draw objects. Layers help you keep objects from running into each other, causing unfortunate, messy results. You organize your entire movie by using layers. For example, if you want to keep some text constant throughout the movie but animate a bouncing dot, you would give the dot its own layer and animate it on that layer. The layer list has room for more layers, and you can add as many layers as you want. (Chapter 6 gives you the lowdown on layers.)

You can lower the bottom edge of the Timeline to make room for more layers. Hover the mouse cursor over the bottom line until you see the two-headed arrow and drag downward.

To the right of Layer 1, you see a bunch of rectangles, each representing a frame. (Actually, before you start using the Timeline, they're just potential frames, like unexposed frames on a roll of film.) By default, each frame lasts ½ of a second. Each layer has its own row of frames because you can have different animations or objects on each layer.

A *keyframe* is a frame that defines some change in your animation. In some animations, every frame is a keyframe. Other animations need keyframes for only the first and last frames.

You don't use the Timeline until you're ready to animate. While you work, however, you should organize your objects on separate layers. Don't worry — you can always move an object from one layer to another.

# Getting Help in a Flash

This book is all that you need to start creating great animations, but we would be remiss if we didn't tell you about the Flash Help system.

To use Flash Help, choose Help⇨Flash Help. You see a window like the one shown in Figure 1-3.

**Figure 1-3:**
The Using
Flash Help
window.

# Multiple Help manuals

Flash Help contains several sections:

- **Getting Started with Flash** contains a basic overview of Flash and creating a Flash movie.

- **Flash Tutorials** is an extensive set of tutorials.

- **Using Flash** is the main Help manual.

- **Flash Samples** contains some specific examples of Flash files, mostly of advanced techniques.

- **Learning ActionScript 2.0 in Flash** is a user's guide for ActionScript, Flash's programming language. (See Chapter 10 to find out more.)

- **ActionScript 2.0 Language Reference** describes the components of the ActionScript programming language.

- ✔ **Using Components** explains how to use components (did you guess?), which we explain in Chapter 10. *Components* are basic Web interface elements, such as check boxes and forms that you can drop into your movie.

- ✔ **Components Language Reference** contains a components dictionary.

- ✔ **Extending Flash** offers help for Flash programmers who want to extend its capabilities.

- ✔ **Flash Lite Developer Guide** explains how to use Flash Professional 8 to develop Flash movies for mobile phones. Flash Lite is a version of the Flash Player for mobile phones.

- ✔ **Learning Flash Lite ActionScript** is about the special version of ActionScript for Flash Lite movies.

- ✔ **Flash Lite 1.x ActionScript Language Reference** is a programming reference for Flash Lite ActionScript.

To search for a term, click the Search button. Then enter the term and click Search. You can choose one of the Help sections from the drop-down list to focus your search more narrowly. You can then choose from the list of topics.

## Finding more help on the Web

Macromedia offers support on its Web site. To access it, choose Help⇨Flash Support Center, which takes you to `www.macromedia.com/support/flash`. There you can search the knowledge base and tutorials for answers to your questions.

# Try It; You'll Like It

Perhaps by now you're getting impatient to try out Flash. Getting started is easy. You collect a few ideas, put together some art, add animation, save your movie, and publish it. Then you view it in a browser either online or offline. That's the gratifying part. In the following sections, you get to try out Flash by working through a basic animation. The rest of the book explains the basic concepts in more detail.

## Conceiving your first animation

Suppose that you want to add an animated logo to a home page that you've already set up. You want the animation to run when the page loads and then stop. Figure 1-4 shows the Rainbow Resources company logo — unanimated, of course — that you can find on this book's Web site, at `www.dummies.com/go/flash8`.

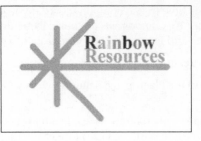

**Figure 1-4:**
A company logo that could stand some animation.

Suppose that you want the word *Rainbow* to fly into your page from the right and the word *Resources* to fly in from the left. At the same time, you want the graphic to rotate 180 degrees. The following section shows you how to create this animation.

## Creating flashy drawings

You can use Flash to create a company logo, but importing one from this book's Web site is simpler. Often, you import existing graphics (such as a company logo) from a file rather than create them from scratch. (Chapter 3 explains how to import and manipulate graphics.)

If you're going through the steps and make a mistake, choose Edit➪Undo (or press Ctrl+Z/⌘+Z) and try again. You can use Undo repeatedly to undo several steps, if necessary.

To import the Rainbow Resources logo into Flash, follow these steps. (The steps might vary if you're importing some other graphic in a different format.)

1. **Start Flash.**

   See the instructions in the section "Starting Flash on a PC" or "Starting Flash on a Mac," earlier in this chapter, if you need help.

2. **Choose Flash Document from the Create New section of the Startup screen.**

   You see a spanking-new movie on your screen.

3. **Go to www.dummies.com/go/flash8 and download the rainbow.gif file.**

4. **Choose File➪Import➪Import to Stage.**

   The Import dialog box opens.

5. **Browse the dialog box until you find `rainbow.gif` in the location where you downloaded it.**

6. **Click to select `rainbow.gif` and then click Open.**

   If you have difficulty importing the file, copy it to your hard drive and try Steps 3–5 again.

   You see the logo on your screen. You need to break the logo into pieces and make it a vector graphic so that you can animate sections of it separately.

7. **Choose Modify➪Bitmap➪Trace Bitmap.**

   The Trace Bitmap dialog box appears.

8. **In the Trace Bitmap dialog box, set the color threshold to 100, the minimum area to 1, the curve fit to Pixels, and the corner threshold to Many Corners. Click OK in the Trace Bitmap dialog box.**

   In our example, we chose to use settings that reproduce the bitmap as faithfully as possible. Flash creates a vector graphic and breaks up the graphic into individual components. The entire graphic, however, is selected.

9. **Click anywhere outside the graphic to deselect it.**

You've got your logo! Now you need to set it up for animation.

### Turning your objects into symbols

In the logo that you imported in the preceding section, each letter is a separate object, which can get pretty confusing. Each line in the logo's design is also separate. But you want your words to stay together — and the little design, too. So you must combine each word and the logo into a symbol. A *symbol* helps keep objects together and is required for some kinds of animation. (See Chapter 7 for the scoop on symbols.)

To turn the words and the logo into symbols, follow these steps:

1. **To get a better view of your image, click the Zoom Control drop-down list (at the upper-right corner of the Stage area) and choose 200%.**

   If you don't see the Zoom Control drop-down list, choose Window➪ Toolbars➪Edit Bar to display it.

   Use the scroll bar to scroll the words of the logo into view, if necessary.

2. **Click the Selection tool on the Tools panel if it's not already selected.**

3. **Click the upper-right corner of the word *Rainbow* (just above and to the right of the *w*) and drag to the lower-left corner of the first letter, *R*.**

   Dragging from right to left makes it easier to avoid selecting the logo at the same time. You should see the entire word selected. If not, click outside the word and try again.

4. **Choose Modify⇨Convert to Symbol. In the Convert to Symbol dialog box, click Graphic for the behavior and then click OK.**

   It is normally good practice to name the symbol, but not necessary for this exercise. When you click OK, Flash places a box around the word so that you can see that it's one object.

5. **Repeat the procedure outlined in Steps 3 and 4 with the word *Resources*.**

   In this case, you might want to start clicking and dragging from the upper-left area of the word; then choose Modify⇨Convert to Symbol again and click OK. Now all the letters of the word *Resources* are a single object.

6. **Click the Zoom Control drop-down list and choose 100% so that you can see the entire logo.**

7. **Click above and to the left of the logo and drag to the lower right to select the entire logo.**

8. **Hold down the Shift key and click each word to remove both words from the selection.**

   Now the design portion of the logo is selected.

9. **Press F8 (the keyboard shortcut to create a symbol) and click OK in the Convert to Symbol dialog box.**

   Flash creates a symbol from the lines of the logo's design.

See Chapter 7 to find out more about what symbols are and how to use them. Symbols are important building blocks in Flash movies.

### Putting your graphics on layers

You need to place different pieces on different layers when you're animating. You use layers to organize your movie and keep shapes separate so that they don't interfere with each other. (See Chapter 6 for the complete story on layers.)

To split your three symbols onto three separate layers, you can use a convenient feature of Flash 8: Distribute to Layers. Follow these steps:

1. **Click the Selection tool on the Tools panel if it's not already selected.**

2. **Drag diagonally across the entire logo, including the two words, to select it.**

   You should see two rectangles inside one bigger rectangle. All three objects in the logo are selected.

3. **Choose Modify➪Timeline➪Distribute to Layers.**

   You now have three new layers, named from Symbol 1 through Symbol 3. The three objects of the logo have been distributed to Symbol 1 through 3 and removed from Layer 1.

4. **Click outside the Stage to deselect any objects and choose 100% from the Zoom Control drop-down list.**

You're now ready for the animation process.

## Making graphics move

We explain earlier in this chapter that your goal is to have the word *Rainbow* fly in from the right and the word *Resources* to fly in from the left. You also want the graphic to rotate 180 degrees at the same time. What you see now is how the animation will end — the last frame of the movie.

Follow these steps to create the last frame of the movie and save the file:

1. **For *each* of the three symbol layers, click frame 30 of the Timeline and choose Insert➪Timeline➪Keyframe.**

   You can find out more about keyframes in Chapter 9.

2. **Choose File➪Save and pick a location where you save other documents that you create.**

   We don't recommend saving the file in the Flash 8 program folder — it might get lost among your Flash program files.

3. **Give your movie a name, such as *Movie of the Year,* and click Save.**

   Flash creates a file named `Movie of the Year.fla`. Flash adds `.fla` for you because that's the filename extension for Flash movies.

Go back and create the beginning of your movie. Flash can fill in all the blanks in between. Follow these steps to create the beginning of the movie and the animation:

1. **If the Property inspector isn't already open, choose Window⇨ Properties⇨Properties to open it.**

   If the Property inspector is open but collapsed, click the arrow at the left end of its title bar to expand the panel.

2. **Select the word *Rainbow*. Click the first frame of the Timeline in the highlighted row.**

   When you select the word *Rainbow,* you can tell which layer it is on by looking at the highlighted layer.

3. **Press and hold down the Shift key while you drag the word to the right, just off the Stage into the gray area.**

   You might need to use the horizontal scroll bar or choose a lower zoom percentage from the Zoom drop-down list to see the gray area. Pressing Shift keeps the object from moving up or down while you drag to the right. By clicking the first frame and moving the word, you set its position at the beginning of the animation.

4. **Click the word *Rainbow*'s layer, anywhere between the first and the 30th frame.**

5. **On the Tween drop-down list of the Property inspector, choose Motion.**

   You now see a solid arrow and a light blue color on the Timeline between the first and 30th frames. Choosing Motion from the Tween drop-down list creates animation that moves the symbol from the position in the first frame to its position in the next keyframe, which is frame 30 in this movie.

6. **Repeat Steps 2–4 for the word *Resources*. When you move the word *Resources,* hold down the Shift key and drag the word to the left, just off the Stage.**

7. **Select the logo design and click the first frame of the Timeline in the highlighted row.**

8. **Choose Modify⇨Transform⇨Rotate 90° CW to rotate the design 90 degrees clockwise.**

9. **Repeat the Modify⇨Transform⇨Rotate 90° CW command to rotate the design a total of 180 degrees.**

10. **Click the logo's highlighted layer, anywhere between the first and 30th frames, and choose Motion from the Tween drop-down list of the Property inspector.**

11. **If necessary, drag the horizontal scroll box until the Stage is in the center of your screen.**

    Otherwise, you won't be able to see the entire animation — and you don't want to miss this one!

12. **Click the first frame of any layer.**

    Your screen should look like the one shown in Figure 1-5.

13. **Press Enter (Return) and watch the animation. (Start writing your Academy Awards acceptance speech.)**

14. **Save your movie again by choosing File⇨Save.**

## Publishing your first animation for posterity

You can't watch the animation in a Web browser until you publish it and insert it into an HTML document. To do so, follow these steps:

1. **Click the Stage to change the display of the Property inspector.**

   You should see the Settings button next to the Publish label.

2. **Click the Settings button in the Property inspector.**

   The Publish Settings dialog box opens.

**Figure 1-5:** Before you run the animation, *Rainbow* appears to the right and *Resources* to the left, and the line logo is rotated.

3. **Click the HTML tab.**

4. **Deselect the Loop check box in the Playback section.**

   We want the animation to play only once.

5. **Click the Publish button and then click OK to close the dialog box.**

   With scarcely a blip, Flash publishes your movie and creates two files, one named `Movie of the Year.swf` (assuming you used that name) and `Movie of the Year.html`. They're in the same folder as your `.fla` movie file. `Movie of the Year.swf` is the file that your browser reads to play the animation. `Movie of the Year.html` contains the HTML code required to display your movie on a Web page.

6. **Open your Web browser.**

7. **Choose File⇨Open (or Open File) and find `Movie of the Year.html` (or whatever you named your movie file).**

   You might need to click Browse and navigate to the file.

8. **Double-click the file.**

   Your browser opens the HTML document and reads its instructions to play the Flash movie.

9. **Sit back and watch it roll.**

   Don't blink or you'll miss it. (If you do miss it, click the Refresh or Reload Current Page button in your browser.) You can see the movie in Figure 1-6.

10. **When you finish watching the movie, close your browser.**

You can find the Movie of the Year files (`.fla`, `.html`, and `.swf`) in the Ch01 folder on this book's Web site, `www.dummies.com/go/flash8`.

## Exiting Flash

When you finish creating something in Flash, choose File⇨Exit (Windows) or choose Flash⇨Quit (Mac).

**Figure 1-6:**
The Movie of the Year animation in detail.

# Chapter 2

# Your Basic Flash

*T*his chapter starts with an overview of the process of creating animation in Flash. We then discuss some tools and features that are fundamental to using Flash efficiently.

As you find out in this chapter, you use movie properties to set the screen size and color, frame rate, and measurement units for the Flash movie as a whole. We also discuss the Library and how it's a storehouse for images, symbols, and sound. Templates enable you to create great movies without much work. Finally, near the end of this chapter, we explain how you can print a Flash movie.

## Looking at the Big Picture

When you use Flash to create animation for your Web site, you generally go through several steps of construction. The steps might vary in their order, depending on your situation. After you know the basics, you can start getting creative and make your Web site rock. Here's a typical path to add animation to an existing Web page:

1. **Think about it.** Noodle around, maybe make some doodles on a napkin, collect a few ideas, and choose one or all of them.

2. **Set up your movie.** Flash lets you choose the size and color of the Stage, the speed of animation (number of frames per second), and other general parameters that affect the entire Flash movie. See the next section of this chapter for details.

3. **Add some graphics.** You have to decide whether you want to create graphics in Flash, create them in another graphics software package, or import existing graphics. Your choice partly depends on how artistic you are, whether you have other software available to you, and whether you can find the right graphics elsewhere. You can also use a combination of sources, which is a common practice. (See Chapter 3 for some suggestions on great places to get graphics.)

4. **Lay out your graphics the way you want your animation to start.** Here's where you might want to scale, rotate, or otherwise fiddle with your graphics. (Chapter 4 has more on transforming your graphics.)

5. **Add some text.** Using Flash is a great way to get terrific text onto your Web site. Add text (also called *type*); then reshape it, make it transparent (if you don't want to be too obvious), add other effects, and move it where you want it. (Check out Chapter 5 for typography tips.)

6. **Organize your text and graphics by using layers.** Layers help you keep track of what each graphic and text object does while you organize everything into a powerful, coherent statement. Layers keep your animations from going bump in the night and getting entangled. Create as many layers as you need and transfer your existing graphics and text to those layers. (See Chapter 6 for further details on layers.)

7. **Turn a graphic into a symbol and multiply it all over the Stage.** Making objects into symbols is a way to keep them from merging with other objects while they merrily animate. You also use symbols to keep the file size down and to enable animation, as well as for interactivity, especially buttons. (Turn to Chapter 7 for more info on symbols.)

8. **Design some buttons.** You know those buttons you click on Web sites all the time? The coolest ones are made in Flash. You can even use movie clips to create animated buttons. (Chapter 8 has more on buttons.)

9. **Animate!** You can create your animation frame by frame or let Flash fill in the animation between your first and last frames, which is called *tweening*. Flash can tween motion, shapes, colors, and transparency, which means that you can create some real magic. (See Chapter 9 for more on animation and the section in Chapter 1 where we step you through your first animation.)

10. **Get interactive.** You want to start a relationship with your Web viewers, so you can create buttons, frames, and symbols that respond to your viewers' actions. This is probably the most complex functionality of Flash, but we make most of it seem easy. (Turn to Chapter 10 for additional info on interactivity.)

11. **Make it louder! Make it move!** Who wants a quiet Web site? Add sound to your movies or your buttons. You can also add a video file. (Check out Chapter 11 for more on sound and video.)

12. **Publish your magnum opus.** Flash makes getting your movie to your Web site easy by creating both the Flash Player (`.swf`) file and the HyperText Transfer Language (HTML) code for your Web page. Flash has other options, too, so you can publish to other formats if you want. (Chapter 12 explains how to put it all together, and Chapter 13 is all about publishing your animation.)

Congratulations! You've completed your first Flash Web animation — in fantasy, at least. The following sections cover some details about how to get started.

# Setting the Stage

Before you create graphics and animate them — all that fun stuff — you need to make some decisions about the structure of your entire movie. You should make these decisions before you start because changing midway can create problems.

The first step is to decide on the size and color of your Stage and other fundamental settings. Make sure that the Property inspector is open (choose Window⇨Properties⇨Properties). When the Stage is active (just click the Stage), the Property inspector looks like Figure 2-1.

**Figure 2-1:**
You can change movie properties in the Property inspector.

# Choosing the Stage color

You can set the color of the Stage to create a colored background for your entire movie. Like with other settings, you need to consider the context of the Web page that will contain the Flash movie. For example, you might want to match the color of your Web page's background. If your Flash movie will constitute the entire Web page, set the Stage color to the color you want for the Web page background. You can also color the Stage to create a mood for your animation.

To set the Stage color, click the Background color swatch in the Property inspector. Flash opens the Color palette. Click the color that you want.

## Specifying the frame rate

In the Frame Rate text box, specify how many frames that a Flash movie plays each second, and then press Enter (Windows) or Return (Mac). A faster rate allows for smoother animation but might present a performance problem on slower computers. Chapter 9 explains more about this setting. The Flash default is 12 fps (frames per second), which is a good starting point. But changing the frame rate midstream in the creation process changes the rate of all the animation in your movie, which might not give you the results that you want.

## Setting the Stage size and adding metadata

The Size button displays the current size of the Stage. By default, Flash uses a Stage size of 550 pixels wide by 400 pixels high. To determine the proper setting, you need to know how your Flash movie will fit into your Web page or site. The default fits on almost everyone's browser screen. You might, however, want to fit your movie into a small corner of a Web page: for example, placing an animated logo in a top corner of a page. In that case, make the Stage smaller.

To change the Stage size, click the Size button to open the Document Properties dialog box, as shown in Figure 2-2. Type the dimensions that you want in the width and height text boxes.

**Figure 2-2:**
The Document Properties dialog box sets the movie's overall parameters.

**Document Properties**

Title:

Description:

Dimensions: 550 px (width) x 400 px (height)

Match: ○ Printer ○ Contents ⦿ Default

Background color:

Frame rate: 12 fps

Ruler units: Pixels

Make Default    OK    Cancel

Flash offers two shortcuts for setting the Stage size in the Document Properties dialog box:

- ✔ **Match Printer:** Click this option to set the Stage size according to the paper size set in the Page Setup dialog box (choose File⇨Page Setup). (For the Mac, the Print Margins dialog box, which you access by choosing File⇨Print Margins, also affects the paper size.) Flash sets the size of the Stage to the maximum possible area of the paper minus the margins. Later in this chapter, in the section "Printing Your Movie," we cover this dialog box in more detail.

- ✔ **Match Contents:** Click this option to set the Stage size to the contents of the Stage. Of course, for this to work, you need some objects on the Stage. Flash creates a Stage size by placing equal space around all sides of the entire contents of the Stage. If you want to create the smallest possible Stage, place your objects in the upper-left corner and then click Match Contents.

To change the units used for measuring the screen and objects, choose a unit from the Ruler Units drop-down list.

You can add *metadata* to your movies. The metadata is information embedded in the movie that search engines can find. You can include a title in the Title text field that describes your movie. In the Description text field, add keywords and descriptions of your movie's content that you would like to be available when people search in a browser. For more information, see the section on adding Web search information to your Flash movie in Chapter 12.

Click the Make Default button to make your settings the default for all your new Flash movies. However, the Title and Description fields don't become defaults; you need to specify them individually for each movie.

When you're done setting document properties, click OK to close the dialog box.

# Grabbing a Graphic

The first step when creating animation for your Web site is usually to create or import graphics. First, you should know a little about the different kinds of graphics that you can use in a Flash movie.

## Understanding vectors and bitmaps

If you know enough about graphics to understand the difference between bitmap and vector graphics, feel free to skip this section. (We hope you always feel free.)

*Bitmaps* are created with lots of dots. Put them all together, and you get a picture. On-screen, they're displayed as *pixels*. As you can imagine, it can take a large file to store the information about all the dots in a bitmap. Another problem with bitmaps is that they don't scale up well. If you try to enlarge a bitmap, it starts to look grainy because you see all those dots (as in the left example shown in Figure 2-3).

**Figure 2-3:**
Bitmaps
lose focus
when
enlarged
(left); vector
graphics
remain
sharp and
clear (right).

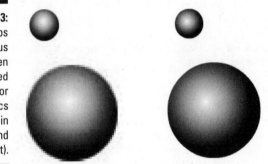

*Vector graphics* are defined with equations that specify lines, shapes, and locations. Blank space doesn't have to be recorded, and the equations are particularly efficient at storing information. As a result, file sizes are usually smaller than bitmap file sizes.

Vector graphics are infinitely scalable, either up or down. No matter how big you make your graphic, it always looks perfect, as shown in the right example in Figure 2-3. In fact, your graphic might even look better when it's larger because the curves are smoother.

Flash creates vector-based graphics. The small size of the files means that Flash Player files load and play super-fast on a Web page. As you undoubtedly know, fast file-loading means that your Web page viewers don't have to wait a long time to see your effects. That's the advantage of Flash. Nevertheless, you can create great graphics with bitmaps that you can't duplicate with vector graphics, and we explain how to import bitmaps in Chapter 3.

## *Finding graphics*

Okay, so you've doodled and played around with some ideas for your Flash animation and perhaps jotted down a few notes or maybe even made a few sketches. You're ready to start building your Flash animation. A logical place to start is to collect some of the graphics that will serve as building blocks in this process.

Where do you get them? You have several choices:

- ✔ Create your graphics from scratch (if you feel artistic) by using the Flash drawing tools that we describe in detail in Chapter 3.
- ✔ Create graphics in another graphics software package, such as Fireworks or FreeHand.
- ✔ Import graphics from archives of art available on this book's Web site, from other places on the Web, or from digital (or scanned) photographs — perhaps your own.
- ✔ Combine any or all of these approaches.

You can also import video files. If you want to add video to your Flash movies, see Chapter 11 for detailed instructions.

## *Going to the Library*

Every graphic that you create in Flash is precious and deserves to be archived in style. Each movie file that you create has a Library. The Library saves the following types of objects so that they never get lost:

- ✔ Graphic, movie clip, and button symbols
- ✔ Sounds
- ✔ Imported bitmap graphics (but not vector graphics that you create in Flash)
- ✔ Imported video files

You'll find yourself going to the Library often. Figure 2-4 shows a Library containing several types of symbols plus a sound and a bitmap.

To go to the Library of the current movie file, choose Window➪Library. You can also press Ctrl+L (Windows)/⌘+L (Mac). When you open the Library, Flash creates a new window or adds the Library panel to the set of panels that are already open.

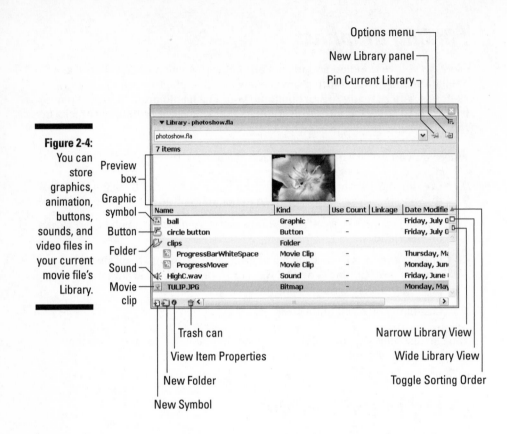

Options menu
New Library panel
Pin Current Library

**Figure 2-4:**
You can store graphics, animation, buttons, sounds, and video files in your current movie file's Library.

Preview box
Graphic symbol
Button
Folder
Sound
Movie clip

Trash can
View Item Properties
New Folder
New Symbol

Narrow Library View
Wide Library View
Toggle Sorting Order

To use any object in the Library, follow these steps:

1. **Select the layer on which you want to put the object or create a new layer for the object.**

2. **Click the point on the Timeline where you want the object to start or appear.**

   The point that you click on the Timeline (in Step 2) must be a keyframe. Chapter 9 explains keyframes in detail.

3. **Click and drag the object from its listing in the Library to the Stage.**

   You can also select an object from the listing or drag its image from the preview box.

You can drag items to the Pasteboard, the gray area around the edge of the Stage, until you're ready to use them.

### Using folders

A Flash movie can contain dozens or even hundreds of symbols, so you need to keep them organized. Flash provides several features to keep you from tearing out your hair.

You can, and should, organize your symbols into folders if you have more than a few. To create a new folder, follow these steps:

1. **Click the New Folder button at the bottom of the Library panel.**

   Flash creates a new folder.

2. **Type a name that describes the type of symbols that you want to put into the folder.**

   For example, you could create a folder named Intro and another one named Conclusion.

3. **Press Enter (Windows) or Return (Mac).**

To put symbols into a folder, drag them to the folder. You can also move symbols from one folder to another — just drag them. Note that folders exist just to help keep you organized. You can move symbols from one folder to another without affecting your movie.

To keep your symbol list from getting unwieldy, you can collapse folders. A collapsed folder doesn't display its contents. As soon as you need to see what's inside, you can expand the folder. Double-click a folder to either collapse or expand it.

To quickly see the structure of your folders, click the Library's Options menu. Choose Collapse All Folders. You can also choose Expand All Folders to see everything in the Library.

### More Library housekeeping

By default, Flash alphabetizes items in the Library by name. You might, however, have different ideas. You can sort from A to Z (ascending) or from Z to A (descending). You can also sort by any of the columns in the Library. To change the direction of sorting (for any column in the Library), click the Toggle Sorting Order button in the upper-right corner of the list (Windows only). To sort, click the heading of the column that you want to sort by. (On the Mac, you can click the column heading again to change the sort order.)

You can resize the Library panel by dragging its lower-right corner. Or you can click the Wide Library View or Narrow Library View button to grow or shrink its width, respectively (refer to Figure 2-4). You can resize any column by dragging the column heading's divider left or right.

To rename any Library item, double-click the item's name, type the new name, and press Enter or Return. Don't worry — the original filenames of imported files remain unchanged at their original location.

To duplicate an item, select the item. Then right-click (Windows) or Control+click (Mac) and choose Duplicate. To delete an item, select the item and click the Trash can.

If you want to find out which items in the Library you aren't using, look in the third column (Use Count) for items with a zero use count. To make sure that the use count is accurate, click the Library's Options menu and choose Keep Use Counts Updated or Update Use Counts Now. After you know which items you aren't using, you can delete them.

You can update imported bitmaps and sounds if the original files have changed. Select the file and choose Update from the Options menu of the Library panel.

### Using the Libraries of other movies

After you place objects in a file's Library, you can use those objects in any other Flash movie that you create. Just open the movie and display its Library panel, and its Library's contents are available for you to use in your current movie.

Choose File⇨Import⇨Open External Library to open the Library of another Flash movie that isn't open.

You can now switch among the Libraries of open movies by using a drop-down list at the top of the Library panel.

When you have libraries open from more than one Flash file, you can copy symbols or anything else in a Library from one movie to another by simply dragging them from one Library to another. Choose the Library that you want to use, select an item, and drag it into the other Library. Easy!

To create a new symbol that goes directly into the Library (rather than on the Stage), choose New Symbol from the Library Options menu in the upper-right corner (refer to Figure 2-4). You're transported to symbol-editing mode, where you can create your symbol as you normally would. To return to your main movie, choose Edit⇨Edit Document. For more information on creating and editing symbols, see Chapter 7.

### Exploring the Flash stock Library

Flash comes with two Libraries that contain a basic assortment of button symbols. They are well done, so they're worth looking through. Choose Window⇨Other Panels⇨Common Libraries and choose Buttons.

# Using a Template

To help you create Flash movies more easily, Flash 8 comes with a few templates for common types of movies. Instructions are included on the templates. To create a Flash movie from a template, choose File⇨New and click the Templates tab. In the New from Template dialog box (see Figure 2-5), select a category, select one of the templates, and then click OK.

**Figure 2-5:** Use the New from Template dialog box to create a Flash movie from a template.

You can choose from the following template categories (although Flash Professional offers some additional categories):

- ✔ **Advertising:** You can choose from a number of ad sizes. These templates simply contain a Stage of the ad size that you choose.

- ✔ **Global Phones:** This creates movies for certain types of supported phones.

- ✔ **Japanese Phones:** This creates movies for certain types of Japanese phones.

- ✔ **PDAs:** You can create content for several types of PDAs.

- ✔ **Photo Slideshows:** This template creates a slide show of photos.

- ✔ **Presentations:** Create your own presentation. Just add the desired text and graphics to each frame.

- ✔ **Quiz:** Create a quiz, complete with several types of question formats and answer feedback. This template's instructions are fairly involved.

When you open a new movie from a template, you should save it as a movie. This way, the template is unchanged, and you are free to make any changes that you want.

You can also save movies as templates. If you create a movie that you want to reuse in many variations, choose File➪Save as Template to open the Save as Template dialog box, as shown in Figure 2-6.

**Figure 2-6:** The Save as Template dialog box saves your movies as templates.

Type a name, choose a category, and enter a description for your template. Then click Save. From now on, you can open your template just like any of the templates that come with Flash, just as we describe. Using templates can save you lots of work!

To create your own category for templates, type a category name in the Category list box instead of choosing one of the existing categories from the list.

# Printing Your Movie

Usually, you don't print your movies — you publish them on the Web. But you might want to collaborate on a movie with others who don't have Flash. (How unenlightened of them!) Or, you might just want to analyze a movie on paper, tack your animation frames on the wall, and rearrange their sequence. In this type of situation, you can print your animation frame by frame.

To print a movie, follow these steps:

1. **To set page margins, choose File➪Page Setup (Windows) or File➪ Print Margins (Mac).**

   The Page Setup (Windows) or Print Margins (Mac) dialog box appears, as shown in Figure 2-7.

**Figure 2-7:**
Use the
Page Setup
dialog box
to specify
how to print
your Flash
movie.

2. **In the Margins section, set the margins.**

   You can probably keep the default margins.

3. **Select the Center check boxes to center the printing horizontally (L–R) and vertically (T–B) on the page.**

4. **In the Layout section, click the Frames drop-down list and decide whether to print only the first frame or all frames.**

5. **Click the Layout drop-down list in the Layout section to choose from the following options:**

   • **Actual Size:** Lets you choose a scale. This option prints one frame to a page.

   • **Fit on One Page:** Fits one frame on a page, scaling it to fit the paper.

   • **Storyboard – Boxes:** Places several thumbnail sketches of your movie on a page. You can specify how many frames that you want in a row in the Frames text box. You might need to experiment to get the right result. In the Frame Margin text box, enter in pixels the space between the boxes. The Storyboard – Boxes option places each frame in a box.

   • **Storyboard – Grid:** Creates a grid of lines for your storyboard rather than individual boxes around the frames. This option is just a matter of aesthetics — don't get too hung up over these choices.

   • **Storyboard – Blank:** Leaves out the boxes or grid and just prints all your frames in the storyboard. You have the same Frames and Frame Margin settings as for the other storyboard options.

6. **If you chose a Storyboard option, select the Label Frames check box (Windows) or Label (Mac) to give each frame a number.**

7. **On a Mac, when you finish setting your options, click OK; then choose File⇨Page Setup.**

   In Windows, you skip this step because you already opened the Page Setup dialog box in Step 1.

8. **Select the size of the paper; (Windows only) define the paper source in the Paper section.**

   Usually you can leave this section as is because it's based on your printer's default settings.

9. **In the Orientation section, select Portrait (taller rather than wider) or Landscape (wider rather than taller).**

10. **(Mac only) In the Format section, choose your printer from the drop-down list.**

11. **When you finish setting your options, click OK.**

12. **(Windows only) If you chose a storyboard option, choose File⇨ Print Preview to preview your movie to ensure that you like the setup. Click the Close button to return to the regular display.**

13. **To print, choose File⇨Print.**

   Alternatively, you can press Ctrl+P (Windows) or ⌘+P (Mac).

Figure 2-8 shows an example of the storyboard with the grid option. The storyboard shows four frames across with a portrait orientation.

You can find out more about the Flash Player's special printing capabilities in Chapter 13.

**Figure 2-8:** You can print a storyboard of your movie that displays a thumbnail sketch of each frame.

# Part II
# 1,000 Pictures and 1,000 Words

## The 5th Wave By Rich Tennant

"Well, it's not quite done. I've animated the gurgling spit-sink and the rotating Novocaine syringe, but I still have to add the high speed whining drill audio track."

## In this part . . .

Graphics are the basis of animation. Before you can make anything move, you need to create the graphics that form the building blocks of your animation. Chapter 3 describes all the types of graphics that you can use, from basic shapes created in Flash to sophisticated imported bitmap graphics. The Flash tools are quite capable, and you can create exciting effects with gradient fills, softened edges, and transparency. The Flash editing features, as we describe in Chapter 4, offer more opportunities to create great-looking graphics — including skewing objects, using the Distort and Envelope options, and manipulating fills every which way.

In Chapter 5, you find ways to say great things with flexible text options and formatting. You can even break up text and animate it, letter by letter. To keep all the pieces of your animation from going completely out of control, you see how to use layers to organize your movie animation in Chapter 6. You can use special layers to guide animation along a path and hide objects behind a mask.

# Chapter 3

# Getting Graphic

*I*n this chapter, you get down to the details of creating your own graphics in Flash. The Flash graphics tools (found on the Tools panel) offer you the capability to easily create interesting and professional-looking shapes. Of course, you can also import graphics created in other programs.

After you master all the techniques for drawing and editing, you can create some very cool graphics. If you're new to Flash, take the time to try out all the tools and techniques until you feel comfortable with them.

For a handy reference to the Tools panel, which we refer to throughout this entire chapter, see the Cheat Sheet at the front of this book.

## Sharpening Your Pencil

The Flash Pencil tool is designed to be used like a real pencil to create free-hand shapes. Whenever you want to create a shape not available from other Flash tools (such as the circle and square), you can use the Pencil. But the Pencil tool goes beyond a regular pencil's capabilities by incorporating cool features that smooth or straighten what you draw. In addition to those features, the Pencil also includes the *shape-recognition* feature (perfect for those who are less artistic). Draw something that approximates a triangle, and Flash forgivingly perfects it for you. In this section, we explain exactly how to use this tool.

 To start, click the Pencil tool on the Tools panel. To draw without changing the Pencil modifier, move the cursor onto the Stage, click, and draw. After you release the mouse button, Flash modifies the shape according to the active modifier setting, as we explain in the next section.

## Setting the Pencil modifier

When you choose the Pencil tool, the Options area below the Tools panel changes to display the drawing mode modifier for the Pencil tool.

The Pencil modifier has three drawing modes:

- ✔ **Straighten:** Straightens lines and converts sloppy squares, rectangles, circles, ellipses, and triangles to perfect ones.
- ✔ **Smooth:** Smoothes out curved lines, eliminating unsightly bumps and lumps. You can specify the amount of smoothing.
- ✔ **Ink:** Slightly smoothes and straightens your curves and lines but leaves them mostly the way that you drew them.

In Figure 3-1, you see a right-pointing arrow. Suppose that you have already drawn the horizontal line and now want to create the arrow's point. See how the point looks before and after Flash modified it by using the Straighten drawing mode to create perfectly straight lines.

**Figure 3-1:**
Use the Straighten mode of the Pencil tool to draw straight lines.

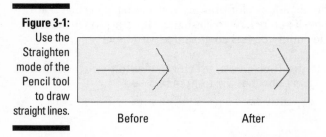

Before                    After

Suppose that you want to animate some waves on your Web site. You start to draw the outline of the waves. Figure 3-2 shows how the waves look before and after Flash smoothes them out by using Smooth mode.

# How to set smoothing and shape-recognition preferences

You can tell Flash just how much you want it to smooth or straighten curved lines when you draw with the Pencil tool. Choose Edit⇨ Preferences (Windows) or Flash ⇨Preferences (Mac) and click the Drawing category. From the Smooth Curves drop-down list, select one of the following options:

- ✔ **Off:** Flash doesn't smooth or straighten at all.

- ✔ **Rough:** Flash smoothes or straightens only slightly, honoring your own work as much as possible.

- ✔ **Normal:** Flash smoothes or straightens a medium amount. Normal is the default setting.

- ✔ **Smooth:** Flash smoothes and straightens more so that you get fewer bumps and jolts.

In the same way, you can tell Flash how picky you want it to be in recognizing lines, circles, ovals, squares, rectangles, and arcs (90 degrees and 180 degrees). For lines, select Off, Strict, Normal, or Tolerant from the Recognize Lines drop-down list. Normal is the default. Use Tolerant if you're a klutz; use Strict (or even Off) if you don't want Flash fiddling too much (or at all) with your work.

For other shapes and arcs, select an option from the Recognize Shapes drop-down list. You have the same Off, Strict, Normal, and Tolerant options.

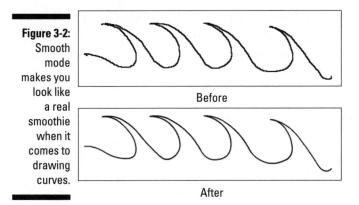

**Figure 3-2:** Smooth mode makes you look like a real smoothie when it comes to drawing curves.

Before

After

For more complex shapes, Ink mode helps you look good without taking away too much of your own authorship.

## *Setting the stroke type*

While drawing with the Pencil tool (and any of the other drawing tools), you can also control the type of *stroke* (line style), its *width* (also called *height* or *weight*), its cap (ending), and how it joins with other strokes. To modify stroke settings, follow these steps:

1. **Click the Pencil tool to make it active.**

2. **Open the Property inspector by choosing Window⇨Properties⇨ Properties.**

   The Property inspector appears, as shown in Figure 3-3. As we explain in Chapter 1, the Property inspector changes depending on which tool is active and which part of the Flash window you're using.

**Figure 3-3:**
Use the Property inspector to control line type and width.

Stroke Height    Stroke Style

Stroke Color

3. **Click the Stroke Style drop-down list to display the available line styles and select a new line style from the list.**

   You can choose from seven line styles, including dashed and dotted lines.

4. **To change the line width, type a new weight in the Stroke Height text box and press Enter or Return or drag the slider bar to the value that you want.**

   The first available stroke width on the Stroke Style drop-down list is Hairline, which creates a hairline-width line. Flash measures *weights* (widths) of other line types in points.

   You can now create a line up to 200 points wide. A point equals ½ of an inch. You can create lines with *caps,* which are line endings, as we explain in Step 5, next.

5. **Click the Cap drop-down list and select one of the styles:**

   • **None:** The end is square with no added ending.

   • **Round:** A rounded cap is added to the end of the line. The length of the cap is half the line's width.

   • **Square:** A squared cap is added to the end of the line. The length of the cap is half the line's width. See Figure 3-4.

   Strangely, when you draw a line that crosses another line, both lines are changed to round caps, regardless of the cap style that you select.

**Figure 3-4:**
I drew these lines to be 100 pixels long, but the bottom two have round and square caps, so they're longer.

6. **If you want, select the Stroke Hinting check box.**

    Stroke hinting makes slight adjustments to avoid blurry horizontal or vertical lines. If your text doesn't look as clear as you'd like, try selecting this option.

7. **Click the Join drop-down list and select one of the styles (see Figure 3-5) to control how lines look when they meet:**

    • **Miter:** A pointed corner.

    • **Round:** A rounded corner.

    • **Bevel:** A squared-off (beveled) corner.

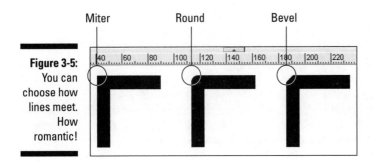

**Figure 3-5:**
You can choose how lines meet. How romantic!

8. **The Scale drop-down box specifies how the thickness of strokes scales if you include them in a symbol. (We discuss symbols in Chapter 7.) From the Scale drop-down list, select an option to control how lines scale:**

- **Normal:** Thickness scales both horizontally and vertically.

- **Horizontal:** Thickness scales horizontally only. This applies to vertical lines, so that they become thicker as you scale them.

- **Vertical:** Thickness scales vertically only. This applies to horizontal lines, so that they become thicker as you scale them.

- **None:** Lines don't become thicker as you scale them.

9. **(Optional) In the Miter text box, you can enter a limit to help prevent beveling a Miter join.**

    When you draw two lines that meet at a sharp angle with a *Miter join* (a sharp point), you might get a bevel instead. Increase the value in the Miter text box to get a nice sharp point where the two lines meet.

You can create custom line styles, as well. In the Property inspector, click the Custom button. In the Line Style dialog box that opens, you can create your own designer line styles.

## Setting the color

 When using the Pencil, you can set the color of the stroke in the Property inspector or in the Colors section of the Tools panel. In either location, click the Stroke Color box to open the Color palette and then select a color.

We explain more about using colors in the section "A Rainbow of Colors," later in this chapter.

# Creating Shapely Shapes

In the preceding section, we explain that you can draw shapes by using the Pencil tool. You can also draw lines, rectangles, squares, ovals, and circles by using the shape tools. Use these tools when you want more control over your shapes — for example, when you want to draw perfect circles, perfect squares, and straight lines.

## Line up

 To draw a line, choose the Line tool from the Tools panel. Click the Stage at the desired starting point of the line and drag to the ending point. Then release the mouse button. To keep your lines at multiples of 45 degrees, press Shift while dragging. Flash creates the line at the 45-degree angle closest to your drag line.

When you use the Line tool, you can modify the line weight, style, and color in the same way as for the Pencil tool, as we discuss in the preceding section.

# Be square

To draw a rectangle, choose the Rectangle tool from the Tools panel. Click the Stage at one corner of the rectangle and drag to the opposite corner. Then release the mouse button. To create a square, press Shift as you drag.

When you click the Rectangle tool, you can modify the line weight, style, and color of the rectangle in the same way that you can modify a line when you use the Pencil tool. You can't see the effect of caps when you create a rectangle because it's a closed shape; however, if you later cut out part of the rectangle, the remaining lines take on the cap you specified.

Unlike lines, rectangles contain *two* objects: the *fill* (the area inside the stroke) and the *stroke* (the outline of the rectangle).

Flash provides the following tools for adjusting the settings for rectangles:

- ✔ **Fill Color:** Determines the color that fills the inside of the rectangle. You can click the Fill Color box — either in the Property inspector or in the Colors section of the Tools panel — and select one of the colors from the palette that opens. You can also select from the gradients displayed at the bottom of the palette. (See the section "A Rainbow of Colors," later in this chapter, for details about customizing colors and gradients.)

- ✔ **Stroke Color:** Determines the color of the stroke (the outline) of the rectangle. Click the Stroke Color box — either in the Property inspector or in the Colors section of the Tools panel — and select a color from the palette.

- ✔ **Black and White:** Sets the stroke color to black and the fill color to white. Click the Black and White button in the Colors section of the Tools panel.

- ✔ **No Color:** Sets either the stroke color or the fill color (whichever tool is pressed) to no color. You have to click either the Stroke Color box or the Fill Color box before you click the No Color box.

- ✔ **Swap Colors:** Switches the stroke and fill colors.

- ✔ **Round Rectangle Radius modifier:** Creates a rectangle with rounded corners. (It's located in the Options section of the Tools panel.) Click this tool to open the Rectangle Settings dialog box, where you can set the radius of corners in points; then click OK to close the dialog box. The rectangle that you draw has nicely rounded corners.

You can also specify the dimensions of the rectangle in advance. Select the Rectangle tool, press Alt (Windows)/Option (Mac), and click the Stage. The Rectangle Settings dialog box opens, but this time it includes Width and Height text boxes that you can use to get exactly the size rectangle that you want. When you click OK, the rectangle appears immediately. You can then move it to the location that you want.

If you want to create a rectangle with no fill, choose the Rectangle tool, open the Fill Color box, and click the box with the diagonal line in the upper-right corner of the Color palette. To create a rectangle with a fill but no outline, choose the Rectangle tool, click the Stroke Color tool, and choose the box with the diagonal line at the top of the palette.

## Be an egg

To draw an oval, choose the Oval tool from the Tools panel. Click the Stage at one corner of the oval and drag to the opposite corner. (Ovals don't really have corners, but you get the idea after you try one or two.) Then release the mouse button. To create a perfect circle, press and hold Shift while you drag.

After you click the Oval tool, you can change the line color, type, and weight in the same way as we describe in the "Setting the stroke type" section, earlier in this chapter, for the Pencil tool. You can set the colors as we describe in the preceding section on drawing rectangles.

You can specify the exact width and height of the oval. Select the Oval tool, press Alt (Windows)/Option (Mac), and click on the Stage. The Oval Settings dialog box opens. Use the Width and Height text boxes to specify the size that you want, and click OK to create the oval.

# Mixing and Matching Shapes

After you create shapes on the Stage, you need to understand what happens when two objects touch. It's a little weird, but you soon see how flexible the Flash drawing tools are. Two basic rules exist about objects that touch.

On the other hand, Flash 8 has a new object-drawing model that lets you keep your objects whole. We discuss both scenarios in the following sections. (If you're trying to follow the next two sections and the objects you draw have blue boundaries around them, you're using the object-drawing model. To turn the object-drawing model on and off, click the Object Drawing button in the Options section of the Tools panel.)

## *Cutting up shapes*

The first rule is that when you use the Pencil or Line tool to draw a line that intersects any other shape or line, the line acts like a knife to cut the other shape or line. The line that you draw is also cut into segments. You don't see the effect until you try to select or move one of the objects. Suppose that you want to draw a broken heart. You can draw the breaking line by using the Pencil tool. You now have several objects, and you can easily move apart the two halves of the heart. In the second heart (see Figure 3-6), we erased the line and separated the halves of the heart.

**Figure 3-6:**
Intersect
any shape
with a line,
and the line
splits the
shape and
is itself
segmented.

## *Placing objects on top of each other*

The second rule about objects that touch is that when you place one shape on top of another, the top shape replaces whatever is beneath it. Again, you can see the results only when you try to select or move the shapes. But now it gets a little complicated:

- ✔ If the two shapes are the same color, they merge together into one combined shape.
- ✔ If the two shapes are different colors, they remain separate.

Figure 3-7 shows a circle and a triangle on the left. They are the same color. On the right, you can see the result after moving the circle down over the triangle. Presto! It's an ice cream cone. If you try to select the shape, it's now one object.

**Figure 3-7:**
Build
complex
shapes by
combining
basic
shapes of
the same
color.

When you combine shapes of different colors, you create cutouts. Rather than add the shapes together, the top shape just replaces the area beneath it. Figure 3-8 shows how you can create a cutout. We display a grid on the Stage (find more about that in Chapter 4) so that you can see that the image on the right is a cutout.

**Figure 3-8:**
A cutout.
There's a
hole in the
bucket!

To create a cutout effect, follow these steps:

1. **Create two separate shapes of different colors.**

2. **Move one shape on top of another shape.**

3. **Deselect the shape that you moved by clicking anywhere off the shape.**

4. **Select the top shape again and drag it away from the bottom shape to create the cutout.**

See Chapter 4 for details on selecting and moving objects.

## Keeping objects safe and secure

You can now use the *object-drawing model* to keep your objects safe from cutups, replacements, and cutouts.

The object-drawing model is new for Flash 8. When you draw using this model, objects maintain their integrity — no dishonest objects here! Other objects on top of or beneath these objects do not cut up, cut out, or merge with them.

To draw any object with the object-drawing model, follow these steps:

1. **Choose any drawing tool from the Tools panel.**

2. **Click the Object Drawing modifier in the Options section so that the button has a white area around it (Windows) or the button darkens (Mac).**

   You click the modifier again to turn off the Object Drawing modifier.

3. **Draw your object.**

   Your object now has a blue rectangular bounding box around it. This bounding box is similar to the one you see when you turn objects into a symbol (as we explain in Chapter 7) or group objects (see Chapter 4 for more information).

If you change your mind and don't want your object to stay separate from touching objects, select the object and choose Modify➪Break Apart.

# Creating Curves with the Pen

The Pen lets you draw *Bezier* curves, also called splines. Bezier curves are named after the French mathematician Pierre Bézier, who first described them. By using the Pen tool, you can create smooth curves that flow into each other. You can also create straight lines.

You can set preferences for the Pen tool by choosing Edit➪Preferences (Windows) or Flash➪Preferences (Mac) and clicking the Drawing category. We suggest enabling Show Pen Preview to display a preview of the line or curve while you draw. This setting helps you get a better idea of what the result will be. Click OK when you finish setting your preferences.

To create a line or curve, choose the Pen tool from the Tools panel. What you do next depends on whether you want to draw a straight line or a curve. The following sections show you how to draw both.

## Drawing straight lines

To draw a straight line with the Pen tool, follow these steps:

1. **To create a line segment, click the start point and then click the end point.**

2. **Continue to add line segments by clicking additional points.**

3. **Double-click to complete the process. You can also Ctrl+click (Windows) or ⌘+click (Mac) anywhere off the line.**

   Flash previews segments in a color that depends on the layer you're working on — see the color of the square next to the current layer as shown on the Timeline. (Chapter 6 explains layers in full.) When you choose another tool, Flash displays Beziers in the current stroke color.

Close a figure by pointing near the start point. You see a small circle. Click the start point, and Flash closes the figure. Flash fills in the shape with the current fill color.

## Drawing curves

Drawing curves with the Pen tool involves a couple of steps, depending on the complexity of the curve that you want to create. To draw a curve with the Pen tool, follow these steps:

1. **Click where you want to start and drag the mouse in the desired direction and distance for the start of the curve, as shown in Figure 3-9(a). Then release the mouse button.**

   You see a *tangent line* that defines both the direction and length, as shown in Figure 3-9(b).

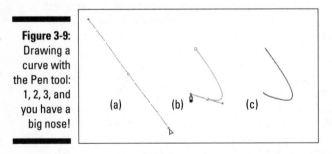

**Figure 3-9:**
Drawing a curve with the Pen tool: 1, 2, 3, and you have a big nose!

(a)  (b)  (c)

2. **To create one curve, move the mouse cursor to the desired end of the curve; then double-click to end the curve, as shown in Figure 3-9(c).**

   If you set preferences to show a preview of the curve (as we explain earlier in the section "Creating Curves with the Pen"), you also see a stretchy line attached to your mouse cursor that previews the shape.

3. **To continue to draw curves, again click and drag in the desired direction, release the mouse button, and move the mouse cursor to wherever you want the end of the next curve to be. Double-click to end the curve.**

For both lines and curves, you can press and hold Shift to constrain the lines or curves (the tangent lines) to 45-degree angles.

Drawing curves with the Pen tool takes practice, but you soon get the hang of it.

# Getting Artistic with the Brush

The Brush tool lets you create artistic effects that look like painting. You can adjust the size and shape of the brush, and if you have a pressure-sensitive pen and tablet, you can adjust the width of the stroke by changing the pressure on the pen.

 To paint with the Brush tool, select the tool on the Tools panel and then click and drag anywhere on the Stage. Press and hold Shift while you brush to keep your strokes either horizontal or vertical. The brush doesn't have a stroke (line) color. The brush creates only fills. Use the Fill Color drop-down list in the Property inspector or in the Colors section of the Tools panel to select a fill color.

When you choose the Brush tool, the Brush modifiers appear in the Options section of the Tools panel, as shown in Figure 3-10. We discuss the Object Drawing modifier (shown here in Figure 3-10) earlier in this chapter, in the "Keeping objects safe and secure" section.

**Figure 3-10:**
The brush modifiers control the size and shape of the brush as well as how the brush relates to existing images.

Options

Object Drawing ———————— Lock Fill

Brush Mode ————

Brush Size ————

Brush Shape ————

Use Pressure ———————— Use Tilt

## Brush Mode modifier

The Brush Mode modifier determines how the brush relates to existing objects on the Stage. Here are your choices for brush mode. (Figure 3-11 shows some examples.)

- **Paint Normal:** You just paint away, oblivious to anything else. Use this setting when you don't need to worry about other objects.

- **Paint Fills:** You paint fills and empty areas of the Stage. The paint doesn't cover lines. Note that your lines seem to be covered while you paint, but when you release the mouse button, they reappear.

- **Paint Behind:** You paint behind existing objects, but only blank areas of the Stage. While you paint, the brush seems to cover everything, but when you release the mouse button, your existing objects reappear. You can messily paint over your objects, knowing that they won't be affected.

- **Paint Selection:** You paint only a filled-in area that you previously selected. While you paint, your existing objects are covered, but they reappear when you release the mouse button. You don't need to worry about painting within the lines because Flash fills only the selected area.

- **Paint Inside:** You paint inside lines. Only the fill where you start brushing is painted. Paint Inside also paints an empty area on the Stage if that's where you start brushing. Again, at first the paint seems to cover up everything, but when you release the mouse button, Flash keeps your paint nice and neat, inside the lines — like every little kid learns in kindergarten.

## Brush Size drop-down list

Click the Brush Size drop-down list and select a size from the list of circles. This list defines the width of the brush. If you use a brush mode that helps you draw neatly, such as Paint Selection, you don't need to be too concerned with the size of the brush. On the other hand, if you're creating an artistic effect by using Paint Normal mode, the width of the brush is important.

## Brush Shape drop-down list

Flash offers several brush shapes you can choose from. Click the Brush Shape drop-down list and choose one of the shapes. Each shape produces a different effect, especially when you paint at an angle — you just need to try them out to see what works best. Figure 3-12 shows a honey jar drawn with various brush shapes.

Original corn

Corn with worms
— Paint Normal

Corn with bad kernels
— Paint Fills

**Figure 3-11:**
Set the
brush mode
when using
the Brush
tool to get
the effect
you want.

Corn with background
— Paint Behind

Sheath with gray gradient
— Paint Selection

Corn with bad kernels
— Paint Inside

**Figure 3-12:**
Each brush
shape
creates a
different
effect —
especially at
the ends of
the stroke.

## Pressure and Tilt modifiers

If you have a pressure-sensitive pen and tablet, Flash also displays a Pressure modifier so that you can vary the width of your strokes according to the pressure that you put on your pen while you draw. Click the Use Pressure button (refer to Figure 3-10) to turn on this feature.

Flash fully supports pressure-sensitive pens and adds some unusual features, such as the ability to use the opposite end of the pen to erase — just like a real pencil. Figure 3-13 shows this type of pen and tablet.

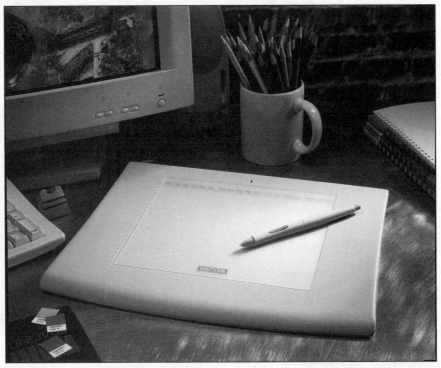

**Figure 3-13:** This Wacom pen and tablet set is easier to draw with than a mouse and enables you to easily vary the brush width as you draw.

*Photo courtesy of Scott Rawlings of Wacom*

A pressure-sensitive pen works together with a tablet to help you draw in Flash. The tablet tracks the movement and pressure of the pen while you draw. You can also use the pen as a mouse to choose menu and dialog box items. In other words, if you want, you can use the pen for all your Flash work. Alternatively, you can use the pen and tablet just for drawing and use the mouse when you want to work with menus and dialog boxes.

The Tilt modifier varies the angle of your brush stroke when you vary the angle of the stylus on the tablet. For example, holding the stylus straight up and down produces a different-shape brush stroke from the one that you get if you hold the stylus at a 45-degree angle to the tablet.

Use the Tilt modifier for fine control over your brush strokes. Click the Use Tilt button in the Options section of the Tools panel to turn on this feature. You see the effect most clearly with a large brush size and one of the narrow brush shapes. When you start to draw, change the angle of the stylus to the tablet. Watch the cursor shape turn, giving you a hint as to the shape of the brush stroke. Try brushing at a few angles to see how this works.

See the section "A Rainbow of Colors," later in this chapter, for an explanation of the Lock Fill modifier, one of the brush tool's modifiers.

## Brush smoothing

Smoothing brush strokes is similar to smoothing pencil strokes. You can finely adjust how much your brush strokes are smoothed after you finish drawing them. You can set smoothing anywhere from 0 to 10.

To set brush smoothing, follow these steps:

1. **Click the Brush tool and open the Property inspector (choose Window⇨Properties⇨Properties).**
2. **Click the Expand arrow at the lower-right corner.**
3. **Use the Smoothing text box or slider to set a new value.**

   The default value is 5. The lower values change your strokes less. Therefore, if you set the Smoothing to 0, the brush stroke is closest to what you actually drew. Lower values create more vectors, resulting in a larger file size for your movie. The higher values smooth and simplify your strokes more. A setting of 10 creates strokes that are smoother.

# Pouring on the Paint

The Paint Bucket creates fills that fill shapes with color. You might want to fill an enclosed area that you created with the Line or Pencil tool. You can also fill enclosed shapes created with the Pen or Brush tool, as we explain earlier in this chapter.

The Paint Bucket is also handy for changing existing fills. You can change the color as well as fiddle around with gradient and bitmap fills. (See Chapter 4 for more on editing fills.)

To use the Paint Bucket, choose it from the Tools panel. Set the color by clicking the Fill Color tool and selecting a color. Alternatively, you can use the Fill Color drop-down list in the Property inspector.

Flash can fill areas that aren't completely closed. The Gap Size modifier (in the Options section of the Tools panel) determines how large of a gap Flash will overlook to fill in an almost enclosed area. Choices range from Don't Close Gaps to Close Large Gaps. Because *small* and *large* are relative terms, you might have to experiment to get the result that you want. After you choose an option from the Gap Size modifier, click any enclosed or almost enclosed area to fill it, as shown in Figure 3-14.

**Figure 3-14:**
You can fill areas that aren't completely closed by using the Gap Size modifier.

After you use the Paint Bucket to fill a shape created with another tool, you can delete the outline of the shape and keep just the fill.

## Strokes, Ink

You use the Ink Bottle tool to create an outline on an existing shape. You can also use the Ink Bottle tool to change an existing line (also called a *stroke*).

To use the Ink Bottle tool, click it on the Tools panel. Click the Stroke Color tool to select a color. Use the Property inspector, as we explain earlier in this chapter (in the discussion of the Pencil tool) to choose a line thickness and line style. Then click anywhere on the shape. If the shape has no existing line, Flash adds the line. If the shape has a line, Flash changes its color, width, or style to the settings that you specified in the Property inspector.

# A Rainbow of Colors

Flash offers you lots of color options. You can work with the solid colors that come with Flash. By default, Flash uses a palette of 216 colors that are Web-safe, which means that they look good on all Web browsers and monitors. Or, in these days when most computers can displays millions of colors, you can create your own colors.

## Solid citizens

When you choose either the Stroke Color or Fill Color tool, Flash opens the *current Color palette,* which is the active set of colors that Flash uses.

### Creating new colors or editing existing colors

Flash provides two ways for you to specify your own colors:

✔ Choose the Stroke Color or Fill Color tool from the Tools panel and click the Colors Window button in the upper-right corner of the palette to open the Color dialog box.

✔ Choose Window➪Color Mixer to open the Color Mixer panel.

These two methods duplicate each other; here, we explain how to use the Color Mixer panel, as shown in Figure 3-15.

Stroke Color
Fill Color
Fill style

No Color
Black and White
Swap Colors
Color specification
text boxes
Transparency
(alpha) value

Options menu

Color space

Brightness
control

Hex text box

Current/
previous
color box

**Figure 3-15:**
Use the
Color Mixer
panel to
create your
own colors.

If you select an object before you use the Color Mixer panel, the object's color changes immediately when you change the color in the Color Mixer panel.

To create a new color or edit an existing color, follow these steps:

1. **Click the menu icon in the upper-right corner of the Color Mixer panel to open the pop-up menu; then choose the color mode.**

   *RGB* specifies a color according to red, green, and blue components; *HSB* specifies a color by hue, saturation, and brightness. You can also define a color by using *hexadecimal notation,* which is the color system used on the Web: Just type the hexadecimal code in the Hex text box of the Color Mixer panel.

2. **Click the Stroke Color or Fill Color icon to specify which color you want to change — stroke or fill.**

   Click the icon to the left of the Stroke Color or Fill Color box — not the box itself, because if you click the box, you open the Color palette.

3. **Type the color specs in the text boxes, use the sliders to drag to the desired color, or find a color in the color space that's close to the one that you want, and then click that color.**

4. **Set the level of opacity/transparency (also called *alpha*) by using the Alpha slider or by typing a number in the Alpha box.**

   A setting of 0% is completely transparent; 100% is opaque.

5. **If you want to create a new color swatch, click the Options menu icon in the upper-right corner of the panel and choose Add Swatch.**

   Flash adds the new color to the Color palette so that you can access it from the Stroke Color or Fill Color boxes on the Tools panel, the Property inspector, or the Color Swatches panel.

### Managing colors

If you've added or changed colors, you can save this new palette. (A *palette* is a set of colors.) You can then save the palette for use in other Flash movies or import a Color palette from another Flash movie (so that you don't have to bother creating the colors again). Color palettes are saved as .clr files and are called *Flash Color Set* files. To save a color palette, choose Save Colors from the Color Swatches option menu. (Choose Window⇨Color Swatches to open the Color Swatches panel and click the option menu icon in the upper-right corner of the panel to display the menu.) In the Export Color Swatch dialog box, choose a location for the file, name it, and click Save.

Macromedia Fireworks and Adobe Photoshop use Color Table files (ACT files), and Flash can import and save these as well.

To import a Color palette that you've saved, use the option menu of the Color Swatches panel. Choose Add Colors if you want to append this imported palette to an existing palette. Choose Replace Colors if you want the imported palette to replace an existing palette. You can use the same Color Swatches panel option menu to manage your Color palettes. Choose from the following options:

✔ **Duplicate Swatch:** Creates a duplicate of a swatch. Do this when you want to create your own color and use an existing color as a basis.

✔ **Delete Swatch:** Deletes a color.

✔ **Load Default Colors:** Replaces the active Color palette with the Flash default palette.

✔ **Save as Default:** Saves the active Color palette as the default palette for any new Flash movies that you create.

✔ **Clear Colors:** Clears all colors except black and white — for when you really want to start from scratch.

✔ **Web 216:** Loads the Web-safe, 216-color palette.

✔ **Sort by Color:** Sorts the display of colors by luminosity.

## Gradient colors

So you're bored with solid colors and want something more interesting. *Gradients* are combinations of two or more colors that gradually blend from one to another. Flash can create gradients of as many as 16 colors — quite a feat. Gradients are always used as fills. The gradient can be linear or *radial* (concentric), as shown in Figure 3-16. Because the figure isn't in color, it can't begin to show you the glory of gradients.

**Figure 3-16:** Linear and radial gradients make your graphics much more interesting than plain solid colors.

Linear gradient      Radial gradient

Flash offers a few standard gradients that you can find at the bottom of the Color palette. But you often need a more customized look, and Flash has the tools to create just about any gradient that you want.

**TIP**

Radial gradients look best on curved objects. A circle suddenly looks like a sphere when you fill it with a radial gradient. Radial gradients give the impression of light highlights if you put white at the center of the gradient. Linear gradients look best on straight objects.

To create your own gradient, follow these steps:

1. **Choose Window⇨Color Mixer to open the Color Mixer panel (refer to Figure 3-15). Then choose Linear or Radial from the Fill Style drop-down list.**

   You see a gradient bar with color pointers that specify the colors of the gradient and where the gradient changes from one color to the next.

   If you select a fill before you use the Color Mixer panel, the object's fill color changes immediately when you change the gradient in the Color Mixer panel.

2. **To use an existing gradient as a starting point, click the Fill Color box on the Tools panel and choose a gradient from the bottom of the Color palette.**

   You can also choose Window⇨Color Swatches to open the Color Swatches panel and choose a gradient from the bottom of the Color palette there.

3. **To specify the color for each color pointer, click and hold the pointer and then release the mouse button (this is like a long mouse click); when the color swatches appear, select a color.**

   You can click the Fill Color box and select an existing color from the Color palette or specify a new color by using the methods that we describe in the earlier section, "Creating new colors or editing existing colors."

   Note that when you click a pointer, its point turns black to indicate that it's the active pointer. The square beneath the point displays the color pointer's current color.

4. **To change the number of colors in the gradient, add or delete color pointers.**

   To add a color pointer, click where you want the pointer to appear, just below the gradient bar. To delete a color pointer, drag it off the gradient bar.

5. **To adjust where the color changes, drag a color pointer to the left or right.**

6. **To add control over how colors are applied to a selected shape beyond the gradient, select one of the following *overflow modes* from the Overflow drop-down list:**

   - **Extend:** Extends the last or outermost gradient color past the end of the gradient.

   - **Reflect:** Fills the shape by mirroring the gradient pattern.

   - **Repeat:** Repeats the gradient from beginning to end.

Overflow modes are new for Flash 8. To use these effects, fill a shape with a gradient and then use the Gradient Transform tool to reduce the size of the gradient so that it no longer completely fills the shape. (We discuss the Gradient Transform tool in Chapter 4.) Then try out the three overflow modes to see the results. The overflow modes are only supported in the Flash 8 player.

Select the Linear RGB check box to create a gradient that complies with Scalable Vector Graphics (SVG) standards. SVG is an XML language for describing 2-D graphics.

7. **To save the gradient, click the menu icon in the upper-right corner of the Color Mixer panel and choose Add Swatch.**

The new gradient now appears in the Color palette of the Fill Color box on the Tools panel and in the Color Swatches panel. Go ahead and fill something with it!

You can also move a gradient's center and focal points, change its width and height, rotate it, scale it, skew it, and tile it. See Chapter 4 for more on editing gradients.

## Bitmap fills

You can create the coolest, weirdest fills by importing a bitmap graphic and using the bitmap to fill any shape. For a hypothetical Web site protesting genetically engineered foods, for example, we could find a bitmap of a bug (representing the Bt bacteria genetically engineered into corn) and use it to fill a graphic of corn. Figure 3-17 shows the result.

**Figure 3-17:**
You can fill any shape with a bitmap, repeated over and over and over. . . .

To use a bitmap graphic to fill a shape, follow these steps:

1. **Create the object or shape that you want to fill.**

2. **Choose File⇨Import⇨Import to Stage.**

   The Import dialog box opens.

3. **In the Import dialog box, choose the bitmap that you want to use as the fill and then click Open/Import.**

   The bitmap appears on the Stage. If necessary, move it to the desired location.

   We explain more about importing graphics in the section "The Import Business — Using Outside Graphics," at the end of this chapter.

4. **Choose Modify⇨Break Apart.**

   Flash breaks the bitmap into separate areas of color.

5. **Click the Eyedropper tool on the Tools panel.**

6. **Click the bitmap on the Stage.**

   Notice that the Fill Color tool on the Tools panel now shows a tiny picture of your bitmap. Flash also automatically switches you to the Paint Bucket tool so that you can immediately fill an object.

7. **Click inside the object that you want to fill.**

   Flash fills it with the bitmap. The bitmap is repeated over and over in an effect called *tiling*.

If you've already imported a bitmap, you can fill an object with the bitmap by using the Color Mixer panel. Follow these steps:

1. **Choose Bitmap from the Fill Style drop-down list.**

   Bitmaps in the movie appear as small tiles at the bottom of the Color Mixer panel.

2. **Click the Fill Color box if it isn't already selected.**

3. **Select the bitmap from the small bitmap tiles.**

4. **Choose the Paint Bucket tool from the Tools panel.**

5. **Click inside a closed object on the Stage.**

   You may need to scale the bitmap. See the section on transforming fills in Chapter 4 for details.

For either method of choosing a bitmap, you can choose the Brush tool (instead of using the Paint Bucket tool) and then brush with the bitmap. Use a thick-enough brush size so that the bitmap shows clearly.

## Locking a fill

Flash has another trick up its sleeve for gradient or bitmap fills. A *locked fill* looks as though the fill is behind your objects and the objects are just uncovering the fill. As a result, if you use the same fill for several objects, Flash locks the position of the fill across the entire drawing surface rather than fixing the fill individually for each object. Figure 3-18 shows an example of a locked fill. In this figure, you see some windows and portholes filled with a locked bitmap of the sky. Doesn't it look as though the sky is really outside the windows?

**Figure 3-18:**
When you lock a fill, the fill's pattern continues across the Stage, but appears only where you use it.

 To lock a fill, choose the Brush tool or the Paint Bucket tool with a gradient or bitmap fill, as we explain in the two preceding sections. Then click the Lock Fill modifier in the Options section of the Tools panel. Start painting where you want to place the center of the fill and continue to other areas.

# Drawing Precisely

If drawing in Flash seems too loosey-goosey to you, you need to know about a few features that can help you draw more precisely. Other programs do offer more precise tools, but Flash might have the tools that you need.

## The ruler rules

To help you get your bearings, you can choose View⇨Rulers to display the Flash ruler along the top and the left side of the Stage, as shown in Figure 3-19.

**Figure 3-19:**
Display the
ruler to help
you draw
more
precisely;
for more
control,
drag guides
onto the
Stage.

To give yourself more room to work while you create drawing objects on the Stage, you can hide the Timeline by choosing Window⇨Timeline. Do the same to display the Timeline again when you need to work with layers or start animating your work.

By default, the ruler is measured in *pixels*. Computer screens are measured by how many pixels they display horizontally and vertically. Pixels are useful for Web site work because Web browsers work with only this unit. A pixel, however, is not a fixed physical size because it depends on the resolution capacity and settings of your screen. You might find it easier to think in inches or millimeters.

You can set the ruler to the unit of measurement that is most helpful to you. Choose Modify⇨Document to open the Document Properties dialog box. From the Ruler Units drop-down list, choose one of the units (pixels, inches, points, centimeters, or millimeters) and click OK.

When the ruler is displayed, lines appear on the top and side rulers whenever you drag an object — either while creating it or editing it. For example, when you drag to create a rectangle, you see a line on each ruler telling you where you started and where you ended up. If you're moving the rectangle, Flash displays two lines on each ruler indicating the outside dimensions of the rectangle. You can easily move the rectangle one inch — or 50 pixels — to the left by looking at the lines on the top ruler.

## Using guides

Guides help you lay out the Stage more precisely. *Guides* (refer to Figure 3-19) are horizontal and vertical lines that you can use as drawing aids while you work. Don't worry — guides never appear in the published Flash Player file.

To use the guides, you must display the rulers, as we describe in the preceding section. To display guides, choose View⇨Guides⇨Show Guides. But that action simply turns on the Guides feature; you still don't see anything!

To display the guides, you need to drag them from the rulers. Drag from the left ruler to create a vertical guide, and drag from the top ruler to create a horizontal guide.

To customize the guides, choose View⇨Guides⇨Edit Guides to open the Guides dialog box, where you can choose the guide color or clear all the guides. To force objects to *snap to* (attach themselves to) the guides, select the Guides check box in the Guides dialog box. You can use the Snap Accuracy drop-down list in the Guides dialog box to choose how precisely Flash snaps to the guides.

To remove an individual guide, drag it back to its vertical or horizontal ruler. To lock the guides so that they don't move while you work, choose View⇨ Guides⇨Lock Guides.

## Working with the grid

You can display a grid on the Stage to help you draw more accurately and to gauge distances. The grid exists only to guide you — it never appears when the movie is printed or published on a Web site. Simply displaying the grid doesn't constrain your objects to points on the grid. Use the grid by itself when you want a visual guide for sizing, moving, and laying out the Stage.

To display the grid, choose View⇨Grid⇨Show Grid. Use the same command to hide the grid again. You can set the size of the grid squares. Choose View⇨ Grid⇨Edit Grid to open the Grid dialog box. You can also change the color of the grid lines here.

You can change the units of measurement used for the grid by choosing Modify⇨Document. In the Modify Document dialog box, select the unit that you want from the Ruler Units drop-down list and click OK.

## Snapping turtle

When you want even more precision, you can turn on snapping. *Snapping* tells Flash to snap objects to the intersections on the grid or to other objects. Usually, you want the grid on when you use snapping so that you can see the snap points.

To turn on snapping, choose the Selection tool and click the Snap modifier in the Options section of the Tools panel or Choose View➪Snapping➪Snap to Objects. To snap to the grid, choose View➪Snapping➪Snap to Grid. Use the same method to turn snapping off again.

Snapping pulls your cursor to the grid points and to existing objects while you work. You can take advantage of snapping both while drawing new objects and editing existing objects. When you have snapping on and select an object, Flash displays a small, black circle and snaps that circle to the grid points.

### Setting snap-to-grid preferences

 You can get downright picky about how Flash snaps to grid points. Do you want the end of a line (for example) to always snap, or should it snap only if it's close to a grid point or existing object? To set your preferences, choose View➪Grid➪Edit Grid. From the Snap Accuracy drop-down list, select one of the options, which range from Must Be Close to Always Snap.

### Setting snap-to-objects preferences

Because snapping applies to objects as well as grid points, you can separately set how Flash snaps to objects. Choose Edit➪Preferences (Windows) or Flash➪Preferences (Mac) and click the Drawing category. Click the Connect Lines drop-down list and select Must Be Close, Normal, or Can Be Distant. Although Flash calls this the Connect Lines setting, it affects rectangles and ovals as well as lines that you draw with the Line and Pencil tools.

This setting also affects how Flash recognizes horizontal and vertical lines and makes them perfectly horizontal or vertical. For example, the Can Be Distant setting adjusts a more angled line than the Must Be Close setting.

## Pixel, pixel on the wall

If the grid isn't precise enough, you can snap to pixels. Choose View➪ Snapping➪Snap to Pixels to toggle snapping to pixels on and off. If Snap to Pixels is on, when you zoom in to 400 percent or higher, Flash automatically displays the pixel grid. With Snap to Pixels on, all objects that you create or move snap to the pixel grid.

 When Snap to Pixels is on, you can press the C key to temporarily turn off pixel snapping. In the same situation, you can press the X key to temporarily hide the pixel grid (but not while you're in the process of drawing).

You can also precisely align existing objects. For more information, see Chapter 4.

# The Import Business — Using Outside Graphics

So maybe you're the lazy type — or totally without artistic talent — and you really need help. Flash hasn't given up on you completely. Rather than create your own graphics, you can use the work of others. Although Flash creates vector-based graphics, it can import both bitmap and vector graphic files.

When using others' artwork, be careful about copyright issues. For example, some graphics available on the Web can be used for personal, but not commercial, purposes. Most Web sites that offer graphics for downloading have a written statement explaining how you can use their graphics.

## Importing graphics

To import a graphic file, follow these steps:

1. **Choose File⇨Import⇨Import to Stage.**

   The Import dialog box opens.

2. **In the dialog box, locate and choose the file that you want.**

3. **Click Open/Import to open the file.**

   The file appears on the Stage. If the file is a bitmap, it also goes into the Library. To import a graphic file directly into the Library without displaying it on the Stage, choose File⇨Import⇨Import to Library.

A cool feature of Flash is its capability to recognize and import sequences of images. If the image file that you choose in the Import dialog box ends with a number and other files in the same folder have the same name but end with consecutive numbers (for example, an1, an2, and so on), Flash asks whether you want to import the entire sequence of files. Click Yes to import the sequence. Flash imports the images as successive frames on the active layer so that you can use them as the basis for animation. (Chapter 9 explains more about frames and animation.)

Table 3-1 provides a list of the types of files you can import into Flash.

| Table 3-1 | Files That Flash Can Import | |
|---|---|---|
| *File Type* | *Windows* | *Mac* |
| Adobe Illustrator (.eps, .ai) through version 10 | X | X |
| All PostScript, including Acrobat PDF (.eps, .pdf, .ai) | X | X |
| AutoCAD DXF (.dxf); 2-D only | X | X |
| Bitmap (.bmp) | X | X* |
| Enhanced Metafile (.emf) | X | |
| Flash Player 6/7 (.swf) | X | X |
| FreeHand (.fh*); versions 7 to 11 | X | X |
| FutureSplash Player (.spl) | X | X |
| GIF/animated GIF (.gif) | X | X |
| JPEG (.jpg) | X | X |
| MacPaint (.pntg)* | X | X |
| Photoshop (.psd)* | X | X |
| PICT (.pct, .pic) | | X |
| PNG (.png) | X | X |
| QuickTime image (.qtif)* | X | X |
| Silicon Graphics Image (.sgi)* | X | X |
| Targa (.tga)* | X | X |
| TIFF (.tif)* | X | X |
| Windows Metafile (.wmf) | X | |

*Only if QuickTime 4 or later is installed

You can also simply copy and paste graphics. From the other application, copy the graphic to the Clipboard; then return to Flash and choose Edit⇨ Paste. However, in some cases, you might lose transparency when using this method. See Chapter 13 for details on exporting objects.

## Using imported graphics

Vector graphics from any drawing program become a grouped object that you can use like any other Flash object. The .wmf format, which is a Windows

vector graphics format, also imports in this way. These formats work especially well when imported into Flash. You can sometimes find .wmf graphics
in clip art collections and on the Web.

You can import text from a text editor, and Flash turns it into a Flash text
object so that you can edit and format it within Flash. See Chapter 5 for more
on text.

When you import a bitmap graphic, you often need to take some steps before
you can use the graphic in your Flash file. You can manipulate your graphics
in several ways to make them more Flash friendly:

- **Delete the background:** In many cases, Flash imports not only the shape
  you want, but also a rectangular background that you don't want. To get
  rid of that background, deselect the imported object, select just the rectangular background, and press Delete. If that doesn't work, read on.

- **Ungroup the graphic:** Ungrouping separates grouped elements into individual elements. Ungrouping retains most of the features of your graphic.
  Select the graphic and choose Modify⇨Ungroup. If you find that you still
  can't work with your graphic properly, read the next item.

- **Break apart the graphic:** Break imported graphics to separate them into
  ungrouped, editable elements. Breaking apart is useful for reducing the
  file size of graphics that you import. Breaking apart converts bitmaps to
  fills, converts text to letters and outlines, and breaks the link between an
  Object Linking and Embedding (OLE) embedded object and its source
  application. In other words, the Break Apart command is a powerful tool.
  Select the graphic and choose Modify⇨Break Apart. You may have to
  repeat the process to break the graphic completely apart.

- **Trace the bitmap:** Flash can work magic. If you want total control within
  Flash, convert a bitmap to a vector graphic.

To trace a bitmap, follow these steps:

1. **Import the bitmap — don't deselect it or perform any other action
   on it.**

2. **Choose Modify⇨Bitmap⇨Trace Bitmap.**

   The Trace Bitmap dialog box opens.

3. **In the Color Threshold text box, type a number to represent the
   threshold.**

   The higher the number, the fewer the colors you get in the final vector
   graphic. For close results, try a value of 10.

4. **In the Minimum Area text box, type a number to represent the number
   of nearby pixels that Flash considers when assigning a color to a pixel.**

   For greatest fidelity, try a value of 1.

5. **From the Curve Fit drop-down list, select an option to represent how smoothly Flash draws the outlines.**

   For the most exact results, select Pixels.

6. **From the Corner Threshold drop-down list, select an option to represent how Flash reproduces sharp edges.**

   For sharpest results, choose Many Corners.

7. **Click OK to close the Trace Bitmap dialog box, and then deselect the graphic to see the result.**

When you import a bitmap graphic, Flash places the graphic in the current movie's Library. For best results, don't delete the original graphic from the Library, even if you have modified it. Flash continues to refer to the graphic after you have converted it to a symbol. (Chapter 2 explains all about the Library. See Chapter 7 for our total wisdom on symbols.)

Whether you created your graphics in Flash or imported them, you probably need to edit them in many ways. Chapter 4 explains the details of editing objects.

# Chapter 4

# You Are the Object Editor

*T*his chapter tells you all you need to know about editing objects. You can manipulate objects in a zillion ways to suit your artistic fancy. The Flash editing tools can give you precisely the results that you want. Sometimes you need to edit because you made a mistake (rarely, of course), but often editing is just part of the creation process. You might also find that you have to alter imported graphics so that they fit into the scheme of things.

## Selecting Objects

Before you can edit any object on the Stage, you need to select it. Flash offers many ways to select objects. After you get the hang of using the Flash selection tools, you'll find them efficient and easy to use.

## *Selecting with the Selection tool*

To select an object, click the black Selection tool and click the object. That sounds pretty basic. But just when you thought it was safe to skip the rest of this section, we add some ifs and buts, so read on.

What is an *object?* If you draw a shape that includes an outline (also called a *line* or a *stroke*) and a fill, such as a filled-in circle, you have two objects — the outline and the fill.

Most of these selection pointers don't work when you use the object drawing model for creating objects. When you use the object drawing model to draw an object, such as a rectangle, both the stroke and the fill are considered one object, so you can't select the stroke or the fill individually.

Here are some pointers for selecting objects:

✔ **If the object doesn't have an outline and is just a fill,** you're home free. Click the object with the Selection tool, and it's selected.

✔ **If the object has an outline and a fill,** clicking the fill selects only the fill. The outline remains deselected. To select both the fill and the outline, double-click the object.

✔ **To select the entire object,** you can use the Selection tool to create a selection box. Click at one corner and drag to an opposite corner, making sure that the bounding box completely encloses the object or objects that you want to select, as shown in Figure 4-1.

✔ **To select just an outline,** click the outline with the Selection tool. Still, you never know when an outline is really several objects, like the one in Figure 4-1, which is made up of several curves. To select the entire outline, double-click it.

**Figure 4-1:**
You can
create a
bounding
box by
using the
Selection
tool to
select one
or more
objects.

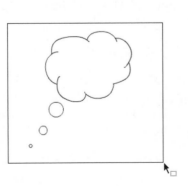

✔ **To select several unconnected objects,** select one object, press and hold the Shift key, and select additional objects. When you press Shift, you can add to already selected objects and select as many objects as you want.

To deselect selected objects, click any blank area.

So you're happily drawing away, using the various drawing tools. Then you want to select one of the objects, but you forget to change to the Selection tool. Oops! You draw another object by accident. Immediately, choose Edit⇨ Undo. Then use one of the Flash arrow shortcuts:

✔ Press the V key to switch to the Selection tool.

✔ To temporarily switch to the Selection tool while you're using another tool, hold the Ctrl (Windows) or ⌘ (Mac) key while you select an object or objects.

## Lassoing your objects

For you rodeo types, you can lasso your objects so that they can't escape. The Lasso tool creates a customized select area and selects everything inside. Use the Lasso tool when you want to select a number of objects that are near other objects that you want to remain free.

To lasso objects, click the Lasso tool on the Tools panel.

To lasso freehand, make sure that the Polygon Mode modifier (in the Options section of the Tools panel) is not selected. Click anywhere on the Stage and drag around the objects that you want to select. Flash creates a selection area while you drag. Release the mouse button close to where you started it to close the lasso's loop, as shown in Figure 4-2.

**Figure 4-2:**
Lasso
freehand to
select only
the objects
you want.

You might find that freehand lassoing is somewhat hard to control. If you tend to inadvertently cut across objects rather than glide around them, use the Polygon Mode modifier to draw straight-line polygons instead — like a lasso with a very stiff rope.

To lasso by using straight lines, follow these steps:

1. **Click to choose the Lasso tool.**
2. **Click the Polygon Mode modifier in the Options section of the Tools panel.**
3. **Click where you want the first line of the polygon to start.**
4. **Click again where you want the first line to end.**
5. **Continue to click, creating line segments as you go.**
6. **Double-click when you finish lassoing the objects.**

## Selecting everything in one fell swoop

Suppose that you want to select or deselect all objects at one time. Flash has some handy shortcuts to help you do that:

✔ **To select everything:** Press Ctrl+A (Windows) or ⌘+A (Mac). Or choose Edit➪Select All. The Select All command selects all objects on all layers except for objects on locked or hidden layers. (See Chapter 6 for an explanation of layers.)

✔ **To select everything on one layer:** Click the layer name.

✔ **To deselect everything:** The easiest method is to click off the Stage or on any blank area of the Stage. Alternatively, you can press Ctrl+Shift+A (Windows) or ⌘+Shift+A (Mac). Or choose Edit➪Deselect All. The Deselect All command deselects all objects on all layers.

To lock a group or symbol so that it can't be selected or edited, select the group or symbol and choose Modify➪Arrange➪Lock. To unlock a group or symbol, choose Modify➪Arrange➪Unlock All. (See the section "Getting Grouped," later in this chapter, to find out about groups. Chapter 7 is all about symbols.)

# Moving, Copying, and Deleting

The most common changes that you make to objects are to move them, copy them, and delete them. Usually, moving, copying, and deleting are straightforward tasks, but Flash has a few tricks up its sleeve, so keep on truckin'.

## *Movin' on down the road*

Before you can move, you have to select. After you select your object or objects, place the mouse cursor over any selected object until your cursor displays the dreaded four-headed arrow. (Okay, most people don't dread it at all.) Then click and drag to wherever you're going. Press Shift while you drag to constrain the movement to a 45-degree angle.

### *Moving precisely with Snap Align*

When you drag an object, you notice vertical and horizontal dashed lines when your object approaches existing objects. This Snap Align feature displays temporary dashed lines when you move objects to show you when the edges of objects are aligned, both vertically and horizontally, with existing objects.

Snap alignment is great for quickly aligning two objects without using the Align panel. While you drag a selected object, the dashed lines appear when you move an object in alignment with an existing object, as shown in Figure 4-3. You also see the lines when you drag an object close to any edge of the Stage.

**Figure 4-3:**
Snap
alignment
visually
displays
alignment
between
objects
while you
move them.

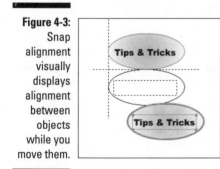

To turn on snap alignment (although it is on by default), choose View➪ Snapping➪Snap Align. You see a check mark next to the Snap Align item. Repeat the process to turn off snap alignment.

You can customize your snap alignment settings. Choose View➪Snapping➪ Edit Snapping to open the Edit Snapping dialog box. Then click the Advanced button to expand the dialog box. Figure 4-4 shows the expanded dialog box.

In the Edit Snapping dialog box, you can also turn on snap alignment for the centers of objects, for easy centering of objects. Mark both check boxes in the Center Alignment section of the Edit Snapping dialog box.

**Figure 4-4:**
The Edit
Snapping
dialog box
makes your
snap
alignments
snap to your
orders.

Flash assumes that a border exists around the edge of the Stage. To change
the border width, type a different number in the Stage Border text box. To
change the accuracy for alignment between objects, type a number in the
Horizontal and Vertical text boxes in the Object Spacing section of the dialog
box. Click OK when you're done to close the dialog box.

You can also use the grid and turn on the snapping feature for moving and
copying objects. (See Chapter 3 to find out about the grid and snapping.) For
example, you can attach one object to another by moving your first object until
it snaps to the second, using the small black circle at the cursor as a guide.

The snap align feature aligns objects by their edges. Object snapping aligns
objects by their transformation point. See the section "Changing the
Transformation Point," later in this chapter for more information.

You can also use the four arrow keys on your keyboard to move a selected
object or objects. Each press of an arrow key moves the selection one screen
pixel in the direction of the arrow. Press Shift plus an arrow key to move the
selection by 10 screen pixels.

### Moving with the Clipboard

You can move an object by cutting to the Clipboard and pasting if you want
to move the object to another layer, scene, file, or application. After you
select the object or objects, choose Edit⇨Cut. Alternatively, press Ctrl+X
(Windows) or ⌘+X (Mac). Choose another layer or scene or open another file
and do one of the following:

✔ **To paste the selection in the center of the display:** Choose Edit⇨Paste
   or press Ctrl+V (Windows)/⌘+V (Mac).

✔ **To paste the selection in the same position relative to the Stage:** Choose
   Edit⇨Paste in Place or press Ctrl+Shift+V (Windows)/⌘+Shift+V (Mac).

### Moving with the Property inspector

If you want to place objects precisely, use the Property inspector. After you select an object or objects, choose Window➪Properties➪Properties and then click the Expand/Collapse arrow to display the expanded panel, as shown in Figure 4-5.

**Figure 4-5:**
Use the expanded Property inspector to place objects precisely.

Use the X and Y text boxes to specify the location. The X setting specifies horizontal distance; the Y setting specifies vertical distance — both are measured from the top-left corner of the Stage.

### Moving with the Info panel

You can also use the Info panel to specify the X and Y positions of objects. Choose Window➪Info to open the panel, as shown in Figure 4-6. You can use the grid next to the X and Y text boxes to measure either from the upper-left corner or the center of the selection — just click in the desired reference point on the grid. Flash uses the units that you specify in the Document Properties dialog box. (See the section in Chapter 3 on drawing precisely for information on setting the units.)

**Figure 4-6:**
The Info panel.

Remember that moving an object onto another existing object on the same layer either joins it (if the objects are the same color) or cuts it out (if they are different colors) — unless you drew the object in object-drawing mode. See the section in Chapter 3 on mixing and matching shapes for more information.

## Aligning objects with the Align panel

The Snap Align feature, as we explain in the section "Moving precisely with Snap Align," earlier in this chapter, is the quick way to align objects. However, for more options and precision, use the Align panel. The Align panel gives you the tools to line up two or more objects vertically or horizontally and also lets you put equal space between three or more objects. Align and space objects to make your Flash movie look professional, as opposed to something that you might create at 3 a.m. when your vision is too blurry for you to see straight.

To align objects, select the objects and choose Window➪Align to open the Align panel, as shown in Figure 4-7.

Choose the option that you want in the panel to align objects or distribute them. For example, you can align objects along their tops, their left sides, or any other direction. You can match the size of objects by using the Match Size buttons or make the spaces between objects the same with the Space buttons. Experiment with the options in this panel until you get the results that you want.

**Figure 4-7:**
Use the
Align panel
to line up
and evenly
distribute
objects.

To perfectly center one object on the Stage, select it and open the Align panel. Click the To Stage button. Click both the Align Vertical Center and the Align Horizontal Center buttons. Flash centers the object on the Stage. A quicker way is to cut and paste the object because Flash automatically pastes objects at the center of the display (which is at the middle of the Stage if you haven't panned or scrolled the display).

If you use the To Stage button, be sure to deselect it when you're done because it can cause unexpected results the next time you use it.

## Copying objects

After you spend loads of time creating a cool graphic, you might want to copy it all over the place. The easiest way is to clone it directly by dragging. Just select the object and press Ctrl (Windows) or Option (Mac) while you drag. Flash makes a copy and moves it wherever you drag.

You can also copy objects to the Clipboard. Select an object or objects and choose Edit➪Copy or press Ctrl+C (Windows) or ⌘+C (Mac). You can paste the selection on the same layer or move it to another layer, scene, or file by using one of these techniques:

- ✔ **To paste the selection in the center of the display:** Choose Edit➪Paste or press Ctrl+V (Windows) or ⌘+V (Mac).

- ✔ **To paste the selection in the same position relative to the Stage:** Choose Edit➪Paste in Place. If you're on the same layer, scene, and file, you now have two copies, one on top of the other. The new object is selected, so you can immediately drag it to a new location.

Because Flash pastes objects from the Clipboard to the exact center of the display, cutting and pasting is a great technique for centering objects on top of each other. For example, if you want to create two concentric circles, one on top of the other, create the circles in separate locations. Cut and paste the larger circle first, and then the smaller circle. You now have perfect concentric circles, and you can move them together to the desired location. This technique works only if the Stage is at the center of your display — that is, if you haven't scrolled the display.

When you paste a new object, be sure to move the new object right away if it covers an existing object on the same layer. If you deselect the new object, it either joins the existing object (if the objects are the same color) or cuts it out (if they're different colors). Of course, that might be your intention. See the section in Chapter 3 on mixing and matching shapes for more information, including how to avoid the joining and cutout behavior.

## Makin' objects go away

Making objects go away is easy. Just select them and press Delete or Backspace in Windows/Delete or Clear on the Mac.

# Making Shapes More Shapely

Suppose that you created an object and now you want to tweak it a bit. Flash has many techniques to help you perfect your artwork, and you can modify both lines and fills.

# Reshaping shapes and outlines

The Selection tool can do more than select objects — it can also reshape them — as long as you didn't create them using the object drawing model. When you reshape with the Selection tool, you do *not* select the object.

To reshape an outline or a fill, choose the Selection tool and place the mouse cursor near the object or on the edge of the object:

✔ If you see a corner next to the cursor, you can move, lengthen, or shorten an end point, as shown on the left side of Figure 4-8.

✔ If you see a curve next to the cursor, you can reshape a curve, as shown on the right side of in Figure 4-8.

**Figure 4-8:**
The
Selection
tool
modifies
end points
and curves.

Click and drag in the desired direction. Flash temporarily displays a black drag line to show you what the result will look like when you release the mouse button. If you don't like the result, choose Edit⇨Undo — or press Ctrl+Z (Windows) or ⌘+Z (Mac) — and try again.

As with drawing, you might find it helpful to increase the zoom factor. Try editing at 200 or 400 percent.

# Using the Subselect tool

You can use the Subselect tool to reshape individual strokes or fills created by using the Pen, Pencil, Brush, Line, Oval, or Rectangle tools. When you use the Subselect tool, you move *anchor points,* which are small squares that appear on the object. To use Subselect, follow these steps:

1. **Choose the Subselect tool (the white arrow in the Tools panel).**

2. **Click the stroke (outline) or fill shape to display the anchor points on the line or shape outlines.**

3. **Drag the anchor points to modify the shape.**

4. **To change the direction of a curve, click any anchor point to display tangent lines and drag the tangent line handles (the little dots at the ends of the tangent lines).**

The tangent lines indicate the direction of the curve. See the section in Chapter 3 on drawing curves with the Pen tool for information on anchor points and tangent lines.

If you click a graphic with the Subselect tool and points aren't displayed on its edges, you might have grouped the graphic, as we describe later in this chapter, or created it with the object-drawing model, or maybe you didn't create it with the Pen, Pencil, Brush, Line, Oval, or Rectangle tool. In any case, try choosing Modify⇨Ungroup or Modify⇨Break Apart and then using the Subselect tool.

You can also delete anchor points. Flash reshapes the shape without that anchor point. Select the object with the Subselect tool, select an anchor point, and press Delete.

## *Freely transforming and distorting shapes*

For way-cool distortions and reshapings, use the Free Transform tool, with its Distort & Envelope options. The Free Transform tool can work its magic on objects, groups, instances, or text blocks. In addition to its special ability to create distortions, it's flexible enough to move, rotate, scale, and skew objects. Flash also has other tools that rotate, scale, and skew — we cover them later in this chapter.

To use the Free Transform tool, select an object, symbol instance, group, or text block. (See Chapter 7 for more about symbols. We discuss groups later in this chapter.) Click the Free Transform tool in the Tools panel. The object displays a bounding box with handles and a *transformation point,* shown as a circle at the center of the bounding box, as shown in Figure 4-9.

**Figure 4-9:**
We love
the Free
Transform
tool!

You can perform the following commonly used transformations on the selected object:

- ✔ **Move:** Place the cursor on the object itself; when you see the four-headed arrow, click and drag to move the selected object.

- ✔ **Set the center for rotation and scaling:** Place the cursor on the transformation point; when you see the small circle, you can drag the circle at the center of the bounding box to move the transformation point. The *transformation point* is the base point used for the current rotation or scaling operation.

- ✔ **Rotate:** Place the cursor just outside any corner handle; when you see the circular arrow, drag the object to rotate it around the transformation point.

  Press Shift while you drag to constrain the rotation to 45-degree increments. Press Alt (Windows) or Option (Mac) while you drag to rotate around the diagonally opposite corner from your cursor.

- ✔ **Scale both dimensions:** Place the cursor on any corner handle; when you see the broken, two-headed arrow, drag inward or outward. Press Shift while you drag to ensure that the object is scaled proportionally without being distorted.

  You can select as many objects as you want, and Flash scales them all. When you select more than one object, Flash places the handles around an imaginary bounding box that encompasses all the objects. Sometimes you might not get exactly the result you want with this method, so check carefully.

- ✔ **Scale one dimension:** Place the cursor on any side handle; when you see the two-headed arrow, drag inward or outward to scale in the direction that you're dragging.

- ✔ **Skew:** Place the cursor anywhere on the bounding box except on the handles; when you see the parallel lines, drag in any direction. (We cover skewing in more detail in the "Getting skewy" section, later in this chapter.)

In the following sections, you find out about the more exciting transformations that you can create with the Free Transform tool.

### Tapering objects

You can turn a square into a trapezoid by *tapering*. When you taper, you use the Free Transform tool to drag a corner handle. While you drag, the adjoining corner moves an equal distance in the opposite direction, as shown in Figure 4-10. You can taper other shapes, not just squares — but adjoining corners are always simultaneously stretched in opposite directions.

**Figure 4-10:**
Tapering
turns a
square into
a trapezoid.

**Figure 4-10:**
Tapering
turns a
square into
a trapezoid.

 To taper, press Ctrl+Shift (Windows) or ⌘+Shift (Mac) while you drag on a corner handle of the bounding box. You can also use the Distort option of the Free Transform tool: Click the Distort button and press Shift while you drag any corner handle. (This technique is ideal for people who have trouble pressing both Shift and Ctrl or ⌘ at the same time.)

### Distorting objects

For even weirder effects, you can *distort* shapes (objects) — but not symbols, symbol instances, text, or groups. When you distort an object, you change the shape of the bounding box, and the shape gets stretched in the same amount and direction as the bounding box, as shown in Figure 4-11.

**Figure 4-11:**
Drag the
bounding
box into a
new shape;
the object
follows suit.

To distort shapes with the Free Transform tool, press Ctrl (Window) or ⌘ (Mac) and drag either a corner or a side handle on the bounding box. You can also use the Distort option of the Free Transform tool — click the Distort button and drag the handle. To use the menu, choose Modify⇨Transform⇨Distort.

### Stretching the envelope

You can make even more refined changes in the shape of the Free Transform bounding box by using the Envelope modifier. With this option, the bounding box takes on editing points like you see when you use the Pen tool. As you drag the points, tangent lines appear, as shown in Figure 4-12.

**Figure 4-12:**
The oval is like taffy when you push the envelope.

 To use the Envelope modifier, select an object — a shape — but not a symbol, instance, text, or group. Choose the Free Transform tool and the Envelope modifier. Drag any of the points in or out and then drag the end of any of the tangent lines to change the direction of the curve.

To end a free transformation, click anywhere off the selected object.

## Straightening lines and curving curves

Just like you can straighten and smooth strokes by using the Straighten and Smooth modifiers of the Pencil tool, you can straighten and smooth strokes and fills of existing objects. (See Chapter 3 for more about the Pencil tool.)

You can activate the Straighten and Smooth modifiers repeatedly and watch while Flash slightly reshapes your strokes or fills each time. Eventually, Flash reaches a point where it can't smooth or straighten anymore.

 Choose Edit➪Preferences and choose the Drawing category to adjust how Flash calculates the straightening and smoothing. Change the Smooth Curves and Recognize Shapes settings.

 To straighten a stroke, first select the object. With the Selection tool active, click the Straighten Modifier button in the Options section of the Tools panel. Flash straightens out curves and recognizes shapes, if appropriate.

 To smooth a curve, first select the object. With the Selection tool active, click the Smooth Modifier button in the Options section of the Tools panel. Smooth softens curves and reduces the number of segments that create a curve.

## Modifying line endings

 Flash 8 offers line caps that you can choose to customize the ends of lines that you draw. (See the section on setting the stroke type in Chapter 3 for details on caps.) You can also change existing line caps. Select a line and display the Property inspector (choose Window➪Properties➪Properties). Select a new option from the Cap or Join drop-down list.

## *Optimizing curves*

Flash offers a technique called *optimizing* for curves. Optimizing reduces the number of individual elements in a curve. Optimizing reduces the size of your file, resulting in faster download times on your Web site. You can optimize repeatedly, just as you can with smoothing and straightening. Optimizing works best for complex art created with many lines and curves. The visual result is somewhat like smoothing but might be even subtler.

To optimize, select the object or objects and choose Modify⇨Shape⇨Optimize. Flash opens the Optimize Curves dialog box, as shown in Figure 4-13.

**Figure 4-13:**
Optimize to
reduce the
number of
curves.

As you can see in the dialog box, you can choose how much you want Flash to optimize curves. If you mangle your work too much on the first try, undo it and try again with a different setting. You can generally leave the other settings as they are. For a slower but more thorough optimization, mark the Use Multiple Passes (Slower) check box. And it's helpful to see the totals message that shows you how many curves Flash cut out and the percentage of optimization that number represents, so select the Show Totals Message check box. Click OK to optimize.

Be careful to check the results after optimizing. Flash sometimes eliminates small objects that you may want to remain. If you don't like the results of optimizing, choose Edit⇨Undo.

## *Expanding and contracting filled shapes*

You can expand and contract shapes. Expanding and contracting works best on shapes with no stroke (outline) because Flash deletes the outline when executing the command. If you want to expand or contract a shape with a stroke, scale it. We explain scaling later in this chapter in the "Scaling, scaling . . ." section. The advantage of expanding and contracting is that you can specify a change in size in terms of pixels.

To expand or contract a shape, select it and choose Modify⇨Shape⇨ Expand Fill. The Expand Fill dialog box appears, as shown in Figure 4-14. Type a number in the Distance text box, using the units that you have set for the entire movie. By default, movies are measured in pixels. (See the section in Chapter 3 on drawing precisely for the details on setting movie units.)

**Expand Fill**

Distance: 4 px          OK

Direction: ⦿ Expand    Cancel
          ○ Inset

To expand a shape, select the Expand radio button. To contract a shape, select the Inset radio button. Then click OK.

## Softening edges

Softening edges is another shape-modification tool. You can soften edges of a shape to get a graphic to look like you created it in a bitmap image editor, such as Photoshop. Figure 4-15 shows some text before and after its edges are softened. Note that adding softened edges can increase your file size.

**Figure 4-15:**
Soften the
edges of
objects to
create cool
effects.

# FUZZ FUZZ

You can create this effect by breaking apart the text twice before softening the edges. We discuss breaking apart objects later in this chapter; Chapter 5 explains more specifically about breaking apart text into editable shapes.

To soften edges, select the object or objects and choose Modify⇨Shape⇨ Soften Fill Edges. Flash opens the Soften Fill Edges dialog box, as shown in Figure 4-16.

**Figure 4-16:**
The Soften
Fill Edges
dialog box
softens
up your
boss . . . uh,
graphics.

| Soften Fill Edges | ☒ |
| --- | --- |
| Distance: 4 px | OK |
| Number of steps: 4 | Cancel |
| Direction: ⦿ Expand |
| ○ Inset |

To soften edges, follow these steps:

1. **Set the distance, which is the width of the softened edge.**

   The distance is measured in pixels unless you have changed the document units. (See the section in Chapter 3 on drawing precisely for information on setting the units in the Document Properties dialog box.)

2. **Select the number of steps, which means the number of curves that Flash uses to create the softened edge.**

   Try the Flash default first and change it if you don't like the result. You can increase the number to get a smoother effect.

3. **Select either the Expand radio button to create the softened edge outside the shape or the Inset radio button to create the softened edge within the shape.**

4. **Click OK to create the softened edge.**

   Your shape is still selected, so click anywhere outside it to see the result. If you don't like it, press Ctrl+Z (Windows) or ⌘+Z (Mac) and try again using different options.

You can also create soft edges by using gradients that blend into the Stage color or with partially transparent colors. Chapter 3 explains more about using colors. Flash 8 Professional also has a blur filter that you can use on text, movie clip symbols, and buttons. Chapter 7 describes filters.

## Converting lines to fills

Flash offers lots of great ways to fill a shape — for example, with gradients and bitmap images. But what about those boring strokes or outlines? You can convert lines to fills and make them fun, fun, fun. (See Chapter 3 for an explanation of fills, including gradients and bitmap images.)

Mind you, there's not much point in converting a line to a fill if it's so thin that no one would ever see a fill in it. Figure 4-17 shows some waves created with a line (by using the Pencil tool) that is 10 points wide. We converted the line to a fill and then used the Paint Bucket tool to fill the line with a gradient.

**Figure 4-17:**
Change the line to a fill and use the Paint Bucket tool to change the fill.

To convert a line to a fill, select the line and choose Modify⇨Shape⇨Convert Lines to Fills. You don't see any visible difference when you deselect the line, but now you can change the fill to anything that you want.

# Transforming Fills

The Fill Transform tool offers a unique way to edit gradient and bitmap fills. You can perform the following changes to a fill:

- Move its center point.
- Change its width or height.
- Rotate it.
- Scale it.
- Tile it.
- Change the radius of a radial gradient.
- Move the focus of a radial gradient.
- Skew (slant) it.

From this list, you can see that there's no point in fiddling with solid fills. They would look the same no matter what direction, size, or scale they were. (See the section in Chapter 3 on colors for colorful coverage of gradient and bitmap fills.)

To edit a fill, choose the Fill Transform tool. Click any gradient or bitmap fill. Flash places an editing boundary and editing handles around the fill, as shown in Figure 4-18. The editing boundary varies with the type of fill — bitmap, linear gradient, or radial gradient.

**Figure 4-18:**
The Fill Transform tool places an editing boundary around the fill.

After you have a fill with an editing boundary, you're ready to go ahead and fiddle with the fills. Here's how to make changes:

- ✔ **Move the center of the fill:** Drag the center point, marked by a small circle at the center of the fill. You can move a center fill to move the center of a radial gradient, move the stripes of a linear gradient, or place a bitmap off-center.

- ✔ **Move the focal point of a fill:** Drag the focal point, marked by a triangle along the center line of a radial gradient. Moving the focal point can make the apparent direction of light move from side to side in a radial gradient with a lightly colored center.

- ✔ **Change the width of a fill:** Drag the square handle on one side of the editing boundary. To change the height of a fill, drag the handle on the bottom of the editing boundary. If a fill doesn't have one of these handles, you can't edit the fill that way. Changing the width of a linear fill that's perpendicular to the direction of its stripes is the same as scaling the fill — the stripes get wider (or narrower).

- ✔ **Rotate a fill:** Drag the rotation handle, which is a small circle just outside the corner of the editing boundary. On a radial gradient, use the bottom of the three handles on the circumference of the boundary. Figure 4-19 shows a linear gradient rotated 45 degrees.

    When rotating a fill, you can press and hold the Shift key while you drag to constrain the rotation of the fill to multiples of 45 degrees.

- ✔ **Scale a bitmap fill:** Drag the square handle at the corner of the editing boundary — inward to scale down and outward to scale up. To scale a circular gradient, drag the middle circular handle on the editing boundary. Figure 4-20 shows a bitmap gradient at original size and scaled down. Flash tiles the bitmap if you scale down significantly.

WARNING!

If you scale down a bitmap so that you see many tiles, the next time that you want to edit the bitmap, Flash places an editing boundary around each tile so that you have to edit each one individually. That could take a long time! If you want to edit a bitmap in several ways, save scaling down for last.

✔ **Skew (slant) a fill:** Drag one of the rhombus-shaped handles on the top or side of the editing boundary. You can skew only if the fill is a bitmap. Skewing is different from rotating because the bitmap is distorted. Figure 4-21 shows an example of a skewed bitmap.

Later in this chapter, we explain how to rotate, scale, and skew entire objects.

**Figure 4-19:**
Rotate a linear fill to create diagonal fills.

**Figure 4-20:**
You can scale a bitmap fill to make it larger or smaller.

**Figure 4-21:**
You can skew a bitmap fill for really weird results.

# Transferring Properties

You can use the Eyedropper tool to copy outline and fill properties from one object to another. (See the section on bitmap fills in Chapter 3 for instructions on using the Eyedropper tool to create bitmap fills.)

To transfer properties, follow these steps:

1. **Choose the Eyedropper tool.**
2. **Select an outline or a fill.**

   If you select an outline, Flash activates the Ink Bottle tool. If you select a fill, Flash activates the Paint Bucket tool and turns on the Lock Fill modifier. (For more information on the Lock Fill modifier, see the section in Chapter 3 that discusses locking a fill.)
3. **Click another outline or fill.**

   Flash transfers the properties of the original outline or fill to the new object.

# Finding and Replacing Objects

One way to change an object is to change its properties. You can find graphics objects by color or bitmap and then replace the color or bitmap. For example, you can easily change every blue fill or stroke to red if your Web color scheme changes.

You can find and replace according to color, bitmap, text, and font (Chapter 5); sound; or video (Chapter 11). You can also find and replace symbols (see Chapter 7).

To find and replace objects, choose Edit➪Find and Replace to open the Find and Replace dialog box, as shown in Figure 4-22.

From the Search In drop-down list, choose to search in the entire Flash movie document or only in the current scene. (See Chapter 9 for a full explanation of scenes.)

**Figure 4-22:**
The Find and Replace dialog box finds lost sheep and can change their color.

From the For drop-down list, select what you want to find from among the following: text, font, color, symbol, sound, video, and bitmap. The dialog box changes according to the choice that you make. For example, to find and replace a color, follow these steps:

1. **Click the top Color button and select a color that exists in your document.**

2. **Click the Replace with Color button and select the replacement color that you want.**

3. **Mark one or more of the three check boxes — Fills, Strokes, and Text — to define what type of objects you want to find.**

4. **Click Find Next to find the next occurrence of the color or click Find All to find every object with that color.**

5. **To replace the color, click Replace to replace the currently selected object or click Replace All to replace the color of every object.**

6. **Click the Close button of the dialog box to return to your movie.**

Find and Replace is a very efficient way to make mass changes of color, text, symbols, sound, video, or bitmaps.

# Transforming Objects

Earlier in this chapter, in the "Freely transforming and distorting shapes" section, we explain how you can use the Free Transform tool to reshape objects. You can do many of the same tasks by using the Transform command.

To scale, rotate, and flip objects, choose Modify⇨Transform and choose one of the submenu commands. When you scale, rotate, or skew an object, Flash kindly remembers the object's qualities so that you can return the object to the state it was in before you fiddled around with it.

## Scaling, scaling . . .

Most of the time, scaling by using the Free Transform tool (as we describe earlier in this chapter) is the easiest, fastest way to go. Sometimes you might want more precision. You can scale any selected object in the Property inspector. (Choose Window⇨Properties⇨Properties. You might need to expand the Property inspector to its full size by clicking the Expand/Collapse arrow at the lower-right corner.) Change the value in the W (width) box or H (height) box, or change both.

To make sure that the proportions of the object stay the same, click the padlock next to the W and H text boxes so that it looks locked. When you change either the W or the H text box, the other box automatically adjusts proportionally.

For yet more scaling options, select an object and choose Window⇨ Transform to open the Transform panel, as shown in Figure 4-23.

The controls in the Transform panel work only if an object is selected. If you forgot to select an object, you don't need to close the panel; just select an object.

**Figure 4-23:** The Transform panel lets you scale, rotate, and skew objects with precision.

To scale the selected object or objects, type a scale value between 1 and 1000. Any value less than 100 reduces the size of the object, so a value of 10 creates a new object at 10 percent of the original object, and a value of 1000 multiplies the object's size by a factor of 10. Then press Enter or Return.

To make a copy of an object at a scaled size, click the Copy button (the left button in the lower-right corner of the panel). The copy appears on top of the original object but is selected so that you can immediately move it if you want. Figure 4-24 shows an example of how you can use scaling and copying together to create the impression of objects at varying distances. After you make the copy, just move it to a new location.

When you're done, click the Close button of the Transform panel to close it.

**Figure 4-24:** The brain creatures are attacking!

# 'Round and 'round and 'round we rotate

Most of the time, you can probably use the Free Transform tool to rotate objects, as we explain earlier in this chapter. If you want to rotate something by an exact number of degrees, such as 20 degrees, use the Transform panel. Select the object and choose Window➪Transform to open the Transform panel (refer to Figure 4-23).

To rotate the selected object or objects clockwise, type a value between 1 and 359. To rotate counterclockwise, type a value between –1 and –359. Then press Enter or Return.

If you don't like the results, click the Reset button in the lower-right corner of the panel and try again.

To make a copy of an object at a different rotation, click Copy (the left button in the lower-right corner of the panel). The copy appears on top of the original object but is selected so that you can immediately move it.

If you want to rotate a section by 90 degrees quickly by using the menu, follow these steps:

   ✔ **To rotate right (clockwise):** Choose Modify➪Transform➪Rotate 90° CW.

   ✔ **To rotate left (counterclockwise):** Choose Modify➪Transform➪Rotate 90° CCW.

When you rotate, Flash rotates the object around its center. To rotate around a different point on the object, you can convert the object to a group or symbol and change its *registration point,* the point on an object that Flash references when rotating. See the section later in this chapter on changing the registration point.

You can create groovy circular patterns by using the rotate and copy functions, as shown in Figure 4-25. Unless the object you're working with is completely symmetrical, you need to change the registration point.

**Figure 4-25:**
By rotating
and copying
an object at
the same
time, you
can add
flower
power to
your Web
site.

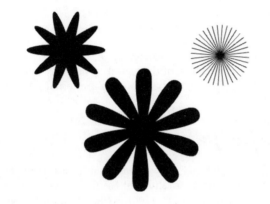

## *Getting skewy*

Skewing is a variation of rotating. Rather than rotate an entire object, you slant it horizontally, vertically, or both. Skewing a square creates a rhombus (diamond). In Figure 4-26, you see a simple arrow before and after skewing.

**Figure 4-26:**
After
skewing, a
boring
arrow looks
like it's in a
hurry.

The easiest way to skew objects is by using the Free Transform tool. Just select an object, choose the Free Transform tool, and drag along one of the sides of the boundary.

Usually, you can eyeball the skewing process. If you want precision or to combine skewing with scaling, use the Transform panel. Select the object and choose Window⇨Transform to open the Transform panel. To skew the selected object or objects, click Skew.

Use the left box to skew horizontally. To skew clockwise, type a value between 1 and 89. To skew counterclockwise, type a value between –1 and –89. Then press Enter or Return.

To skew vertically, type a value in the right text box. Positive values skew clockwise, and negative values skew counterclockwise. If that sounds confusing, just try something out and see whether you like it. If you don't, click Reset (the right button in the lower-right corner of the panel) and try again.

To make a copy of an object at a skewed angle, click the Copy button (the left button in the lower-right corner of the panel). The copy appears on top of the original object but is selected so that you can immediately move it.

## Flippety, floppety

*Flipping* reverses an object so that you have a mirror image of your original object. You can flip both horizontally (left to right or vice versa) and vertically (up to down or vice versa). Flash flips objects about their center so that they stay in their original position on the Stage.

Figure 4-27 shows a curlicue design in its original form, flipped horizontally, and flipped vertically. If you flip an object horizontally and then vertically, you end up with an object that has been mirrored in both directions.

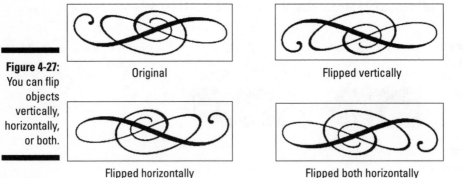

**Figure 4-27:**
You can flip
objects
vertically,
horizontally,
or both.

Original

Flipped vertically

Flipped horizontally

Flipped both horizontally
and vertically

To flip an object, select it and choose Modify⇨Transform⇨Flip Vertical or Flip Horizontal. To flip an object in both directions, flip it in one direction and then in the other.

To create symmetrical objects, you need to change the object's registration point from the center to one side or corner. Later in this chapter, in the section "Changing the Transformation Point," we explain how to use flipping to create symmetrical objects.

# Combining Objects

A new feature in Flash 8 is the ability to combine objects in various ways. You can perform the following actions:

- ✔ **Union:** Combines two objects into one object. The effect is similar to grouping objects, which we cover in the next section of this chapter. (In fact, you can use the Ungroup command to separate the objects again.) Combining two objects puts a boundary around them, like the boundary you see when you use the object-drawing model. To combine objects, select them and choose Modify⇨Combine Objects⇨Union.

   See the section on keeping objects safe and secure in Chapter 3 for more information on how to use the object-drawing model.

- ✔ **Intersect:** Creates a shape that is the intersection of two overlapping shapes. However, this works only with objects that you create by using the object-drawing model. The shape that remains is from the top object.

- ✔ **Punch:** Removes the object on top from an object beneath it and requires two objects that you drew using the object-drawing model. If you put a smaller circle on top of a larger circle, the Punch feature is like punching a hole in the larger circle (but it doesn't hurt). Select two overlapping objects and choose Modify⇨Combine Objects⇨Punch.

- ✔ **Crop:** Creates a shape that is the intersection of two overlapping shapes that you created by using the object-drawing model, but the object that remains is from the bottom object. Select two overlapping objects and choose Modify⇨Combine Objects⇨Crop.

# Getting Grouped

When you know how to create objects, you can get carried away and create so many objects on the Stage that they're hard to manage. You might want to move a number of objects at once. Although you can select them all and move them, that technique might not be enough. For example, you might inadvertently leave behind one piece and discover that it's hard to move that piece in the same way that you moved the rest. That's why Flash provides *grouping*. You select multiple objects and group them once. From then on, you can select them with one click. If you move one of the grouped objects, the rest come along for the ride.

In Flash, grouping has an additional advantage: If you put objects on top of each other, they merge if they're the same color or create cutouts if they're different colors, unless you draw them by using the object-drawing model. One way that you can avoid such friendly behavior and keep the integrity of objects is to group them. (You can also put them on different layers, as we explain in Chapter 6, or turn them into symbols, as we explain in Chapter 7.)

Grouping objects is easy. Select them and choose Modify⇨Group. You short-cut types can press Ctrl+G (Windows) or ⌘+G (Mac). When you group objects and select them, all the objects are surrounded by one blue selection border.

After you group objects, you can ungroup them at any time. Select the group and choose Modify⇨Ungroup. You can also break apart a group. See the discussion later in this chapter on breaking apart objects.

If you want to edit an element of the group without ungrouping first, Flash lets you do so. To edit without ungrouping, follow these steps:

1. **Using the Selection tool, double-click the group.**

    Flash dims other objects on the Stage and displays the Group symbol above the layer list.

2. **Edit any of the group components.**

3. **Return to regular editing mode.**

   Double-click any blank area on the Stage with the Selection tool, click the current scene symbol to the left of the group symbol, or click the Back arrow to the left of the scene symbol. You can also choose Edit⇨Edit All.

# Changing the Transformation Point

When Flash rotates or scales an object, it uses a *transformation point* as a reference. This point is generally the center of the object. For positioning and certain transformations of lines and shapes, Flash uses the upper-left corner. You might find that the point Flash uses isn't suitable for your needs. For example, you might want to rotate an object around its lower-left corner. For a single rotation or scaling of a simple graphic object, use the Free Transform tool and drag the transformation point — the little circle — to the desired location. If you deselect and reselect the object, you see that the circle has returned to its original central position.

Changing the transformation point is useful when you want to create symmetrical objects by flipping. To use flipping to create symmetrical objects, follow these steps:

1. **Select the object.**

2. **Choose the Free Transform tool and drag the transformation point to one edge of the object, from where you want to mirror the object.**

3. **Choose Edit⇨Copy to copy the object to the Clipboard.**

4. **Choose Edit⇨Paste in Place to paste the copy on top of the original.**

5. **Choose Modify⇨Transform⇨Flip Vertical or Flip Horizontal.**

   You see your original and the copy. The copy has been flipped so that it's a mirror image of its original.

6. **(Optional) To create a four-way symmetrical object, group the original and mirrored objects (as we explain in the previous section of this chapter), and change the transformation point to one side of the combined group; then repeat Steps 3 and 4, this time flipping in the other direction.**

Figure 4-28 shows a weird creature created by copying, changing the transformation point, and then flipping.

**Figure 4-28:** Create scary, symmetrical creatures by manipulating the transformation point.

Groups, symbol instances, text, and bitmaps have a *registration point*, which Flash uses to animate and transform these objects. When you use the Free Transform tool to move the circle on these objects, the circle keeps its position even after you deselect and reselect it. To move an object's registration point, follow these steps:

1. **Select a group, symbol instance, text object, or bitmap.**

2. **Choose the Free Transform tool.**

   Flash displays a small circle at the transformation point.

3. **Drag the circle to the desired location.**

4. **Click anywhere else on the Stage to hide the registration point.**

To return the registration point to its original position, double-click it.

# Breaking Apart Objects

With the Break Apart command, you can break apart text, groups, instances of symbols, and bitmaps into separate objects that you can edit individually. To break apart one of these types of objects, select it and choose Modify⇨ Break Apart.

What happens to your objects when you break them apart? Do they splatter all over the Stage? Here's what happens when you break apart the following objects:

- ✔ **Text:** Flash divides the words into individual letters, each one a separate object. If you use the Break Apart command a second time on one of the letters, the letter becomes a shape that you can modify like any other shape.

  Break apart blocks of text and then use the Distribute to Layers command to animate individual letters. For more information, see Chapter 5 about text and Chapter 6 about layers.

- ✔ **Shapes created in the object-drawing model:** The shape loses its object-drawing model status, as if you had drawn it without using the object-drawing model.

- ✔ **Groups:** Flash breaks up the group into its component parts. The result is that same as ungrouping.

- ✔ **Instances of symbols:** The symbol becomes a shape. (Symbols are covered fully in Chapter 7.)

- ✔ **Bitmaps:** Flash converts the bitmap to a fill. You can then erase parts of it.

# Establishing Order on the Stage

Flash stacks objects in the order that you create them. If you draw a circle and then an overlapping square, the square looks like it's on top of the circle because you created it more recently.

If you place an object on top of another object, the two objects become one if they're the same color. If they're different colors, the top object cuts out the underlying object.

One exception is if you use the object-drawing model to draw the objects. Another way to keep the integrity of objects is by grouping them. Symbols also maintain their integrity. (Symbols are covered in Chapter 7.) Groups, object-drawing model shapes, and symbols are always stacked on top of regular objects. Therefore, to move objects above existing groups or symbols, you need to group them or convert them to a symbol. You might also need to turn some imported graphics into a symbol or group before you can move them in the stack.

If you draw an object and it immediately disappears beneath another object, it's often because you tried to draw the object on top of a group or symbol. Group the object or change it to a symbol if it must be on top.

Another way to reorder objects is to put them on different layers. You can then reorder the objects by reordering their layers. (See Chapter 6 for the details.)

As long as you have objects that can maintain their integrity, you can change their stacking order. You can move them up or down in the stack or from the top or bottom of the stack — all within the same layer. To change the stacking order of an object, select the object and choose Modify⇨Arrange. Then choose one of these options:

- **Bring to Front:** Brings the selected object to the tippy-top of the stack.
- **Bring Forward:** Brings the selected object up one level.
- **Send Backward:** Moves the selected object down one level.
- **Send to Back:** Sends the selected object down, down, down to the bottom of the stack.

Figure 4-29 shows an example of two objects stacked in different ways.

**Figure 4-29:**
The big, old-fashioned bitmap star and the small, up-and-coming vector star vying to be in front.

# Undoing, Redoing, and Reusing

Sometimes you do something in Flash and decide that it's a mistake. Oops! For this situation, you can undo actions. You can even redo the actions that you undid. Finally, if you're environmentally conscious, you can reuse earlier actions to avoid wasting any more of your energy.

## Undoing actions

To undo your last action, choose Edit⇨Undo or press Ctrl+Z (Windows) or ⌘+Z (Mac). You can continue this process for a very long time. This is the familiar — and default — type of undo, and Flash calls it *document-level undo*.

To set the number of undo steps that Flash remembers, follow these steps:

1. **Choose Edit⇨Preferences (Windows)/Flash⇨Preferences (Mac) to open the Preferences dialog box.**

2. **Click the General category.**

3. **From the Undo drop-down list, select Document-level Undo.**

4. **In the text box just below the Undo drop-down list, enter the number of undo actions you want Flash to track. (The default is 100, and the maximum is 300.)**

Later in this chapter, in the "Reusing actions" section, we explain another way to undo actions.

## Redoing actions

Maybe you were right the first time. After you undo an action, suppose that you want to redo it. You can do that, too. To redo actions, choose Edit⇨Redo or press Ctrl+Y (Windows) or ⌘+Y (Mac).

If you haven't undone anything, you can use the same command (and keyboard shortcut) to repeat your last action, in which case it's called the Repeat command.

## Using object-level undo and redo

Generally, undos and redos apply to every action you take in Flash. But Flash 8 offers something new — object-level undo and redo.

Object-level undo applies only to editing symbols, which we cover in Chapter 7. When you use object-level undo and redo, Flash remembers actions by symbol. Therefore, when you're editing a symbol, using the Undo command applies only to changes that you made to that symbol, even though you have made other changes to your movie in the meantime. If you use a lot of symbols, object-level undo offers you more flexibility. Object-level redo works in the same way.

You can use only one type of undo and redo at a time. To use object-level undo and redo, choose Edit⇨Preferences (Windows)/Flash⇨Preferences (Mac) and select the General category. From the Undo drop-down list, select Object-level Undo.

You see a message explaining that switching from one type of undo to another will delete your current undo history. Flash can keep track of only one stream at a time. Click OK to close the message and again to close the Preferences dialog box.

Deleting your current history is not generally a problem. But if you are in the middle of a long, complicated experiment and might need to undo many steps, choose another time to switch.

## *Reusing actions with the History panel*

If you make several changes to an object and would like to make the same changes to other objects, you can save time and increase accuracy by saving and reusing the steps for the operations that you perform. Flash tracks the steps in the History panel.

The History panel lists every command that you perform in Flash during one session. When you save and close the file, the history list isn't saved for the next time. To open the History panel, choose Window⇨Other Panels⇨History, as shown in Figure 4-30. The shortcut is Alt+F10 (Windows) or Option+F10 (Mac).

**Figure 4-30:**
The History panel keeps track of everything you do.

You can use the History panel to troubleshoot recent steps, repeat steps, undo steps, or save steps as commands for future use.

By default, Flash records up to 100 steps in the History panel. You can change the number of steps recorded by choosing Edit⇨Preferences (Windows) or Flash⇨Preferences (Mac) to open the Preferences dialog box. On the General tab, change the value for Undo levels. Valid settings are from 2 to 300. If you want to be able to go back and save earlier steps as commands, you probably need to record more than 100 steps.

### Undoing steps

One of the simplest things that you can do in the History panel is to undo one or more operations. You can also undo operations by choosing Edit⇨Undo, but you can see more specific descriptions of the operation (such as Undo Move) in the History panel, such as Move {x:0, y:-103.6}. To view the specifics, right-click (Windows) or Control+click (Mac) any history item and choose View⇨Arguments in Panel. With these details, you can more easily predict the result of undoing an operation.

You undo steps by using the slider on the left side of the History panel:

- **Undo the last operation that you performed:** Drag up the slider one step.
- **Undo several steps:** Drag the slider to the step above the first step that you want to undo.

    For example, if you want to undo three steps, drag the slider up three steps — it's now next to the step previous to the one that you undid. This is the last step that has still been executed. You can also click to the left of a step. The slider scrolls up to that step and undoes all the later steps.

When you undo a step, the History panel displays the step as dimmed.

### Replaying a step

You can repeat any command from any time during a Flash session. For example, if you filled an object with a specific color, you can fill another object with the same color, even if you have done other operations in the meantime.

To replay a step, click the step itself (not the left side of the step above the slider) in the History panel. Then click the Replay button. If you want to replay the step on a different object, first select that object.

### Copying steps

You might want to keep a list of certain steps or use them in a different movie. Select one or more steps in the History panel and click the Copy Selected Steps to the Clipboard button.

To use these steps in another Flash movie, open the movie and choose Edit⇨ Paste. To apply the steps to an object, select the object first.

Flash copies the step or steps as JavaScript code. Therefore, when you paste the step or steps into a word processor or text editor, you see the JavaScript code, which looks more complex than the step listed in the History panel. Usually, you can figure out what it means, even if you don't know JavaScript. For example, `Fill Color: '#0000ff'` appears as `fl.getDocumentDOM().setFillColor('#0000ff');`.

### Saving commands

If you want to save a step or set of steps to use the next time that you open the movie, save a command. Saving a command is even useful if you want to re-execute some steps several times later on in the same session because scrolling back to find the exact steps that you want to reuse can be time-consuming.

To save a command, follow these steps:

1. **In the History panel, select the steps that you want to save.**

   You can drag along the step names (not along the left side, where the slider is). You can also use the usual methods of selecting multiple objects in a list — click the first object, press Shift and click the last, or press and hold Ctrl (Windows)/⌘ (Mac) and click each step that you want to select.

2. **Click the Save Selected Steps as a Command button.**

   This button is in the lower-right corner of the History panel. The Save As Command dialog box opens.

3. **In the Save As Command dialog box, enter a name for the command.**

   You can simply summarize the steps. For example, you might name a command `fill blue, rotate 45`.

4. **Click OK to close the dialog box.**

When you save a command, it appears on the Commands menu. The menu in Figure 4-31 shows the command `fill blue, rotate 45`, which fills any selected shape with blue and rotates the shape 45 degrees. To use that command, you simply select a shape and then choose Commands⇨Fill Blue, Rotate 45. Presto! It's all done. As you can imagine, you can combine complex commands and save them to automate the authoring process of creating Flash movies.

**Figure 4-31:**
Saved
commands
appear
on the
Commands
menu.

| Commands |
|---|
| **Manage Saved Commands...** |
| **Get More Commands...** |
| **Run Command...** |
| fill blue, rotate 45 |

### Clearing the History panel

If you don't want the History panel to record everything you do — perhaps it makes you feel as if you don't have any privacy left anymore — you can clear the history list. Clearing the history list doesn't undo any steps. To clear the History panel, click the options menu and choose Clear History. Click Yes to do so.

For good Commands menu housekeeping, choose Commands⇨Manage Saved Commands to open the Manage Saved Commands dialog box. In this dialog box, you can delete or rename a command. When you're done, click OK to close the Manage Saved Commands dialog box.

# Chapter 5

# What's Your Type?

**In This Chapter**

▶ Creating, editing, and formatting text

▶ Using cool text effects

*W*e assume that occasionally you want to say something on your Web site, so this chapter covers text in all its forms and formats. You can use Flash to create the text for your Web pages if you want (although you don't have to). But if you want flashy text effects, Flash is definitely the way to go.

*Typography* is the art or process of arranging text on a page, and basically that's what this chapter is all about. Many graphics programs call text *type*. We use the words interchangeably here — we don't care what you call it.

## Presenting Your Text

The majority of text on most Web sites is formatted by using HyperText Markup Language (HTML) coding that sets the font, size, and color of the text. Using HTML code is ideal for larger amounts of text because the HTML is simple to code and loads quickly.

For smaller amounts of text that you want to have special formatting or effects, Flash offers more options than HTML. Of course, if you want to animate your text, you can use Flash. For example, an animated logo usually includes not only the graphic art but also the name of the organization, which is, of course, text.

Here are some innovative things that you can do with text:

✔ Rotate, scale, skew, or flip text without losing the ability to edit the text.

✔ Turn text into shapes and modify them any way that you want. However, after you turn text into shapes, you can't edit the text characters by simply typing. Figure 5-1 shows some text that was modified in this way.

✔ Create transparent type.

✔ Create hyperlinked text that sends users' browsers to other Web pages when the users click the text.

✔ Enable viewers to control some aspect of the movie by entering text in a text box

✔ Load text, such as sports scores or current weather, dynamically from a server.

**Figure 5-1:**
You can turn text into a shape and edit it to your heart's content.

## Creating text

Creating text in Flash is simple. Follow these steps:

1. **Click the Text tool on the Tools panel.**

2. **Specify the text starting point on the Stage.**

   • To specify the width of the text, click the Stage in the upper-left corner where you want your text to start and drag to the right until you have the width that you want. Flash places a square block handle in the upper-right corner of the text block.

   • To create a text block that expands while you type, just click the Stage at the desired starting point. Flash places a round block handle in the upper-right corner of the text block.

3. **Start typing.**

   To force a return to the left margin, press Enter or Return.

4. **After you finish typing, click anywhere off the Stage to deselect the text.**

Congratulations — you've just said something! We hope it was worthwhile.

# Editing text

After you type text, it never fails that you want to change it. Editing text is easy in Flash, but first you have to select it. Here are the selection techniques:

- **To edit an entire text block:** Choose the Selection tool and click the text. Flash places a selection border around the text. You can move, rotate, and scale all the text in a text block this way, just as you would with any other object. For example, you can use the Free Transform tool to scale the text.

- **To edit the content of text itself:** Double-click the text by using the Selection tool. (Or choose the Text tool and click the text.) Flash switches you to the Text tool automatically and places the text cursor where you clicked or double-clicked the text, more or less.

- **To select a character or characters individually:** Choose the Text tool and drag across one or more characters. Do this when you want to edit only those characters.

- **To select a word:** Choose the Text tool and double-click any word to select it.

- **To select a string of words or block of text:** Choose the Text tool, click at the beginning of the text that you want to select, and then Shift+click at the end of the desired selection.

- **To select all the text in a text block:** Choose the Text tool, click in a text block, and then press Ctrl+A (Windows) or ⌘+A (Mac).

To change the content of the text, select the characters or words that you want to change, as we explain in the preceding list. Type to replace the selected text. Other text-editing techniques are the same as in your word processor. For example, you can press the Delete key to delete characters to the right of the text cursor or press the Backspace key (Windows) or Delete key (Mac) to delete characters to the left of the cursor.

## Checking spelling

Spell checking works like the spell check in your word processor, so you'll probably find it easy to use. This feature shows Macromedia's commitment to reducing typos on the Web!

The first step is to set up the parameters for spell checking. Choose Text⇨ Spelling Setup to open the Spelling Setup dialog box, as shown in Figure 5-2. In fact, you can't check your spelling until you have opened this dialog box and closed it again; then the Check Spelling item becomes available on the Text menu.

**Spelling Setup**

Document options
- ☑ Check text fields content
- ☐ Check scene and layer names
- ☑ Check frame labels/comments
- ☑ Check strings in ActionScript
- ☐ Check symbol/bitmap names
- ☐ Check current scene only
- ☐ Check single letter text fields
- ☐ Show in Movie Explorer panel
- ☑ Select text on stage

Dictionaries
- ☑ Macromedia
- ☑ American English
- ☐ Brazilian Portuguese
- ☐ British English
- ☐ Canadian
- ☐ Danish
- ☐ Dutch
- ☐ Finnish
- ☐ French
- ☐ German (Classic Spelling)

Personal dictionary

Path: C:\Documents and Settings\Ellen\Application Data\Macrom

[ Edit Personal Dictionary ]

Checking options
- ☑ Ignore non-alphabetic words
- ☐ Ignore words with numbers
- ☐ Ignore internet/file addresses
- ☑ Ignore words in UPPERCASE
- ☐ Ignore words with MIxedCasE
- ☐ Ignore first letter capped words
- ☑ Ignore possessives in words
- ☑ Find duplicate words
- ☑ Split contracted words
- ☑ Split hyphenated words
- ☐ Split words (German, Finnish)
- ☑ Suggest split words
- ☐ Suggest phonetic matches
- ☑ Suggest typographical matches

[ OK ]  [ Cancel ]

**Figure 5-2:**
Use the Spelling Setup dialog box to specify how spell checking works.

The Spelling Setup dialog box has three sections:

- ✔ **Document Options:** Choose which parts of a movie that you want to check. You can also specify whether you want each misspelled word to be highlighted.

- ✔ **Personal Dictionary:** You can change the location of the file that holds words that you add to the dictionary. Click the Edit Personal Dictionary button to add words directly. Otherwise, you add words when you are checking spelling of specific text.

- ✔ **Checking Options:** Set options that define how spell checking works. For example, you can choose to ignore words in uppercase or with numbers.

You can also choose which dictionaries you want to use for checking spelling from the Dictionaries list. When you're done, click OK to return to your movie. You're now ready to check spelling.

To check spelling, you can select text if you want to check just that text or leave all the text deselected to check the entire movie. Choose Text➪Check Spelling to open the Check Spelling dialog box, as shown in Figure 5-3.

**Check Spelling** ⊠

Word not found (text field):

Yeshayah and Eliyah    | Add to Personal |

Change to: | Yeshiva |    | Ignore |

Suggestions: Yeshiva    | Ignore All |
Essay
Yes    | Change |
Dysphasia
Escheat    | Change All |
Elsa
Yves    | Delete |
Ayes

| Setup... |    | Close |

**Figure 5-3:**
The Check
Spelling
dialog box.

If you selected text, Flash checks that text first and then asks you whether you want to check the rest of the document. Click Yes to continue or No to end the spell check. For each misspelled word, you can do one of the following:

✔ Choose one of the suggestions and click Change to change that instance of the word.

✔ Choose one of the suggestions and click Change All to change all instances of the word.

✔ Click Ignore to go to the next misspelled word.

✔ Click Ignore All to ignore all instances of that word and go to the next misspelled word.

✔ Click Delete to delete the word.

✔ Click Add to Personal to add the word to the Personal Dictionary so that it won't appear as misspelled in the future.

To finish spell checking, click Close. You may see a message asking whether you want to start from the beginning of the document. Click Yes to do so. When spell checking is complete, you see a Spelling Check Completed message. Click OK to return to your movie.

### Finding and replacing text

If you need to change all instances of the word *big* to *large,* you're in luck. The Find and Replace feature comes to the rescue. For more information about this feature, see Chapter 4. In that chapter, we discuss this feature in detail and specifically how to find and replace color. Here we explain the steps (which are very similar) for finding and replacing text:

1. **Choose Edit⇨Find and Replace.**

   The Find and Replace dialog box appears.

2. **In the For drop-down list, choose Text.**

3. **In the Search in Text text box, enter the text that you want to find.**

4. **In the Replace with Text text box, enter the replacement text.**

5. **(Optional) Enable one or more of the left three check boxes to define what type of text you want to find: Whole Word, Match Case, and Regular Expressions.**

   *Regular expressions* are formulas that you use to locate specific text patterns in a text string. Regular expressions are beyond the scope of this book, but you can find a good tutorial at www.regular-expressions. info/tutorial.html.

6. **(Optional) Select one or more of the check boxes on the right to define where you want Flash to look for text.**

   - **Text Field Contents** searches text objects.

   - **Frames/Layers/Parameters** looks for frame labels and scene names (see Chapter 9), layer names (see Chapter 6), and component parameters (see Chapter 10).

   - **Strings in ActionScript** looks for text strings in ActionScript.

   - **ActionScript** looks for all ActionScript code.

7. **To edit each object one at a time, select the Live Edit check box.**

   When you use Live Edit, you can't make multiple changes at one time, and your cursor returns to the Stage to directly edit each object.

8. **Click the appropriate button as needed:**

   - Click **Find Next** to find the next occurrence of the text.

   - Click **Find All** to find all occurrences of the text.

   - Click **Replace** to replace the currently selected object.

   - Click **Replace All** to replace all instances of that text.

When Flash finds the specified text, the box at the bottom of the Find and Replace dialog box displays its location and type along with the entire text so that you can see the context of the text that you're replacing. You can resize the Find and Replace dialog box as well as the columns in the list of found items. When you're done, click the Find and Replace dialog box Close button to return to your movie.

# *Setting character attributes*

Of course, you don't always want to use the Flash default font and size for your Web site. Boring! You can set the attributes before you start typing or edit the attributes of existing text. To edit existing text, double-click the text block and then select the characters or words that you want to format. To either set or edit attributes of text, choose Window⇨Properties⇨Properties to open the Property inspector. Figure 5-4 shows the expanded Property inspector when some static text is selected. (Static text is normal text that just sits there and looks pretty.) The Property inspector changes slightly depending on which type of text you select. See "Creating input and dynamic text," later in this chapter, for more information about the various types of text.

**Figure 5-4:**
The Property inspector is the place to liven up your text.

*Setting the font, font size, and font style*

Usually, the first step in formatting text is selecting a font. To select a font for your text, simply pick one from the Font drop-down list on the Property inspector. Flash changes the font of the selected text. You can change the font characteristics that control specific properties of the font, such as size and style:

✔ **To select a font size:** Type a font size in the text box or drag the slider to the desired value.

✔ **To select a font style:** Click Bold, Italic, or both. Flash applies the style to selected text.

You can also select fonts, font sizes, and font styles directly from the Text menu. This menu is devoted entirely to helping you format your text.

Flash 8 offers FlashType, a new method of displaying fonts for extra clarity. FlashType is especially helpful for small font sizes.

You can create vertical text, where letters flow downward instead of across. Okay, so the purpose is mostly for languages that are often written vertically, such as Chinese. Vertical text must be static and can go from either left to right or right to left. (We explain static, input, and dynamic text later in this chapter.) Figure 5-5 shows some vertical text.

**D**
**o**
**w**
**n**

**Figure 5-5:**
Try vertical
text for a
change of
direction.

**w**
**e**

**g**
**o**

To create vertical text, follow the instructions for creating normal text, but before clicking on the Stage to place the text, select the Left-to-Right or the Right-to-Left option from the Change Direction of Text button on the Property inspector (refer to Figure 5-4).

### Specifying text color

Black is the Flash default color, but you have lots of additional options. The first concern is that the text is legible against its background. For example, yellow text looks great in front of a black background, but it's almost invisible against white. Also consider that text is often unreadable in front of complex graphic images, no matter what the color.

To set text color, select the text that you want to change if you've already created the text. In the Property inspector, click the Text Color button (refer to Figure 5-4) to open the Color palette, and select a color. (For more information on colors, see Chapter 3.) If you haven't created the text yet, choose the Text tool, select the color, and then create the text.

To create transparent (or semitransparent) text, select the text and choose Window➪Color Mixer to open the Color Mixer panel. Type a new Alpha percentage and press Enter. A 100-percent alpha setting results in opaque text. Text with a 0-percent alpha setting is completely transparent. A setting of 50 percent results in text that looks somewhat transparent but is still visible. To see the results, deselect the text by choosing the Selection tool and clicking outside the text. You can also set the transparency after you choose the Text tool but before you type anything.

For a nice example of text animation, open `time.fla` from this book's companion Web site at `www.dummies.com/go/flash8`. (If you see a missing font warning, just click the Use Default button.) Then choose Control➪Test Movie from within Flash. *(Thanks to the animation's creator, Stefano Gramantieri, [`gramants@libero.it`] for this movie.)*

### Adjusting kerning and tracking

To get the look that you want, you can adjust the spacing between letters of your text. *Kerning* reduces the spacing between certain letters, such as V and A. Because of the diagonal line on the left side of the A, without kerning, the V and the A might look too far apart. Figure 5-6 shows an example of text with and without kerning.

**Figure 5-6:** The first line uses kerning; the second line doesn't.

# VACATION
# VACATION

By default, Flash uses a font's kerning information, which is embedded in the font definition. Sometimes with smaller font sizes, kerning can make text hard to read, so you can turn it off. Without kerning, text takes up slightly more space. To turn off kerning, select the characters that you want to adjust and clear the Auto Kern check box in the Property inspector.

You can adjust the spacing between all the letters, called *tracking.* Perhaps you need the text to fit into a tight space or you want to stretch it out without changing the font size. Figure 5-7 shows some text two-letter-spacing settings. To change tracking, open the Property inspector (Window➪Properties➪ Properties) and type a value in the Character Spacing text box or drag the slider bar to the desired value.

**Figure 5-7:**
Stretched
and
condensed
text.

Split the scene
and leave it clean

Split the scene
and leave it clean

Split the scene
and leave it clean

Split the scene
and leave it clean

## Hyperlinking text

You can create text that acts as a link to other Web pages. Flash underlines linked text, following the global convention on Web sites. To create text with a hyperlink, follow these steps:

1. **Select the text.**

2. **Choose Window⇨Properties⇨Properties to display the Property inspector.**

3. **In the URL text box, type the URL (Uniform Resource Locator, or Web address) of the Web page that you want to use.**

   The URL Link text box is on the expanded Property inspector. If necessary, click the Expand arrow in the lower-right corner of the Property inspector to display the URL text box. When you complete the URL, a dotted line appears beneath the text to indicate that it's a hyperlink. When your Flash movie appears on a Web site, clicking the hyperlinked text sends users to the URL that you specified.

4. **In the Target drop-down list, choose one of the window targets for the URL. The two most commonly used are**

   • _blank opens the URL in a new browser window.

   • _self opens the URL in the same window and is the default.

## Getting the best text appearance

Flash usually stores outlines of the text in your movie when you publish or export it, so your audience will see your fonts in your movie even if they're not installed on your audience's computer. However, not all fonts displayed in Flash can be stored as outlines when you publish or export your movie.

To test whether Flash can export a font with a movie, choose View⇨Preview Mode⇨Antialias Text. You should see the text become smoother and less jagged. If the text remains jagged, Flash cannot export the text with the movie.

*Anti-aliasing* is a method of making text look smoother — reducing the jaggies that sometimes create stair-like lines on text. Anti-aliasing is especially helpful for smaller font sizes.

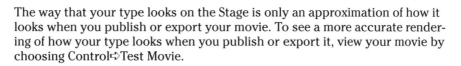

The way that your type looks on the Stage is only an approximation of how it looks when you publish or export your movie. To see a more accurate rendering of how your type looks when you publish or export it, view your movie by choosing Control➪Test Movie.

Flash 8 offers new options to anti-alias text so that it looks smoother, both in Flash and in the Flash player, after you publish your movie. The new anti-aliasing kicks in when you choose the Anti-alias for Readability option from the Font Rendering Method drop-down list in the Property inspector. You also need to choose Flash Player 8 (the default) when you publish your movie.

If you want to use type in a font that Flash can't export, you can break apart the type into shapes, as we describe at the end of this chapter, but this increases the size of your movie file, and you cannot edit the text any more.

If you'd like a space-saving alternative to storing your text as outlines in your Flash movie, you can use Flash's three *device fonts* that the Flash Player always converts to the closest available font on the local computer:

- ✔ _sans: A sans serif font similar to Arial (Windows) and Helvetica (Mac).
- ✔ _serif: A serif font similar to Times New Roman (Windows) and Times (Mac).
- ✔ _typewriter: A font that looks like it has been typed on a typewriter. (Are you old enough to remember what that is?) It's similar to Courier New (Windows) and Courier (Mac).

When you use device fonts, your resulting published movies are smaller, so download time is shorter. With device fonts, your text also might be more legible in text sizes below 10 point. To use device fonts, specify one of the device fonts and then deselect the text. Then select Use Device Fonts from the Font Rendering Method drop-down list in the Property inspector. (This setting applies only to horizontal static text.) When you publish your movie, select the Device Font check box on the HTML tab (Windows only) of the Publish Settings dialog box. Chapter 13 tells more about publishing settings.

## *Setting up paragraph formats*

You can set paragraph attributes such as alignment, margins, indents, and line spacing. Use these settings whenever you type more than one line of text.

### Setting text alignment

You can align text along the left margin *(left justification)* or right margin *(right justification)* of the text block. You can also center text. You can create an even edge along both margins, called *full justification* or *justified text.* By default, text is left justified.

To align text, select it and choose Window⇨Properties⇨Properties to open the Property inspector (refer to Figure 5-4). Then click the Align Left, Align Center, Align Right, or Justify button.

### Setting margins and indents

The *margin* is the space between the text block border and your text. By default, the margin is 0 pixels. You can increase the margin to guarantee some space around the text. You can set only the left and right margins (not the top or bottom ones).

To set the left margin, select the paragraph and click the Edit Format Options button in the Property inspector to open the Format Options dialog box, as shown in Figure 5-8. Type a value in the Left Margin text box or click the arrow and use the slider to specify a value. Then press Tab or Enter (Windows) or Return (Mac) to see the result right away. To set the right margin, use the Right Margin text box.

**Figure 5-8:**
Use the
Format
Options
dialog box
to whip your
text into
shape.

| Format Options | | |
| --- | --- | --- |
| Indent: | 0 px | OK |
| Line spacing: | 2 pt | Cancel |
| Left margin: | 0 px | |
| Right margin: | 0 px | |

Indentation creates an indented first line. It's equivalent to placing a tab at the beginning of a paragraph. (Remember your sixth grade teacher who told you to always start each paragraph with an indent?) To indent the first line, select the paragraph and type a value in the Indent text box in the Format Options dialog box or click the arrow and drag the slider bar.

### Specifying line spacing

Line spacing determines the space between lines. Flash measures line spacing in points ($\frac{1}{72}$ of an inch) because font size is measured in points. For example, if your text is 18 points high and you want to double-space the lines, use a line spacing of 18 points so that a space exactly one line high exists between each line of text. To set line spacing, select the paragraph, then click the Edit Format Options button in the Property inspector to open the Format Options dialog box, and type a value in the Line Spacing text box or click the arrow and drag the slider bar. Press Tab or Enter (Windows) or Return (Mac).

Click OK (Windows) or Done (Mac) when you're done with the Format Options dialog box.

Flash remembers paragraph properties from movie to movie. When you change paragraph properties for one movie, the properties rear their ugly heads in your next movie. If your text automatically indents at the beginning of paragraphs or comes out double-spaced, check out the Format Options dialog box.

## Creating input and dynamic text

You can create three kinds of text in Flash:

- ✔ **Static text:** Regular text that doesn't change or do anything, although you can animate it.

- ✔ **Input text:** Text that viewers can enter, as in a text box. You can use input text for forms and surveys or to interactively create values that affect the movie.

- ✔ **Dynamic text:** Text that changes based on data coming from an external source (such as a Web server), an internal source (such as ActionScript), or input text in the movie (often used for data such as sports scores, current weather, and stock prices).

To choose the type of text, use the Text Type drop-down list in the Property inspector. (It's a good thing the Flash creators didn't call it the Type Type drop-down list.) For an example of input text, see Chapter 8.

Several of the text settings in the Property inspector apply only to input or dynamic text (and therefore don't appear if you use static text):

- ✔ **Instance Name:** This text box appears under the Text Type drop-down list when you select Input or Dynamic text. An instance name identifies the text object so that you can refer to the text in ActionScript. (See Chapter 10 for the scoop on ActionScript.)This is handy because with Input or Dynamic text, the contents of the text field can change while your Flash movie is playing; but if you give your text field an instance name, you can always refer to it by using ActionScript, even though you don't know the contents of the text field ahead of time.

- **Line Type:** Defines how text is displayed.

  - **Multiline** displays the text in multiple lines.

  - **Single Line** displays the text as one line.

  - **Multiline No Wrap** displays text in multiple lines that break only if the last character is a breaking character, such as Enter (Windows) or Return (Macintosh).

  - **Password** displays asterisks.

- **Render Text as HTML:** Preserves formatting, such as fonts and hyperlinks, with certain HTML tags. You need to create the formatting by using ActionScript.

- **Show Border Around Text:** Displays a black border and white background for the text field. This border helps users know where to enter text in an input text block.

- **Selectable:** Enables users to select dynamic text by dragging across it with the mouse. They can then copy it to the Clipboard. Deselect this button to prevent users from selecting dynamic text.

- **Variable:** Type a variable name for the text field. Variable names are used similarly to instance names, but your options are more limited.

- **Maximum Characters:** Specifies the maximum allowable characters that users can input in a text box.

- **Embed:** Opens the Character Embedding dialog box, where you can select options for embedding font outlines. Choose one or more of the options (such as Uppercase and Lowercase). You can press Ctrl (Windows) or ⌘ (Mac) and click several options. Or click the Don't Embed button if you don't want to embed font outlines. When you're done, click OK. The font outlines you chose are exported when you publish the movie to ensure a smooth appearance. Limiting the font outlines you export helps to make the file size smaller.

## Creating Cool Text Effects

Flash wouldn't be worth its salt if you couldn't create some flashy effects with text. You can manipulate text in several ways:

- **Transform text just like other objects.** In other words, you can scale, rotate, skew, and flip type. Figure 5-9 shows an example of skewed text.

**Figure 5-9:**
This text is
skewed to
match the
angles of
the skewed
rectangles,
creating a
3-D effect.

Grapple with enigmas
and master our
mysteries!

Grow your brain with our
brain teasers!
Unravel baffling riddles,
and cut your teeth on
curious conundrums!

Crack our
fascinating
puzzles and
decipher our
codes!

✔ **Convert type to shapes by breaking it apart.** Select the text and choose Modify⇨Break Apart. The first time that you use the Break Apart command, words are broken up into individual letters. Use this command again, and letters are turned into shapes so that you can then edit the text in the same way that you edit shapes. However, you can no longer edit the text as text, so check your words before converting them! Refer to Figure 5-1 for an example of text turned into shapes.

✔ **In the Professional version of Flash, you can apply special graphic effects to text, called *filters*.** Select the text and click the Filters tab of the Property inspector. Click the Plus (+) icon and choose one (or more) of the following filters: Bevel, Drop Shadow, Glow, Blur, Gradient Glow, Gradient Blur, or Adjust Color.

Of course, you can animate text to your heart's content. To animate text, you usually break it apart so that you can move letters individually. You can then use the Modify⇨Timeline⇨Distribute to Layers command to put each letter on a separate layer. After that, you can animate each letter. (See Chapter 9 for the details on animation.)

# Chapter 6

# Layering It On

. . . . . . . . . . . . . . . . . . . . . . . . . . . . . . . . . . . . . . . . . .

## In This Chapter

▶ Creating layers

▶ Modifying layers

▶ Using guide layers

▶ Creating holes with mask layers

. . . . . . . . . . . . . . . . . . . . . . . . . . . . . . . . . . . . . . . . . .

*F*lash lets you organize objects on the Stage in layers. *Layers* keep objects separated from each other. Flash either combines or creates cutouts when two objects overlap if you don't use the object-drawing model (as we explain in Chapter 3). By placing the two objects on different layers, you avoid this behavior yet retain the appearance of overlapping objects. In addition, by rearranging your layers, you can easily rearrange the order of your objects, that is, which objects appear to be on top and which appear to be on the bottom.

Layers are also necessary for error-free animation. To move one object across the Stage in front of other objects, such as a background, you need to put the object on its own layer. If you want to animate several objects across the Stage, put each object on a separate layer.

You can hide layers. Flash doesn't display objects on hidden layers. Hidden layers are great for hiding some objects temporarily while you figure out what to do with all the rest of the stuff on the Stage.

Finally, layers are great places to put sounds and ActionScript code. For example, you can name a layer *Music* and put your music there. Then you can easily find the music if you want to change it. Layers provide a great way to keep the various components of your movie organized. (See Chapter 10 to find out more about ActionScript.) In this chapter, you get all the information that you need to use layers effectively.

# Creating Layers

Flash lists layers at the left side of the Timeline. New movies start out with one layer, named Layer 1. You can, and should, change the name of this layer and new layers to something more descriptive, as shown in Figure 6-1.

**Figure 6-1:** Flash keeps you organized by listing all your layers.

If you're the organized type, you should think about your animation in advance and decide which layers you need. However, animations often don't work out the way you plan, and you might find yourself creating layers after you've created objects. Either way, your method for creating the layer is the same.

To create a layer, click the Insert Layer button at the bottom of the layer list (or choose Insert⇨Timeline⇨Layer). Flash displays the new layer above the active layer and makes the new layer active. To name the layer, double-click its name, type something meaningful, and then press Enter (Windows) or Return (Mac).

## Using layers

Any object that you create goes on the active layer. You can tell which layer is active because it's highlighted and has a pencil icon next to its name (refer to the Rainbow layer in Figure 6-1). To change the active layer, just click any inactive layer's name. You can also click anywhere in the layer's row on the Timeline.

To help make your work easier, Flash automatically changes the active layer to match any object that you select. So, if you're working on a layer that you named *Text* and select a shape on a layer that you named *Shapes*, Flash automatically activates the Shapes layer. Any new objects that you create are now on the Shapes layer. Of course, if that's not the layer that you want, you can switch to any other layer at any time by clicking its name.

If you click a layer to make it active, Flash selects all the objects on that layer that exist in the current frame. (Even if a layer is already active, you can click its name to select all its objects.) This feature is helpful for working with all the objects on a layer and discovering which objects a layer contains. If you don't want all the objects selected, click anywhere not on an object.

Because each animated object needs to be on its own layer, you often need to distribute objects to their own layers. Select the objects and choose Modify⇨ Timeline⇨Distribute to Layers. This command saves lots of work!

## Changing layer states

Besides being active or inactive, layers have three states that determine how objects on that layer function or look; you can show or hide a layer, lock or unlock it, or display objects on a layer as outlines. Use these states to help you organize how you work. The more objects and more layers that you have, the more you need to use these layer states.

To the right of the layer name, you see an eye, a lock, and a box. These aren't mystical symbols. The following sections explain what they are and how to use them.

### Show/Hide

Use Show/Hide (as shown at the left) to hide all objects on a layer (also called *hiding a layer*). Hide a layer to reduce clutter while you work. To hide a layer, click beneath the eye icon on that layer's row. Flash places a red X under the eye icon. All the objects on that layer disappear. Keep in mind, however, that you can't work on a hidden layer. Click the X to get them back again. To hide (or show) all the objects on the Stage, click the eye icon itself.

Don't forget hidden layers because they do appear in your published movies.

To show or hide all layers *except* one, Alt+click (Windows) or Option+click (Mac) beneath the eye icon on that layer's row. You can also right-click (Windows) or Control+click (Mac) on a layer and choose Hide Others from the shortcut menu.

### Lock/Unlock

Use Lock/Unlock to prevent objects from being edited by locking their layers. Lock a layer when you want to avoid changing objects by mistake. To lock a layer, click beneath the lock icon on that layer's row. Flash places a lock in the layer's row. Click the lock to unlock the layer again. The lock disappears, and you can now edit objects on that layer. You can lock *all* layers by clicking the lock icon directly — but remember that you can't work on a locked layer. Click the lock icon again to unlock all the layers.

To lock or unlock all layers *except* one layer, Alt+click (Windows) or Option+click (Mac) beneath the lock icon on that layer's row. You can also right-click (Windows) or Control+click (Mac) a layer and choose Lock Others from the shortcut menu.

### Outlines

Use Outlines to display objects as outlines of different colors. *Outlines* help you see which layer's objects are on because each layer uses a different color, as shown in Figure 6-2. (Okay, you can't *really* see the colors in a black-and-white book, but you can probably tell by the variations in gray that the objects aren't all the same color.) To display outlines, click beneath the Outlines (box) icon on that layer's row. Flash puts a colored box in the layer's row, and all objects on that layer are now shown as outlines in that color. (Text is still filled in, however.) Click the box to display objects on that layer normally. To display *all* layers as outlines, click the Outlines icon directly. Click it again to see your objects as normal. You can work on outlined layers, but all new objects appear as outlines, so telling how they appear when displayed normally is difficult.

**Figure 6-2:**
All the objects on the Stage are shown as outlines except for text that hasn't been broken apart.

*Thanks to Polly Wickstrom, www.tomatotreedesigns.com, for this Flash movie.*

In Figure 6-2, some text has been broken apart for animation and is therefore outlined like other objects.

To display all layers as outlines except for one layer, Alt+click (Windows) or Option+click (Mac) beneath the outline icon on that layer's row.

## Getting Those Layers Right

Good layer housekeeping can help keep you sane. Delete layers that you no longer need. You can rename layers when their content changes; you can copy layers with their entire contents (rather than re-create them from scratch). Here we explain how to keep control over layers.

You can select more than one layer at a time. To select a contiguous group, click the first layer, hold down the Shift key, and click the last layer in the group. To select more than one layer when they're not all together in a group, click the first layer, press and hold Ctrl (Windows) or ⌘ (Mac), and click any additional layers that you want to select.

## Deleting layers

When you work, you might find that a layer no longer has any objects. It's a layer without a purpose in life, so delete it. Select the layer and click the Trash can at the bottom of the layer list. You can also drag the layer to the Trash can.

When you delete a layer, you delete everything on the layer. However, some objects on a layer might not be visible, because you see only what exists on the Stage in the current frame. For example, if you introduce a circle in Frame 15 of a layer named *Circle* but you're in Frame 1, you don't see that circle. Deleting the Circle layer, however, deletes the circle, although you can't see it. (We discuss frames in more detail in Chapter 9.)

To check for objects on a layer, right-click the layer and choose Hide Others from the contextual menu. Click the first frame on the Timeline and press Enter (Windows) or Return (Mac) to run any existing animation. Objects on that layer appear during the animation if they exist.

## Copying layers

You can copy a layer, along with its entire contents, throughout all frames. If you've created a great bouncing ball and now want two balls, copy the layer. You can then modify the position of the second ball throughout the Timeline without having to re-create the ball itself. Now you have two bouncing balls.

To copy and paste a layer, follow these steps:

1. **Click the layer name to select the layer.**

2. **Choose Edit⇨Timeline⇨Copy Frames.**

3. **Click the Insert Layer button to create a new layer.**

4. **Click the new layer to make it active.**

5. **Choose Edit⇨Timeline⇨Paste Frames.**

## *Renaming layers*

Rename a layer whenever you want. By default, Flash names layers *Layer 1, Layer 2,* and so on. When you use a layer, rename it to reflect its contents. To rename a layer, double-click the layer name and type a new name. Then press Enter (Windows) or Return (Mac).

## *Reordering layers*

In Chapter 4, we explain how to change the order of objects on the Stage when they're on the same layer. When objects are on different layers, a new rule applies. The order of the layers indicates the display order of objects on the Stage. Therefore, objects on the uppermost layer on the list are always on top, objects on the second layer appear one level down, and so on. Objects on the last layer on the list appear on the bottom level of the Stage, behind everything else.

In fact, a simple and effective way to control object stacking is to put objects on different layers and then move the layers higher or lower on the layer list. To move a layer, just click and drag it within the layer list to the desired position. Figure 6-3 shows an example before and after moving a layer. The ball and the oval are on different layers. The left image looks a little odd, but when you reorder the layers, their objects are reordered as well, and you can then see a ball and its shadow.

Changing the layer order can help you more easily select and edit objects that are covered up by other objects. Simply drag the layer to the top of the list, and the objects on that list then appear on top. When you finish editing the objects, drag the layer back to its original location.

**Figure 6-3:**
By changing the order of the layers, you change the order of the objects on those layers.

# Organizing layers

Sometimes layers can get out of hand. You might have several layers with sounds on them or several layers for each animation. Tame those layers by putting them into *folders*. A folder holds layers. Instant organization! For example, you can create a Sounds folder and folders for each animation group.

 To create a folder, click the Insert Layer Folder icon below the layer list. You see a new folder just above the active layer. Name the folder in the same way that you name a layer: Double-click it, type the name, and press Enter (Windows) or Return (Mac). You can distinguish a folder from a layer by its folder icon.

After you have a folder, you fill it up with layers by dragging layers into it. Click and drag a layer onto the folder's row until the folder icon darkens, and then release the mouse button. At the same time, the layer's name becomes indented so that you can easily tell that it's in a folder, as shown in Figure 6-4.

**Figure 6-4:**
Put your layers into folders to keep yourself organized.

You can even put folders in folders. Just drag one folder into another. A folder within a folder is a *nested* folder, and the folder that it's in is the *parent* folder.

Here are some other things that you can do with folders:

- **Remove a folder from a folder:** Drag the nested folder above its parent folder.

- **Remove a layer from a folder:** Drag the layer above the folder name or to another location where it doesn't darken a folder.

- **Collapse or expand individual folders:** Click the folder's arrow at the left of its icon.

- **Expand or collapse all folders:** Right-click (Windows) or Control+click (Mac) and choose Expand All Folders or Collapse All Folders from the shortcut menu.

- **Hide or lock an entire folder and its layers:** You can hide or lock a folder just like you hide or lock a layer. (See the section "Changing layer states," earlier in this chapter.) Click beneath the eye (Show/Hide) or lock (Lock/Unlock) icon on the folder's row.

✔ **Reorder folders:** You can change the order of folders, which automatically changes the order of the layers that they contain. Just drag any folder up or down. For more information, see the previous section.

✔ **Copy the contents of a folder to another folder:** To make a quick shortcut for copying layers and their contents, you can copy folders. Collapse the folder and click the folder name. Choose Edit⇨Timeline⇨Copy Frames. Create a new folder. With the new folder active, choose Edit⇨Timeline⇨ Paste Frames.

✔ **Delete folders:** You can delete folders in the same way you delete layers. Select the folder and click the Trash can icon.

**WARNING!**

Deleting a folder deletes all layers in the folder and everything on those layers. Luckily, Flash warns you before you take the plunge.

## Modifying layer properties

You can use the Layer Properties dialog box, as shown in Figure 6-5, to change certain layer properties, such as the color used for the layer's outlines and the layer height. Most settings, however, are easily accessible from the layer list. Select a layer (or a folder) and choose Modify⇨Timeline⇨Layer Properties.

**Figure 6-5:**
The Layer
Properties
dialog box
lets you
fine-tune
layer
settings.

Here's how to use this dialog box to get the most from your layers:

✔ **The Name text box displays the current name of the layer.** You can rename the layer here if you want.

✔ **Change the Show/Hide and Lock/Unlock layer states by marking (or clearing) the appropriate check boxes.** Usually, you change these states directly on the layer list, as we explain earlier in this chapter.

✔ **You can change the type of layer by choosing from the list of layer types.** We cover guide and mask layers later in this chapter.

✔ **You can change the color that Flash uses when the layer is displayed as outlines.** Click the Outline Color swatch and choose another color from the Color palette.

✔ **Select the View Layer as Outlines check box to turn on outlines.** As we explain earlier in this section, you can accomplish this task easily from the layer listing.

✔ **You can change the layer height to two or three times the normal height.** One reason to change the height of a layer is to more easily view sound waves on a layer that contains a sound. Another is to see larger previews of your keyframes in the Timeline — you can turn these on by clicking the drop-down list in the upper-right corner of the Timeline and choosing Preview or Preview in Context from the pop-up menu.

After you finish using the Layer Properties dialog box, click OK.

# Creating Guide Layers

A *guide layer* is a layer that's invisible in the final, published animation. You can use guide layers for several purposes:

✔ **Animation:** You can place a path on a guide layer to control the motion of an object during animation. Figure 6-6 shows a guide layer that contains a motion guide for the skateboarder. When animated, the skateboard does two flips, following the motion guide. (Read through Chapter 9 for the lowdown on how to create a motion guide.)

✔ **Layout:** Although Flash MX 2004 lets you display guides on the screen to help you draw precisely (as we describe in Chapter 3), you can also place gridlines on guide layers to help you lay out the Stage. Graphic designers use these types of gridlines to figure out how to create a balanced, pleasing effect in their art.

✔ **Drawing:** You can import a bitmap graphic onto a guide layer and draw over the graphic on a regular layer by using the Flash drawing tools. This technique of drawing over a graphic can be a big help when creating your artwork.

Of course, you could use a regular layer and then erase whatever you don't want to appear in the final movie. But if you need to go back and make changes, you would have to create the guide layer over again. Using a guide layer gives you the flexibility of keeping the layer in the movie file, knowing that it will never appear in the published animation.

Layers that are hidden appear in the published .swf file, but guide layers don't appear.

**Figure 6-6:**
A guide layer controls the motion of an object during animation.

To create a guide layer, create a new layer. Then right-click (Windows) or Control+click (Mac) and choose Guide from the contextual menu. The layer is now a guide layer. Use the same procedure to convert a guide layer back to a regular layer. The Guide item on the menu is a toggle, so when you click it again, Flash removes the guide status of the layer.

When you use a guide layer as a motion guide, you must link the guide layer to a layer that contains the objects that you want to guide. The layer with the guided objects is called a *guided layer*. In Figure 6-6, the loops are on a guide layer, and the skateboarder is on a guided layer. All objects on a guided layer automatically snap to the path of the motion guide on the guide layer. To link a layer to a guide layer, creating a guided layer, you can do any of the following:

✔ Create a new layer under the guide layer.

✔ Drag an existing layer under the guide layer.

✔ Choose Modify⇨Layer and choose Guided in the Layer Properties dialog box.

Flash indents the guided layer beneath the guide layer to help you see that they're linked. If you want to unlink a guided layer, drag it above the guide layer or choose Modify⇨Timeline⇨Layer Properties and select the Normal option in the Layer Properties dialog box.

# Opening Windows with Mask Layers

A *mask layer* hides every object on its related layers except those inside a filled shape or text object. You can use mask layers to create peepholes or spotlight effects. Figure 6-7 shows a keyhole shape on a mask layer that hides the entire garden scene except for the part within the keyhole. The garden scene is a rectangle much larger than the section displayed through the keyhole.

**Figure 6-7:**
You can use
a mask layer
to create a
hole through
which you
can see
the layer
or layers
beneath.

## Creating a mask layer

To create a mask layer, the object on the mask layer, and the objects behind
the mask layer, follow these steps:

1. **Create the objects that you want to show through the hole in the
   mask layer.**

   These objects can be on one or more layers. Place all the layers that you
   want to be masked next to each other and at the top of the layer list.

2. **Select the topmost layer on the layer list and click the Insert Layer
   button to create a new layer at the top of the list.**

   This layer will become the mask layer.

3. **Create, insert, or import one filled shape, text, or an instance of a
   symbol on the new layer. (See Chapter 7 for more about symbols.)**

   The filled part of the shape, text, or instance becomes the hole — in
   other words, it's transparent. Unfilled portions of the objects become
   opaque, so everything becomes the opposite of its current state.

4. **Right-click (Windows) or Control+click (Mac) the layer's name and
   choose Mask from the contextual menu.**

   Flash turns the layer into a mask layer and locks the mask layer as well
   as the layer just beneath it on the layer list. The masked layer is indented.
   You see the mask effect displayed. (To link more than one layer to the
   mask layer, see the next section, "Editing mask layers.")

## Editing mask layers

Because Flash locks both the mask layer and the layer or layers that are
masked, you cannot edit them. To edit them, click the lock icon above the

layer list. Flash unlocks the layers and removes the mask effect. After you finish editing the layers, lock them again to redisplay the mask effect.

When you create a mask layer, Flash links only the layer directly beneath it to the mask layer. A layer linked to a mask layer is masked. If you place objects that you want to be masked on several layers, you need to change the property of all those layers from normal to masked.

All the layers that you want to be masked must be directly under the mask layer.

You can link a layer to a mask layer in several ways:

- ✔ If you drag a normal layer directly beneath a mask layer, Flash links it to the mask layer in addition to existing masked layers.
- ✔ Right-click (Windows) or Control+click (Mac) the layer and choose Properties. Select the Masked option button in the Layer Properties dialog box.

Similarly, you can unlink a layer from its mask layer by using one of these methods:

- ✔ Drag the linked layer above the mask layer.
- ✔ Right-click (Windows) or Control+click (Mac) the layer and choose Properties. Select the Normal option button in the Layer Properties dialog box.

## Animating mask layers

Mask layers are more fun when you animate them. You can move them, change their sizes, and change their shapes. If you create a keyhole like the one shown in Figure 6-7, you can move the keyhole past the masked layers, revealing what lies beneath while the keyhole moves. You can use the same technique to create an effect of a spotlight moving around a stage, revealing whatever it lights up. The only thing that you can't do is to animate the mask layer objects along motion paths. (Chapter 9 explains how to animate masks along with other objects.) You can create more complex mask animations by using ActionScript. For the steps to do this, see the section on creating animated masks with movie clips in Chapter 10.

Look for `ffd_reveal.fla` on this book's Web site at `www.dummies.com/go/flash8`. To see the mask, open the file and unlock all the layers. *(Thanks to Shane Mielke, one of our top ten designers to watch [see Chapter 16], for this file.)*

# Part III
# Getting Symbolic

"You know, I've asked you a dozen times not to animate the torches on our Web page!"

# *In this part . . .*

**S**ymbols can show you the deeper levels of life, and Flash symbols let you get down deep into the mechanics of animation. In this part, you discover the three kinds of symbols — graphic, button, and movie clip symbols — and how to use them.

Manipulating symbols is a critical feature of Flash. Symbols enable you to easily place duplicate graphics in your movie without significantly increasing the movie's size, and you use symbols when you start to animate. This part of the book also gives you the lowdown on buttons, which are central to the Web lifestyle in the 21st century. Flash lets you create buttons that change when you pass the mouse cursor over them and again when you click them. You can even make animated buttons. Part III provides you with the basis for creating great animations.

# Chapter 7

# Heavy Symbolism

. . . . . . . . . . . . . . . . . . . . . . . . . . . . . . . . . . . . . . . . . . . . .

. . . . . . . . . . . . . . . . . . . . . . . . . . . . . . . . . . . . . . . . . . . . .

*F*lash offers a way to simplify your work, called symbols. A *symbol* can be any object or combination of objects, animation, or a Web button. When you create a symbol, the objects (or animation) become one object. Sounds like grouping, yes? (If you've already read Chapter 4, you know what we mean.) The difference is that Flash stores the definition of the symbol in the Library. From the Library, you can now effortlessly insert multiple copies of the symbol into your movie. Each copy is called an *instance*.

Besides making your life easier when you want to use a set of objects more than once, symbols have another advantage: They significantly reduce the size of your files. Rather than store each instance that you use, Flash stores one definition for the symbol and refers to that definition each time that you display an instance of the symbol. You can place symbols inside other symbols, which is called *nesting*. Used this way, symbols are the building blocks for complex graphics and animation. Motion-tweened animation requires symbols, groups, or text, so you often create symbols when preparing to animate. (Chapter 9 explains tweened animation.)

So, symbols are all-around good guys, and you should use them as much as possible.

## Understanding Symbol Types

Flash offers four types of symbols: graphic, movie clip, button, and font. Each type is made up of a group of objects or animation, but each type has a different purpose. Understanding these types is very important to understanding symbols and Flash animation in general.

## *Using graphic symbols*

*Graphic symbols* are the simplest and most obvious type of symbol. When you create a Flash movie, you create objects on the Stage. Some objects may remain still, such as backgrounds. You animate other objects — after all, what would Flash be without animation? Use graphic symbols for collections of static objects or for simple animation. Figure 7-1 shows a graphic symbol created from several curves and circles.

**Figure 7-1:**
A graphic symbol, created from several objects, has a single selection border.

You create graphic symbols to reduce the size of your file and to make it easier to add multiple copies of a graphic to your movie. Symbols are stored in the Library and are available to not only the movie in which you created them but also any other movie. Therefore, using symbols is a good way to store graphic images for use in Flash movies. You don't have to re-create the wheel.

Flash ignores sounds and ActionScript inside graphic symbols. ActionScript code (which we explain in detail in Chapter 10) is the key to creating interactive movies. For that reason, use graphic symbols only when the animation is simple.

## Using movie clip symbols

A *movie clip* is like a movie within your movie that you can manipulate by using interactive controls (created with ActionScript, which you can read about in Chapter 10). Movie clips are crucial for complex animation and especially interactive animation. A movie clip has its own Timeline independent of the movie's main Timeline. For example, you can go to a movie clip at any point in the movie, play it, and then return to where you left off on the Timeline. You can also attach movie clips to buttons. We explain how to create movie clips in this chapter; Chapter 8 discusses using movie clips with buttons. Chapter 9 covers using movie clips in animation, and Chapter 10 explains how to use and control movie clips by using interactive controls.

Flash comes with several *components,* which are special movie clips that allow you to add user interface elements — such as radio buttons, check boxes, and scroll bars — to your movies. Choose Window➪Components and drag one of your choices to the Stage. Then choose Window➪Component Inspector to set the parameters of the component. For example, you can insert a list box and then add all the items (called *labels* on the Component Parameters panel) that you want on the list. For more information on components, see Chapter 12.

## Using button symbols

Button symbols create *buttons* — those little graphics that you click on Web pages to take you to other pages on the site or the Internet. In Flash, you can use buttons in the same way, but you can also use buttons to interact with your site. For example, you can let viewers decide whether they want to see a movie — when they click the button, the movie starts. You can also use advanced scripting to create buttons that control interactive games and other viewer activities. However you want to use buttons, button symbols are the way to start. You can add movie clips and interactive controls to buttons. Find out all about buttons in Chapter 8.

## Using font symbols

A *font symbol* exports a font for use in multiple Flash movies. This is great whenever you use the same font in more than one Flash movie on a Web site: Your audience needs to download the font information only once instead of every time for every single Flash movie. This makes your Flash movies smaller and the user's loading time faster. We show you how to use font symbols in Chapter 12.

# Creating Symbols

For graphic symbols and button symbols, usually you create the objects that you need and then turn them into a symbol. The same is true of movie clips if they are static and you use ActionScript to control them. However, when you use a movie clip as a type of animation, you either create an animation on the Stage and then convert it to a movie clip symbol; or create the movie clip symbol, create the initial objects, and then create the animation.

In the next few sections, we explain the various ways of creating symbols, for whichever purpose you want to use them. Each type of symbol has its own icon that's used in the Library. The following table shows what type of symbol each icon represents:

| *Symbol* | *What It Represents* |
| --- | --- |
| | Movie clip |
| | Button |
| | Graphic |

## Creating symbols from existing objects

To create a symbol from unanimated objects you've already created, follow these steps:

**1. On the Stage, select the objects that you want to convert to a symbol.**

**2. Choose Modify⇨Convert to Symbol or press F8.**

The Convert to Symbol dialog box opens, as shown in Figure 7-2.

**Figure 7-2:**
The Convert to Symbol dialog box.

```
Convert to Symbol                                       ☒

  Name:  Symbol 1|                              [   OK   ]

  Type:  ○ Movie clip   Registration: ░░░      [ Cancel ]
         ○ Button
         ⊙ Graphic                             [ Advanced ]
```

**3. In the Name text box, type a name for the symbol.**

A common convention is to name the symbol in a way that's unique and also indicates the symbol type. For example, help_btn could be the name for a button symbol that will become a Help button on a Web site.

4. **From the Behavior list, select the type of symbol that you want to create: graphic, button, or movie clip.**

5. **Click OK to create the symbol and close the Convert to Symbol dialog box.**

The objects that you selected become one object, indicated by a single selection border around all the objects. Flash also stores the symbol in the Library. (Chapter 2 explains how to use the Library.)

## Creating empty symbols

Rather than create a symbol from existing objects, you can create an empty symbol and then create the objects for the symbol. If you know in advance that you want to create a symbol, you can use this method.

To create an empty symbol, follow these steps:

1. **With no objects selected, choose Insert⇨New Symbol.**

The Create New Symbol dialog box opens.

2. **In the Name text box, type a name for the symbol.**

3. **From the Behavior list, select the type of symbol you want to create — graphic, button, or movie clip — and then click OK.**

Flash switches to symbol-editing mode, which we describe in the section "Editing symbols," later in this chapter.

4. **Create the objects or animation for the symbol in the same way that you do in regular movie-editing mode.**

5. **Choose Edit⇨Edit Document to leave symbol-editing mode and return to your movie.**

Your new symbol disappears! Don't worry — Flash saved the symbol in the Library. To insert an instance of the symbol on the Stage, see the section "Inserting instances," later in this chapter.

## Converting an animation to a movie clip symbol

You can create a movie clip symbol by converting regular animation to a movie clip. Use this method when you already have the animation created on the Timeline.

To convert an animation on the Stage to a movie clip symbol, follow these steps:

1. **On the layer listing, select all frames in all layers containing the animation by clicking the first layer and pressing Shift while you click the last layer in the group.**

   Alternatively, you can press Ctrl (Windows) or ⌘ (Mac) and click additional layers.

2. **On the Timeline, right-click (Windows) or Control+click (Mac) and choose Copy Frames to copy all the frames of the animation to the Clipboard.**

   Alternatively, you can choose Edit➪Timeline➪Copy Frames.

3. **With no objects selected (click off the Stage to be sure that no objects are selected), choose Insert➪New Symbol.**

   The Create New Symbol dialog box opens.

4. **In the Name text box, type a name for the movie clip.**

5. **From the Behavior list, select Movie Clip as the type of symbol.**

6. **Click OK to close the Create New Symbol dialog box.**

   Flash switches to symbol-editing mode so that you can edit the symbol.

7. **Click the first frame of the Timeline to set the start of the movie clip symbol.**

8. **Choose Edit➪Timeline➪Paste Frames to paste the animation into the Timeline and create the symbol.**

9. **To return to the main movie and Timeline, choose Edit➪Edit Document.**

10. **To delete the animation from the main movie (now that you've saved it in a movie clip), select all layers as you did in Step 1 and choose Edit➪Timeline➪Remove Frames.**

    You can delete the animation from the main movie because your Library now has a movie clip that contains that animation. When you choose the movie clip in the Library panel, you can click the small Play button to play the animation in the Library panel's window.

## Creating a symbol by duplicating a symbol

One more way to create a graphic, button, or movie symbol is to duplicate an existing symbol. To duplicate a symbol, follow these steps:

1. **Open the Library (choose Window➪Library).**

2. **Select the symbol that you want to duplicate.**

3. **Click the Options menu in the upper-right corner of the Library window and choose Duplicate.**

   Flash opens the Duplicate Symbol dialog box.

4. **In the Name text box, type a name for the duplicate. Select the type of symbol that you want to create if you want a different kind from the original.**

5. **Click OK to close the dialog box and create the duplicate symbol.**

# Modifying Symbols

Flash is a master of flexibility, and sometimes you need to make changes. Of course, you can change symbols after you create them. Here we explain the procedures you need to know.

## Changing the properties of a symbol

You might need to change a symbol's properties. For example, you might create a graphic symbol and then realize that you need it to be a movie clip. Or you might want to change the font used by a font symbol. No problem!

To change the properties of a symbol, follow these steps:

1. **Choose Window➪Library to open the Library.**

2. **Right-click (Windows) or Control+click (Mac) the symbol's icon (not its name) and choose Properties from the menu.**

   The Symbol Properties dialog box opens.

3. **If the symbol is a graphic, button, or movie clip, select the type of symbol that you want from the Behavior list and click OK. If the symbol is a font, change the font or its size or style as you desire and click OK.**

Look on our companion Web site at www.dummies.com/go/flash8 for ffd_reveal.fla — a good example of a short movie with lots of symbols. *(The Flash movie is courtesy of Shane Mielke. You can see the full Web site at www.pixelranger.com.)*

## Editing symbols

An *instance* is a copy of a symbol that you insert into your movie. Part of the power of symbols lies in their control over instances. If you edit a symbol,

Flash updates all instances of that symbol in the movie. You can change a symbol once and save yourself the time of creating the same change for every instance of that symbol. For that reason, it's worthwhile to make a symbol every time that you want to use a certain shape or group of shapes more than once.

You can edit a symbol in three different modes:

- ✔ **Edit in Symbol-Editing Mode:** Switches you to symbol-editing mode. You see only the symbol. Right-click a selected symbol and choose Edit.

- ✔ **Edit in Place:** Lets you edit a symbol while still viewing other objects on the Stage. Other objects are dimmed while you edit the symbol. Right-click a selected symbol and choose Edit in Place.

- ✔ **Edit in a New Window:** Opens a new window where you can edit your symbol. You see only the symbol. Right-click a selected symbol and choose Edit in New Window.

The value of editing in place is that you can see how your change works with the rest of the objects that you have on the Stage. For example, if you want to make your symbol bigger, you may need to make sure that it doesn't obscure some nearby text. If you have lots of stuff on the Stage, however, editing in symbol-editing mode or in a new window can help you focus more easily on the symbol itself.

To edit a symbol, follow these steps:

1. **Select any instance of the symbol on the Stage.**

2. **Right-click (Windows) or Control+click (Mac) the instance and choose Edit, Edit in Place, or Edit in New Window. (Choosing Edit puts you into symbol-editing mode.)**

   Flash displays the symbol name above the Timeline. If you choose Edit in Place, other objects are dimmed, as shown in Figure 7-3.

   This kaleidoscope animation is in the Ch07 folder on the companion Web site at www.dummies.com/go/flash8.

3. **Edit the symbol in any way you want.**

4. **After you finish editing (from Edit or Edit in Place), click the scene name to the left of the symbol name or choose Edit➪Edit Document; from a new window, click the Close button.**

   You are now back in your main movie.

**Figure 7-3:**
One symbol,
which
includes
a wedge
and some
circles,
is being
edited.
Other
objects are
dimmed
because
Flash is
in edit-in-
place mode.

# Using Symbols from Other Movies

After you create a symbol and store it in the Library, you can use that Library in any other movie. You can also open the Library from any other movie and use its symbols in your current movie.

If the other movie is open and its Library is open, you can access that movie's Library from within your current movie. Libraries of any open movie are available from any other open movie. Just choose that other movie from the drop-down list at the top of the Library palette. (Choose Window➪Library to open the Library.)

To use a symbol from the Library of another movie that is closed, follow these steps:

1. **Choose File➪Import➪Open External Library.**

   The Open as Library dialog box opens.

2. **Select the movie file.**

3. **Click Open.**

   Flash displays the Library of the other movie in a new Library window.

The new Library might hide your current movie's Library. Just drag it by its grabber in the upper-left corner of the panel window under the current Library until it docks there. In the new Library, many Option menu items and icons are disabled to prevent you from making changes in the other movie's file.

When you have more than one Library open, the background of the listing of open movies is white. The background of Libraries from other, unopened movies is gray. So you can look at the background to quickly see which Library is which.

To use a symbol from the other Library, drag it onto the Stage. When you do this, Flash places a copy of the symbol in the current movie's Library. (See Chapter 2 for more information about the Library.)

You can also update or replace any graphic, button, or movie clip symbol in your movie's Library with the content of a symbol from any other Library on your hard drive or network. Accessing a symbol in this way is called *author-time sharing* of symbols or assets. On the other hand, you can also share symbols or assets at *runtime,* after you have uploaded your movie. A *font symbol* is a special type of symbol that you use at runtime. We explain runtime shared libraries (which can include sounds) in Chapter 12.

When you share a symbol while you're creating a movie (during *authoring*), the symbol in your current movie keeps its original name, but the contents take on the properties of the symbol that you're sharing. If you have already replaced a symbol and the outside symbol changes (because it has been edited), use author-time sharing to update the symbol in your current drawing to match the symbol's new properties.

To update or replace a graphic, button, or movie clip symbol in your movie with the properties of another symbol, follow these steps:

1. **Open the Library (choose Window⇨Library) and select the symbol that you want to update or replace.**

2. **From the Library menu, choose Properties.**

   The Symbol Properties dialog box opens.

3. **Click Advanced, if necessary, to see the expanded dialog box. In the Source section, click Browse.**

   The Locate Macromedia Flash Document File dialog box opens.

4. **Navigate to the movie (.fla) file that contains the symbol that you want to use. Select it and click Open.**

   The Select Source dialog box opens. You see a list of the symbols in the movie that you selected.

5. **Choose a symbol and click OK.**

    When you choose a symbol, you see a preview in the preview box, so you can easily find the symbol you want. When you click OK, you're back in the Symbol Properties dialog box.

6. **In the Source section of the Symbol Properties dialog box, select the Always Update Before Publishing check box if you want to automatically update the symbol if the original has changed.**

    Enable this check box to create a link between the source symbol and the symbol in your current movie.

7. **Click OK.**

You now have a symbol in your Library that has its original name but looks like the symbol that you chose from the other movie.

## Using the Flash Library

Flash comes with three common libraries that you can use. To access these libraries, choose Window➪Common Libraries and then select one of the libraries. Flash includes buttons, learning interactions (interface items for creating online courses), and classes (building blocks for developing ActionScript applications). These libraries are also a good place to pick up ideas and see what you can create in Flash.

## Using the Flash For Dummies Library

The Flash libraries contain some good examples, but they miss many basic shapes and simple objects, some of which are hard to draw in Flash. We decided to fill in the gaps! We created a library of art, geometric shapes, and fun shapes that you can use in your movies, with some new shapes designed especially for this edition. The *Flash For Dummies* Library is named Flash 8 For Dummies Library.fla. You can find it at www.dummies.com/go/flash8.

To use this library, go to www.dummies.com/go/flash8 and download Flash For Dummies Library.fla. In Windows, download it to the Program Files\ Macromedia\Flash 8\en\Configuration\Libraries folder on your hard drive. On the Mac, download it to the Applications/Macromedia Flash 8 /Configuration/Libraries folder on your hard drive.

After that, you can always open this library the same way you open other common libraries: Choose Window➪Common Libraries➪Flash 8 For Dummies Library.fla. We hope you enjoy it!

# Working with Instances, for Instance

After you create a symbol, you can use it in many ways. You can insert it in your movie, inside other symbols, or even in other movies. Each copy of the symbol is called an *instance*. You can change the properties of an instance so that it differs from its parent symbol. For example, you can change the color of an instance — the original symbol remains unchanged.

## Inserting instances

To insert an instance of a symbol, follow these steps:

1. **Choose Window⊏Library (Ctrl+L or F11 for Windows or ⌘+L or F11 for the Mac) to open the Library, as shown in Figure 7-4.**

**Figure 7-4:**
Insert an instance of a symbol by dragging it from the Library.

2. **Choose the layer where you want the instance to be placed.**

3. **Click a keyframe on the Timeline where you want the instance to be placed.**

   Flash places instances only in keyframes. If you don't select a keyframe, Flash puts the instance in the first keyframe to the left of the current frame. (See Chapter 9 for more about keyframes.)

4. **Drag the symbol from the Library to the Stage.**

When you insert a graphic instance, you need to consider how it fits within your entire animation. For example, the instance might be the starting point for some animation, or it might be part of the background that remains static throughout the animation. Perhaps you want the instance to suddenly appear at some point in the animation. If the instance contains animation, you need to insert it at its proper starting point. (Chapter 9 explains how to copy graphics across any number of frames to create a static background and covers the entire topic of animation in detail.)

A movie clip instance, on the other hand, takes up only one frame on the Timeline. It plays and loops automatically unless you create ActionScript code to control it. (Chapter 10 talks about ActionScript.)

## Editing instances

A symbol's children don't have to be carbon copies of their parents, thank goodness. Instances of a symbol can differ from their parent symbol by color, type, and play mode. You can also rotate, scale, or skew an instance, leaving the parent symbol unchanged.

When you edit an instance, Flash remembers the changes. When you edit the symbol, Flash doesn't forget those changes. Suppose that you create a red circle graphic symbol, and then you create several instances of it and change one instance to pink. Then you edit the (still red!) circle symbol to change it to an oval. All the instances are now ovals, but the one you turned pink is still pink. The instance's shape has been updated, but the pink color remains.

In the Property inspector (choose Window⇨Properties⇨Properties), you can change an instance's color (or tint), brightness, or transparency, giving you some very useful control over the appearance of your instances. To change an instance's color, brightness, or transparency, follow these steps:

1. **Select the instance.**

2. **Choose Window⇨Properties⇨Properties to open the Property inspector.**

3. **From the Color drop-down list, select one of these options:**

   - **None:** Adds no color effect.

   - **Brightness:** Changes the lightness or darkness of the instance.

   - **Tint:** Changes the color of the instance.

   - **Alpha:** Changes the opacity/transparency of the instance.

   - **Advanced:** Changes both the color and the alpha at one time.

4. **Make the desired changes, as we explain in the next few sections.**

   You see the changes that you make in the Property inspector immediately in your selected instance.

### Changing brightness

When you choose Brightness from the Color drop-down list, a slider and a text box appear. Type a brightness percentage or drag the slider and see the result immediately in the symbol instance. High brightness makes the image light, and 100-percent brightness makes the instance disappear. Low brightness makes the image dark so that 0-percent brightness turns the instance black.

### Changing tint

When you choose Tint from the Color drop-down list, you can pick the color and then the amount of the color (the tint), by percentage, that you want to apply. Figure 7-5 shows the controls for this option. You can pick a color by clicking the Tint Color button and choosing from the color swatches or type red, green, and blue values (if you know them).

**Figure 7-5:**
Changing
color and
tint used on
a symbol
instance.

Specify the percentage of the color that you want to apply by typing a value in the percent text box or by clicking the drop-down arrow and dragging the slider to choose a percentage. When the percentage is set to 100%, the instance completely changes to the color that you specified. If the percentage is set to 0%, Flash leaves the instance unchanged.

The Flash method of specifying a color gives you great flexibility and precision. You can choose a color and use the tint control to create a meld of the current color and your chosen color.

If you want to stick to the 216 Web-safe color palette, just select a color swatch from the ones displayed when you click the Tint Color button and then slide the tint control all the way up to 100%.

### Changing transparency

Choose Alpha from the Color Effect drop-down menu to change the transparency of an instance. (*Alpha* enables levels of transparency, and you can think of the term as somewhat synonymous to *opaqueness*.) Use the slider or type a value in the text box. A value of 0 means that your instance becomes completely transparent — in that case, when you return to the Stage, all you see is the selection border and the small plus sign that marks the symbol's registration point. When you deselect the instance, you see absolutely nothing! (Chapter 4 explains more about a symbol's registration point, including how to move it. See the section on groups.)

 Partial transparency lets your background show through. A partially transparent instance blends in with your background, creating a softer effect. However, transparency is a complex feature and can slow down the loading and playing of a movie.

### Changing color and transparency at the same time

Select Advanced from the Color Effect drop-down menu to change both the color and the transparency at the same time by using red, green, and blue values. The Settings button appears on the Property inspector. Click Settings to open the Advanced Effect dialog box. Figure 7-6 shows the controls, which are complex.

**Figure 7-6:**
The
Advanced
Effect
dialog box.

> **Advanced Effect**
>
> Red = ( 55% ⌄ x R) + 0 ⌄
> Green = ( 55% ⌄ x G) + 69 ⌄
> Blue= ( 55% ⌄ x B) + 115 ⌄
> Alpha = ( 100% ⌄ x A) + 0 ⌄
>
> OK   Cancel

Use the controls on the left to specify the color or transparency as a specific percentage of the current value. Use the controls on the right to change the color or transparency to a specific, absolute amount. Flash then calculates the new color value by multiplying the current value by the percentage that you specified and then adding the value from the right side. As you can see, this method provides lots of control — but it might make you crazy first.

 To simply change both the color and the transparency of an instance, use the Tint controls to change the color and then just change the left Alpha setting in the Advanced Effect dialog box.

### Adding filters and blends

 In the Professional version of Flash only, you can apply special graphic effects to buttons and movie clips, called *filters*. Select the text and click the Filters tab of the Property inspector. Click the Plus (+) icon and choose one (or more) of the following filters: Bevel, Drop Shadow, Glow, Blur, Gradient Glow, Gradient Blur, or Adjust Color.

You can also apply new *blend modes* to movie clips in Flash 8 Professional. Blend modes determine how movie clips that overlap blend with each other at the point of overlap. To apply a blend, select a movie clip instance and adjust the color and transparency as we explain in the previous sections. Then choose a blend mode from the Blend drop-down list in the Property inspector.

### Changing an instance's type

The instance type — graphic, movie clip, or button — comes from the symbol type, but you might want to change it. For example, if you created some animation and saved it as a graphic symbol, you might want to use it as a movie clip. Rather than change the symbol type, you can change only the type of the instance that you have inserted.

To change the instance type, follow these steps:

1. **Select the instance.**

2. **Choose Window⇨Properties⇨Properties to open the Property inspector.**

3. **From the Instance Behavior drop-down list, select one of the following types:**

   - **Graphic:** If the graphic contains animation, select Graphic in the Behavior drop-down list and then determine how the animation will run in the Options for Graphics drop-down list on the Property inspector. You have three choices:

     *Loop* plays the animation contained in the instance over and over during the frames occupied by the instance.

     *Play Once* plays the animation one time from the frame that you specify.

     *Single Frame* displays any one frame of the animation. In other words, the animation doesn't play; you specify which frame the movie displays.

   - **Button:** Select the Button option to determine how the button is tracked in the Tracking Options section. From the Options for Buttons drop-down list, select Track as Button when you're creating single buttons. Select Track as Menu if you're creating pop-up menus.

   - **Movie Clip:** Select the Movie Clip option and specify an Instance name in the Name text box. You use this name with certain ActionScript controls so that you can refer to and control the instance. (For more information about ActionScript, see Chapter 10.)

### Replacing an instance

Suppose that you create a complex animation with bouncing bunnies all over the Stage. Suddenly your boss decides that some of the bouncing bunnies should be bouncing squirrels instead. Meanwhile, you had already edited all the bunnies to make them different sizes and colors. You need a way to replace some of the bunnies with squirrels without losing their sizes and colors.

To replace an instance, follow these steps:

1. **Create the squirrel symbol (or whichever new symbol you need).**

   Flash stores the new symbol in the Library.

2. **Select an instance of the bunny — that is, your original instance — on the Stage.**

3. **Choose Window⇨Properties⇨Properties to open the Property inspector.**

4. **Click the Swap button to open the Swap Symbol dialog box.**

5. **In the dialog box, select the squirrel or any other symbol.**

6. **Click OK to swap the symbols and close the Swap Symbol dialog box.**

   Flash retains your color effects and size changes but changes the symbol.

Unfortunately, you must repeat this process for all the bunnies that you want to change on the Stage, but it's better than reinserting all your instances and re-creating the instance changes.

If your boss actually wants you to change ALL the bunnies to squirrels, your job is much simpler. Just edit the bunny symbol (as we describe in the "Editing symbols" section, earlier in this chapter) to replace the bunny image with a squirrel. Then all the instances of that symbol instantly change to squirrels yet retain the color effects and size changes that you gave them while they were still bunnies.

Duplicate a symbol when you want to use one symbol as a springboard for creating a new symbol. Follow the instructions in the "Creating Symbols" section, earlier in this chapter. Make any changes that you want to the new symbol and place instances on the Stage.

### Breaking apart an instance

You can break apart an instance into its component objects. The original symbol remains in the movie's Library. You might want to use the instance as a starting point for creating a completely new symbol, or you might want to animate the components of the symbol so that they move separately. Other instances remain unchanged.

To break apart an instance, select it and choose Modify⇨Break Apart. If an instance contains symbols or grouped objects within it, you can use the Break Apart command again to break apart those internal objects as well.

# Chapter 8

# Pushing Buttons

*W*hen you view a Web page, you see buttons that you can click to move to other pages or sites. These buttons are graphical images, but they're hyperlinks as well. If you start to pay attention to these buttons, you see that some of them change when you pass your mouse cursor over them. They change again when you click them. Sometimes they make a sound when you click them.

Flash can create these types of buttons and more. You can animate Flash buttons, for example, so that they move or rotate when viewers pass over or click them. You can add interactive controls (actions) to buttons so that passing over or clicking them starts other movies or creates other effects.

In this chapter, you find out how to create buttons that look the way you want. You also discover how to make more complex buttons that include sounds, movie clips, and simple ActionScript. To discover more about ActionScript and interactivity, see Chapter 10.

## Creating Simple Buttons

Before you create a button, stop and think about what you want the button to accomplish on a Web page and how you want it to look. Web page designers often create a series of similar buttons that lead to various Web pages. This similarity creates a coherent style to the page. Buttons often include some text to identify the button's purpose.

But you can use buttons for lots of other more advanced purposes than navigating to Web pages. A button can stop music, indicate a choice in a survey or game, or be dragged around on a puzzle or game Web page.

A *button* is a symbol that responds when a user clicks it. (See Chapter 7 for the lowdown on how to create and edit symbols.) In this chapter, we cover the entire process of creating buttons.

## Understanding button states

A button has four states that define characteristics of the button:

- ✔ **Up:** Defines what the button looks like when the mouse pointer is not over the button. The viewer initially sees the Up state of a button.

- ✔ **Over:** Defines what the button looks like when the pointer is over the button (but it hasn't been clicked).

- ✔ **Down:** Defines what the button looks like when the button is clicked.

- ✔ **Hit:** Defines the area of the button that responds to the mouse. The user doesn't see this area — it's invisible. When you pass the pointer over the hit area, the pointer is considered to be over the button. When you click anywhere in the hit area, the button works.

Figure 8-1 shows a button in its four states. A typical, simple button might show a lit-up effect for the Over state and an indented look (as though the button is pressed in) for the Down state. In this example, the Down state moves the highlight to the right, giving the impression of movement when the user clicks the button.

**Figure 8-1:**
The four states of a button: Up, Over, Down, and Hit.

Up    Over

Tips &+Tricks    Tips &+Tricks

Tips &+Tricks    Tips &+Tricks

Down    Hit

**TIP**

Radial gradients are useful for creating a lit-up or pushed-in look. Use a light color or white to create the appearance of a highlight. Use a dark color or black to create an indented look. Just changing the color of the fill (often to a lighter color) is often enough to make it seem lit up.

**ON THE WEB**

The button shown in Figure 8-1 is on the companion Web site at `www.dummies.com/go/flash8`. Look for `capsule.fla` in the Ch08 folder. To try out the buttons in this movie, choose Control➪Test Movie.

## *Making a basic button*

To create a simple button, follow these steps:

1. **Choose Insert⇨New Symbol to open the Create New Symbol dialog box.**

2. **In the Name text box, type a name for the button.**

3. **In the Behavior section, choose the Button option and click OK.**

   You're now in symbol-editing mode. Flash displays the special Timeline for buttons, with four frames: Up, Over, Down, and Hit, as shown in Figure 8-2. Note the dot in the Up frame, indicating that the frame is a keyframe. (For more information about keyframes, see Chapter 9.) The word *Up* is highlighted, indicating that the Up frame is active.

**Figure 8-2:**
The Flash symbol-editing mode for buttons displays a Timeline with four frames.

4. **Create the graphic for the Up state.**

   You can use the Flash drawing tools, an imported graphic, or an instance of a symbol. You can create as many layers as you want for the button. For an animated button, use a movie clip symbol. We explain how to create an animated button in the "Adding a movie clip to a button" section, later in this chapter.

   If you want the button image for the four states to be in the same place, place the graphic in the center of the display and build the other states in the center as well. To do this, cut and paste the graphic. (See Chapter 4 for more about centering objects on the display.) If the button images aren't in the same place, the button appears to shift when the viewer passes the cursor over, or clicks, the button.

5. **Right-click (Windows) or Control+click (Mac) the Over frame and choose Insert Keyframe from the contextual menu.**

   Flash inserts a keyframe in the Over frame of the button. You can also choose Insert⇨Timeline⇨Keyframe or press F6. The graphic for the Up state remains on the Stage.

6. **Create the graphic for the Over state.**

   You can use the graphic for the Up state as a starting point and change it (or leave it the same if you don't want the button to change when the mouse pointer passes over the button). You can also delete the graphic and put a new one in its place. If you have more than one layer, place a keyframe on each layer before creating the artwork for that layer.

7. **Right-click (Windows) or Control+click (Mac) the Down frame and choose Insert Keyframe from the contextual menu.**

8. **Create the graphic for the Down frame.**

   Repeat as in Step 6.

9. **Right-click (Windows) or Control+click (Mac) the Hit frame and choose Insert Keyframe from the contextual menu.**

10. **If necessary, create the shape that defines the active area of the button.**

    This shape should completely cover all the graphics of the other state. Usually, a rectangle or circle is effective. If you ignore the Hit frame, Flash uses the boundary of the objects in the Up frame, which might be what you want.

    If you use text for the button, viewers have to click the letters precisely unless you create a rectangular hit area around the text. To cover an area of text, create a filled-in shape on a new layer.

11. **Click the scene name above the layer list (or the Back arrow to the left of the scene name) to return to the regular Timeline and leave symbol-editing mode.**

12. **If the Library isn't open, choose Window⊃Library and drag the button symbol that you just created to wherever you want it on the Stage.**

    You just created a button!

A button is a symbol, but when you want to place a button on the Stage, you must drag the button from the Library to create an instance of the symbol. See Chapter 7 for a full explanation of symbols and instances.

## Putting Buttons to the Test

After you create a button, you need to test it. You can choose from a couple methods.

The fastest way to test a button is to enable it. An enabled button responds to your mouse as you would expect — it changes as you specified when you pass the mouse over it and click it. To enable the buttons on the Stage, choose Control⊃Enable Simple Buttons. All the buttons on the Stage are now enabled.

Have fun with your button! Pass the mouse over it, click it, and watch it change.

After you test your button, suppose that you want to select the button to move it. You try to click it to select it, and it only glows at you, according to the Down frame's definition. Choose Control➪Enable Simple Buttons again to disable the buttons. Now you can select a button like any other object. In general, enable buttons only to test them.

However, if you really want to select an enabled button, you can do so with the Selection tool by dragging a selection box around it. You can use the arrow keys to move the button. If you want to edit the button further, choose Window➪Properties➪Properties to open the Property inspector and edit the button's properties, as we explain in Chapter 7.

If you have other animations on the Stage, you can play an animation with the buttons enabled. Choose Control➪Play or press Enter (Windows) or Return (Mac). By playing the animation, you can see how the buttons fit in with the rest of your movie.

Another way to test a button is to test the entire movie. Choose Control➪Test Movie. Flash creates an .swf file just as it would if you were publishing the movie based on default publishing settings. Any animation plays, and you can test your buttons as well. When you're done, click the Close box of the window.

If your button contains movie clips, you must use this method of testing the button because the animation doesn't play on the Stage.

# Creating Complex Buttons

Buttons can do more than just change color or shape. You can enhance a button in three ways:

- ✔ **Add a sound:** For example, you can add a clicking sound to the Down frame of a button so that users hear that sound when they click the button.
- ✔ **Add a movie clip:** To animate a button, you add a movie clip to it. You can animate the Up, Over, and Down frames, if you want.
- ✔ **Add an action (interactive control):** To make a button do something, you need to add an action to it by using ActionScript. Actions are covered in Chapter 10, but we discuss some of the basic concepts here.

## Adding a sound to a button

For fun, you can add a sound to a button. Usually, sounds are added to the Over or Down frame — or both, if you want. Chapter 11 explains lots more about sound, but in this section, we explain how to add a simple sound to a button.

Look in the Ch08 folder of the companion Web site at www.dummies.com/go/ flash8 for click.wav. You can add this sound to the Down frame of a button.

To add a sound to a button, follow these steps:

1. **Create the button symbol.**

2. **Choose File⇨Import⇨Import to Library to open the Import dialog box.**

3. **Select the sound file (in .wav, .aiff, or .mp3 format) and click Open.**

   Flash stores the file in the Library.

4. **Choose Window⇨Library to open the Library.**

5. **If you aren't in symbol-editing mode, double-click the button's icon in the Library to enter symbol-editing mode.**

6. **Click the plus sign at the bottom of the layer list to add a new layer.**

   See Chapter 6 for a full explanation of layers.

7. **Name the new layer *Sound* or something similar.**

8. **In the new layer, right-click (Windows) or Control+click (Mac) the frame where you want to place the sound — for example, the Down frame — and choose Insert Keyframe from the contextual menu.**

9. **Choose Window⇨Properties⇨Properties to open the Property inspector.**

10. **From the Sound drop-down list, select the sound file that you want.**

    Flash lists all the sounds that you have imported into the Library. When you select the sound file, you see the sound wave indicator on the sound's layer in the frame where you inserted the sound, as shown in Figure 8-3.

**Figure 8-3:**
When you add a sound to a button, the sound wave appears in the Timeline.

| Timeline | ⇦ | 🎬 Scene 1 | 👆 bn_capsule |
|---|---|---|---|
| | 👁 🔒 ▢ | Up | Over | Down | Hit |
| 🗹 Sound | 🖉 • • ▢ | ∘ | ▯ | • | ▯ |
| 🗹 Layer 1 | • • ▢ | • | • | • | • |

11. **From the Sync drop-down list of the Property inspector, select Event.**

    To see the Sync drop-down list, you need to click the Expand arrow at the lower-right corner of the Property inspector.

The Event setting synchronizes the sound to the occurrence of an event: in this case, the clicking of the button. Event is the default setting.

12. **Click the scene name in the upper-left area of the layer list or the Back arrow to the left of the scene name.**

    Flash returns you to the regular Timeline and leaves symbol-editing mode.

13. **Drag the button symbol that you just created from the Library to wherever you want the button on the Stage.**

    You're done! Now test the button as we explain in the earlier section, "Putting Buttons to the Test."

Be sure to look in Chapter 11 for more information on adding sounds to buttons and movies.

If you've already added the sound to another movie, choose File⇨Import⇨ Open External Library and choose the other movie. Click the desired keyframe and drag the sound from the Library to anywhere on the Stage. Flash places the sound in the selected keyframe.

## Adding a movie clip to a button

If you think that simple buttons are b-o-r-i-n-g, you can animate them. To animate a button, you must create a movie clip symbol and then insert the movie clip into one of the frames. Generally, button animation is localized in the area of the button. If you want to make an elaborate button, you can animate all three frames — Up, Over, and Down.

To add a movie clip to a button, you must first create the movie clip. Chapter 7 explains how to create a movie clip symbol, and Chapter 9 explains how to create the animation to put in the movie clip.

For the following steps, you can use the movie clip that we provide in the Ch08 folder of the companion Web site at www.dummies.com/go/flash8. Open flower power.fla. It's a blank movie whose Library contains the symbols necessary to create a button with a movie clip.

If you've never created a button, review the steps in the section "Making a basic button," earlier in this chapter. Then, to create a button with a movie clip, follow these steps:

1. **If you're using the movie file included on the Web site, open flower power.fla; otherwise, open any new movie file.**

2. **Choose Insert⇨New Symbol to open the Create New Symbol dialog box.**

3. **In the Name text box, type a name for the button.**

4. **In the Behavior section, choose the Button option and click OK.**

5. **Create the graphic for the Up state.**

   If you're using the movie from the Web site, choose Window⇨Library and drag to the Stage the graphic symbol named *Flower*. Click anywhere on the Stage to make it active, and press the arrow buttons on the keyboard (left, right, up, and down, as necessary) to center the flower symbol's registration point (shown by a little plus sign) exactly over the registration point (also a plus sign) on the Stage (see Figure 8-4). You can also cut and paste the symbol to center it. The flower graphic symbol is static, not animated.

6. **Right-click (Windows) or Control+click (Mac) the Over frame and choose Insert Keyframe from the contextual menu.**

   Flash inserts a keyframe.

7. **Create the graphic for the Over state.**

   For this example, delete the graphic on the Stage (it's still there from the Up frame) and drag the movie clip called *Flower Rotating* to the center of the Stage. Click the Stage and use the arrow keys to perfectly center the flower. The Flower Rotating movie clip animates the flower by rotating it.

8. **Right-click (Windows) or Control+click (Mac) the Down frame and choose Insert Keyframe from the contextual menu.**

9. **Create the graphic for the Down state.**

   In this example, delete the graphic on the Stage and drag the Flower Light graphic symbol to the exact center of the Stage.

10. **Right-click (Windows) or Control+click (Mac) the Hit frame and choose Insert Keyframe from the contextual menu.**

11. **Use the Rectangle tool and drag a square to cover the entire area of the symbol, leaving the symbol on top; use the Selection tool to select and delete the symbol, leaving only the square.**

    If you don't perform this step, viewers must place the mouse cursor exactly over one of the petals to see the animation. By defining the Hit frame as a square, placing the cursor anywhere within that square activates the button. Your screen should look like Figure 8-4, shown with the Up frame active.

12. **Click the scene name (Scene 1) above the layer list to return to the regular Timeline.**

13. **Drag the button symbol that you just created from the Library to wherever you want the button placed on the Stage.**

    Congratulations! You have just created a button with a movie clip.

To test the button that you just created, choose Control➪Test Movie. Place the cursor over the button, click the button, and watch the animation. If you used the Flower Power movie from the Web site, first save the file on your computer by choosing File➪Save As and choosing a location on your hard drive. When you test this movie, the flower rotates when you pass the cursor over it and also lightens. When you click the flower, it seems to freeze. When you're done, click the Close box of the window.

If you want to see the final result of the preceding steps, check out `flower power final.fla` in the Ch08 folder on the companion Web site at `www.dummies.com/go/flash8`.

## Adding an action to a button

A button doesn't do anything except look pretty until you give it the proper instructions. For example, a button can link you to another Web page or start a movie. You find out about ActionScript in Chapter 10, but in this section, we explain the basic principle of adding an action to a button — in this case, an action that links the user to another Web page.

You can add an action for a button in two ways. Both methods have advantages and disadvantages. We explain both ways next.

### *Adding an action directly to a button*

The most direct method is to add the ActionScript directly to the button. This method is very intuitive, because the code is right there in the button. However, if you have lots of code in lots of different buttons (and perhaps movie clips as well), you might have a hard time troubleshooting problems. Opening each button and looking at the ActionScript could be difficult.

Put the ActionScript directly on the button if you want the simplest method and you won't be adding a lot of code to your movie. For the maximum simplicity, use the Behaviors panel.

To add an action to a button by using the Behaviors panel, follow these steps:

1. **If you haven't already done so, drag an instance of the button onto the Stage. If the button isn't selected, select it.**

2. **Choose Window⇨Behaviors to open the Behaviors panel.**

   We explain the Behaviors panel in Chapter 9.

3. **Click the plus sign and choose whichever category and subcategory contains the action that you want.**

   In our example, choose Web and then choose Go to Web Page.

4. **Depending on the behavior that you chose, complete the information in the dialog box.**

   In our example, complete the URL, as shown in Figure 8-5. When typing the Uniform Resource Locator (URL), follow the same rules that you would to create any hyperlink on your Web site. For example, usually you can use local URLs (referring just to the page, for example) for other pages on the same Web site, but you need absolute URLs (that is, complete URLs, starting with `http://`) for hyperlinks to other sites.

**Figure 8-5:**
The Go to URL dialog box.

5. **(Optional) You can change the Open In drop-down option, which determines how the URL opens.**

   For example, `_blank` opens a new browser window, and `_self` displays the URL in the same window.

**6. Click OK.**

Figure 8-6 shows the Behaviors panel with the `Go to Web Page` action. Note that the top line of the ActionScript says that the event is `On Release`, which means that the button works when the mouse button is released.

**Figure 8-6:**
The Behaviors panel.

| Event | Action |
|-------|--------|
| On Release | Go to Web Page... |

bn_myflower

**7. If you want, select another event by clicking the event and selecting from the drop-down list.**

See Chapter 10 for a list of button events and how they work.

To view the ActionScript that you created, select the button and open the Actions panel (choose Window➪Actions). You can type ActionScript directly in the Actions panel if you're familiar with the proper syntax. For more information, see Chapter 10.

You can add your button to an existing Web page. In such a case, the button might be the only Flash element on the page. You can also include buttons as part of an environment completely created in Flash. Either way, buttons are a valuable piece of the Flash arsenal.

For a gorgeous example of a button, as shown in Figure 8-7, look for `nav_button.fla` on the companion Web site at www.dummies.com/go/flash8. Open the `.fla` file and choose Control➪Test Movie to see how the button works. Right-click (Windows)/Control+click (Mac) the button (not the entire symbol) and choose Actions to see the Get URL action attached to this button. *(The* `nav_button.fla` *file is courtesy of Jeremy Wachtel, Vice President of Project Management at Macquarium Intelligent Communications —* www.macquarium.com*.)*

### Adding an action to the Timeline

You can add an action for a button by placing the action on the Timeline, usually in the first frame. This method is more difficult than the method we describe in the preceding section, because you need to know some ActionScript. However, if you put all your ActionScript on the Timeline, it's very easy to find because all the code is in one place. Click the frame — you usually create a special layer just for your actions — and when you open the Actions panel, you see all the ActionScript there.

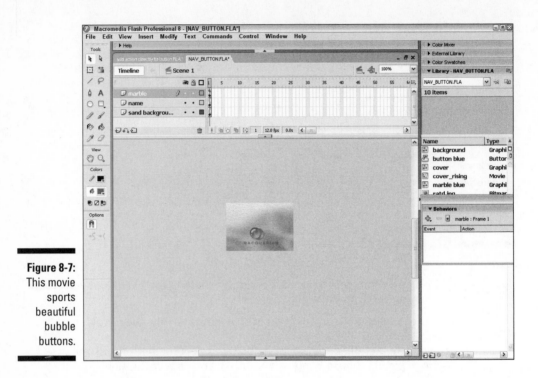

**Figure 8-7:**
This movie
sports
beautiful
bubble
buttons.

To place ActionScript for a button on the Timeline, follow these steps:

1. **If you haven't already done so, drag an instance of the button onto the Stage. If the button isn't selected, select it.**

2. **Open the Property inspector (choose Window➪Properties➪Properties). In the Instance Name text box, enter a name for this instance of the button symbol.**

   The name can't include any spaces. You can use an underscore or hyphen for readability.

   If you see a Frame Label text box, click the button again to deselect any frame on the Timeline.

   Each instance of a button symbol should have a different instance name.

3. **Click anywhere off the Stage to deselect the button.**

4. **Create a new layer, called *Actions*.**

   Chapter 6 explains how to create layers.

5. **Click the first frame of the Actions layer.**

   This instruction assumes that you want the button to appear at the beginning of the movie. If you want the button to appear later on, right-click (Windows)/Control+click (Mac) the frame where you want the button to appear and choose Insert Keyframe. When you click a keyframe of a layer, all actions that you add go in that keyframe and on that layer.

## Testing your button's Get URL action

To properly test a button with a Get URL action, you need to publish your movie, upload it to your Web page, go online, and try it out. You can test the button on your hard drive first, however, so that you can be fairly sure that it will work when you put it on your Web page.

To test your button without publishing it, choose Control⇨Test Movie and click a button with a Get URL action. If you used an absolute (complete) URL, you should have no problem. Your browser should open and display the appropriate Web page. However, a relative (local) URL might not be available.

You can still test a relative URL on your hard drive. Perhaps the relative URL is `tips.html`. Assume that `tips.html` is in the same folder as the Web page containing your Flash button so that you can use this simple local URL.

To test your button's Get URL action, follow these steps:

1. **After creating the button and its Get URL action with a URL of `tips.html` (or whatever is appropriate in your situation), choose File⇨Save to save the movie file.**

2. **Choose File⇨Publish.**

   Flash publishes the file, creating a HyperText Markup Language (HTML) file and an `.swf` file in the same folder as your `.fla` file. (These are default settings. See Chapter 13 for more information on publishing movies.)

3. **To test the button, you need a file on your hard drive with the same URL that you used for your button. Create a file named `tips.html` (or whatever URL you used) on your hard drive in the same folder as your movie.**

   You can use either of two methods:

   ✔ Copy the existing `tips.html` file (if you have it on your hard drive) to the folder containing your movie.

   ✔ Create a new HTML document and save it as `tips.html` in the same folder as your movie. This document can be a dummy document — you can put any text you want in it. For example, you can type **This is a test HTML document**. If you create this document in a word processor, be sure to save it as an HTML document. Otherwise, use the software that you normally use to create HTML documents.

4. **Working offline, open your browser, choose File⇨Open, and open the HTML file for your Flash movie. (It has the same name as your movie.)**

5. **Click your button.**

   You should see `tips.html` displayed. If you don't, go back and check your ActionScript.

6. **Open the Actions panel (choose Window⇨Actions). Type the following ActionScript, substituting your instance name for `bn_myflower1` and the URL you want for the URL in the code you see here:**

```
bn_myflower1.onRelease = function (){
    getURL("http://www.ellenfinkelstein.com", "_self");
};
```

This code references an instance of a button and uses the `onRelease` event so that the button will work as a user finishes clicking the button. Then you create a little function that specifies the URL for the button.

7. **Close the Action panel and save your movie.**

## Creating a button that acts on text input

Here's a more advanced example of a button that uses an action to make a graphic respond to user input. As you can see in Figure 8-8, the example has a text box, a graphic, and a button. The text box is defined as input text, which means that the user can type text in it. (For more information on text, see Chapter 5.) When the user types a number in the text box and clicks the button, the graphic's width changes to the number of pixels specified in the text box. In this way, the user can interactively change the movie. You could use any graphic, and the button could change properties other than width.

**Figure 8-8:**
This movie's button changes the width of the graphic (in pixels) as specified by the number you type in the text box.

Before trying to re-create this example, look on the companion Web site at www.dummies.com/go/flash8 for Wide Frog.fla to see how it works. Open the movie and press Ctrl+Enter (Windows) or ⌘+Return (Mac) to test the movie. Enter a number in the text box and click the button. Then enter a different number and try again. Have fun with it! Follow these steps to create this example:

1. **Create a symbol with a movie clip behavior.**

   This symbol will be the graphic that changes in width. For information on creating movie clips, see Chapter 7.

2. **Open the Library (choose Window⇨Library) and drag an instance of the symbol onto the Stage.**

3. **Open the Property inspector (choose Window⇨Properties⇨Properties). In the Instance Name text box, type a name for the instance.**

   For example, you could name the instance mc_frog_wide. Later, you need to refer to this name.

4. **Click the Text tool. In the Property inspector, select Input Text from the Text Type drop-down list. Drag out a text box on the Stage.**

5. **In the Instance Name text box, type an instance name for the input text box that you created on the Stage.**

   In the sample movie, the variable name is width_txt.

6. **Click the Show Border around Text button in the Property inspector so that the border of the text box is visible when you publish the movie.**

7. **Click the Embed button on the Property inspector to open the Character Embedding dialog box, choose Numerals [0–9] from the list, and click OK.**

8. **Create a button as we describe earlier in this chapter.**

   If you want, put some text on the button to help guide users to click the button. In the example, the word *Go* appears on the button.

9. **Drag an instance of the button onto the Stage.**

10. **In the Property inspector, enter an instance name for the button in the Instance Name text box.**

    In our example, we use the instance name bn_go1.

11. **Create a new layer and call it *Actions*.**

12. **With the first keyframe of the Actions layer selected, open the Actions panel (choose Window⇨Actions).**

13. **In the ActionScript panel, enter the following:**

```
bn_go1.onRelease = function() {
    mc_frog_wide._width= width_txt.text;
};
```

This ActionScript creates a function that operates when the user releases the Go button. It sets the width property of the frog movie clip to the number that the user enters in the text box.

14. **Collapse or close the Actions panel. Add some text that explains to users what to do and make the rest of the Stage look pretty, if you want.**

15. **Save your movie.**

16. **Test the movie! Press Ctrl+Enter (Windows) or ⌘+Return (Mac). Try different numbers and click the button. Make the symbol skinny or fat!**

# Part IV
# Total Flash-o-Rama

The 5th Wave    By Rich Tennant

"Is this really the best use of Flash animation on our e-commerce Web site? A bad wheel on the shopping cart icon that squeaks, wobbles, and pulls to the left?"

# In this part . . .

Moving imagery is the heart and soul of Flash, and in this part you make your Flash creations come to life through the power of animation and video. You find out about moving objects, changing their shape (or *morphing* them), letting Flash create animation for you, and easy ways to integrate video into your Flash extravaganzas.

After you create your movie, you can make it interactive so that the viewer's Web experience is more meaningful and engaging. Flash ActionScript offers infinite potential, so let your imagination soar. We show you how to combine your animation with your symbols and then add actions to script your entire movie.

The world is not silent, and your Flash movies don't have to be either. Find out how to add sounds and music to your movies — from the simplest sound of a button click to the majestic tones of a full-fledged symphony.

# Chapter 9

# Getting Animated

. . . . . . . . . . . . . . . . . . . . . . . . . . . . . . . . . .

## In This Chapter

▶ Understanding animation in Flash

▶ Getting ready to animate

▶ Using Timeline effects to create animations instantly

▶ Animating with keyframes

▶ Using motion tweening

▶ Editing your animation

▶ Managing scenes

. . . . . . . . . . . . . . . . . . . . . . . . . . . . . . . . . .

*I*n this chapter, we explain animation and making your graphics move. Are you ready to plunge into a world where you can make almost anything seem to happen? Hold on to your hats!

We start by explaining the basics of animation, including how to prepare for animation and how to work with the Timeline. Then we go into the specific techniques — Timeline effects, frame-by-frame animation, and tweening — that you can use to create great, animated effects in Flash. We cover both motion and shape tweening and then give you the details of editing your animation. So let's get moving!

## Who Framed the Animation?

The secret of animation in Flash, as in the movies, is that nothing ever really moves. A Flash movie creates the illusion of movement by quickly displaying the sequence of still images. Each still image is slightly different. Your brain fills in the gaps to give you the impression of movement.

One of the great things about Flash is that you can easily create complicated, spectacular extravaganzas of animation. And Flash stores lots of information in super-compact vector format. Because the files are so small, they download quickly. So Flash = spectacular animation + fast download. That's good for your Web site viewers.

Just as in a movie on film, each still image is contained in a frame. Each *frame* represents a unit of time. You create the animation by placing images in the frames. A frame can contain one object or none or many, depending on how crowded a scene you want to create.

Time is your ally in Flash because you have complete control over it. You can look at each individual image in time and tweak it to your heart's content. Then you can step on the gas, play everything back at full speed, and watch everything appear to move.

In Flash, you create animation in three ways:

- ✔ **Frame by frame:** You move or modify objects one frame at a time. This frame-by-frame animation is time consuming but is sometimes the only way to create complex animated effects. This method can certainly satisfy your appetite for total control.

- ✔ **Tweening:** You create starting frames and ending frames and let Flash figure out where everything goes in the in-between frames, which is why it's called *tweening.* Tweening is much more fun and easier than frame-by-frame animation. If you can create the animation that you want by tweening, it's definitely the way to go. Flash offers two types of tweening: motion tweening and shape tweening, both of which we describe later in this chapter, in the section "The Animation Tween."

- ✔ **Timeline effects:** You choose from a list of prebuilt animations, adjust a few settings, and then instantly apply them to your text, graphics, buttons, or movie clips. Flash automatically creates the tweens for you. This cool feature of Flash takes the automatic creation of animation to a whole new level.

In tweening, the starting and ending frames are called *keyframes* because they are the key moments in time that the software uses to calculate the in-between frames. Tweening not only means less work for you but also creates smaller files (which download faster) because you're describing your animations more concisely. In frame-by-frame animation, every frame is a keyframe because every frame defines a change in the action.

## Preparing to Animate

You probably want to get started animating already, but you need to set the stage first so that your animation works properly. Here are the steps that you need to take before you can begin creating your animation:

 1. **Choose Insert➪Timeline➪Layer to create a new layer for your animation and put your starting graphic or graphics on that layer.**

You should always animate each object on a separate layer that has no other objects on it. Otherwise, your animated objects might erase, connect to, or segment other objects . . . with messy results. And your animation probably won't work. Refer to Chapter 6 for more information on layers.

2. **If you plan to use motion tweening, turn your object into a symbol or group; if you plan to use shape tweening, make sure that your object is a shape and not a symbol; and if you plan to do frame-by-frame animation, your graphic can be anything that you want.**

See the section "The Animation Tween," a little later in this chapter, to find out more about motion tweening and shape tweening. Your graphic absolutely must be a symbol instance, a group, or text in order for your motion tweening to work properly. (Refer to Chapter 7 for more about symbols and instances, and Chapter 4 for the lowdown on grouping objects.) For shape tweening, the rule is the opposite of motion tweening. If your graphic is a symbol or a group or both, you can't shape tween it, so for shape tweening just draw a shape by using the drawing tools.

3. **Set a frame rate. (See the later section "Turtle or hare?" for more information.)**

When you animate, you often need to play back your animation during the process. The simplest way is to press Enter (Windows) or Return (Mac), which plays the movie. Sometimes, however, you might want more control — perhaps to play part of your movie. In this case, the Controller is invaluable. The Controller, as shown in Figure 9-1, is a simple toolbar that looks like the controls on a tape recorder. Use it to play, rewind, fast-forward, and stop your animation.

Pressing Enter or Return or using the Controller is a quick way to see your animation, but if you have a movie clip on the Timeline, you won't see the animation within the movie clip until you choose Control➪Test Movie.

**Figure 9-1:**
The
Controller.

Master of the Timeline

The *Timeline* is the map of your animation sequence. If the Timeline isn't visible, choose Window➪Timeline. Each layer has its own Timeline row. The Timeline has its own coding to help you understand the structure of your animation, as shown in Figure 9-2.

Scene name     Playhead (current frame marker)

Folder     Frame label     Keyframe

Empty keyframe

Incomplete tweened animation (no ending keyframe)

**Figure 9-2:**
Use the Flash Timeline to control your animations.

Layers     Shape tween (light green)     Motion tween (light blue)     Unchanged content (light gray, ending with rectangle)

Frame rate     Elapsed seconds

You can undock the Timeline from the main Flash window and resize it. Just grab the Timeline in the gray area below the title bar and to the left of the Eye icon, and drag it to where you want it. Then you can resize it as an independent window by dragging the lower-right corner (Windows) or by dragging the Size box in the lower-right corner (Mac).

Half the power of the Timeline is that it divides motion into *frames* — bits of time that you can isolate and work with — one at a time. The other half of the Timeline's power is that you can organize different components of your animation into different layers.

Always animate one layer at a time.

Click any frame to make it active. Remember to click in the row of the layer containing the graphics that you want to animate. By clicking any frame, you can view your animation frozen in a moment of time.

As you read through the examples and steps in this chapter, you quickly get the hang of working with the Timeline.

Hide the layers that you're not interested in (click beneath the Eye icon) to help you visualize the animation. But don't forget to check the animation with all the layers displayed to see how everything looks together. You should also lock layers when you're finished with them to avoid unwanted changes. Refer to Chapter 6 for further instructions on hiding and locking layers.

## Turtle or hare?

All you need to do to make animation work is to view your sequence of still images over time at high speed. Unless you have a remarkable attention span, one image per second is way too slow. Silent movies were typically 16 or 18 frames per second (fps). With the arrival of talkies, the speed got bumped up to 24 fps for better quality sound. On your television, the speed is roughly 30 images per second.

The smoothness of the playback of your animation depends not only on the frame rate that you specify but also on the complexity of the animation and the speed of the computer that's playing it. Generally, 12 fps is a good choice for Web animation. Luckily, that's the default rate in Flash.

To change the frame rate for your animation, follow these steps:

1. **Double-click the Frame Rate box (which displays a number and the letters fps) at the bottom of the Timeline to open the Document Properties dialog box.**

    Alternatively, you can choose Modify⇨Document.

2. **In the Frame Rate text box, type a new number (in frames per second).**

    You can set only one frame rate for all the animation in your current Flash file, and you should set the frame rate before you start animating.

3. **Click OK to set the new speed and close the dialog box.**

A Flash movie's frame rate represents the maximum speed at which the movie runs. Flash animation has no guaranteed minimum speed. If your animation is lagging or bogging down, increasing the frame rate doesn't help at all; in fact, it might make things worse.

# Creating Animations Instantly with Timeline Effects

You can instantly create complex animations in Flash simply by choosing from a list of Timeline effects and applying one to your art. With Timeline effects, you can use prebuilt animations to make your art spin, shrink, explode, expand, fade in or out, and do many other tricks, with just a few clicks of your mouse.

To add animation by using Timeline effects, do the following steps:

1. **Select an object that you want to animate.**

   You can apply Timeline Effects to a shape, text, a bitmap image, a graphic symbol, a button symbol, a group, or a movie clip.

2. **Choose Insert➪Timeline Effects and the submenus you want.**

   For example, from the Assistants submenu, you can choose Copy to Grid or Distributed Duplicate. From the Effects submenu, you can choose Blur, Drop Shadow, Expand, or Explode. From the Transform/Transition submenu, you can choose Transform or Transition.

   The Effects Settings dialog box opens for the effect that you select. Figure 9-3 shows the effects setting dialog box for the Drop Shadow effect.

3. **In the Effects Settings dialog box, modify any of the default settings if you want to change them and then click OK.**

   The Effects Settings dialog box disappears. Flash automatically creates a new layer. The layer has the same name as the effect but with a number appended corresponding to the number of Timeline effects that you've created so far.

   Flash also automatically puts your object inside a new symbol, which is in turn inside a new graphic symbol that contains all the new tweens and transformations needed for the effect. Flash transfers all this to the new layer.

4. **Choose Control➪Test Movie to view your animation.**

   Your movie is exported to a Flash Player ("swf") window.

5. **To further adjust your Timeline effect, close the Flash Player ("swf") window and click the Edit button in the Property inspector.**

   The Effects Settings dialog box for your Timeline effect reappears.

6. **Repeat Steps 4 and 5 as desired.**

To delete a Timeline effect, follow these steps:

1. **On the Stage, right-click (Windows) or Control+click (Mac) the object with the Timeline effect that you want to remove.**

   A contextual menu appears.

2. **Choose Timeline Effects➪Remove Effect from the contextual menu.**

   The Timeline effect is removed, and the original layer names are restored.

**Figure 9-3:**
You can use
the Drop
Shadow
effect to
automatically
add a
shadow
behind your
graphics.

# Animating with Keyframes

*Keyframes* are the frames that are key to your animation. In frame-by-frame animation, every frame is a keyframe. In tweened animation, only the first and last frames of a tween are keyframes. By creating keyframes, you specify the duration and therefore the speed of an animated sequence.

To create a keyframe, select a frame on the Timeline and choose Insert➪ Timeline➪Keyframe. For faster service, right-click (Windows) or Control+click (Mac) a frame on the Timeline and choose Insert Keyframe from the contextual menu that appears. You can also press F6.

You can change the display of the appearance of frames on the Timeline by clicking the Frame View button in the upper-right corner of the Timeline. This action brings up the Frame View pop-up menu. With this menu, you can

- Set the width of frame cells to Tiny, Small, Normal, Medium, or Large.
- Decrease the height of frame cells by choosing Short.
- Turn on or off the tinting of frame sequences.
- Choose to display a thumbnail of the contents of each frame. This is an awesome feature, like unspooling a reel of film. If you choose Preview, the thumbnail is scaled to fit the Timeline frame; if you choose Preview in Context, the thumbnail also includes any empty space in the frame.

## *Frame after frame after frame*

If your animation isn't a simple motion in an easily definable direction or a change of shape or color — and isn't one of the prebuilt Timeline effects — you probably need to use frame-by-frame animation.

If you must, you must. Some complex animations just have to be created frame by frame. The basic procedure is simple.

To create an animation by using the frame-by-frame technique, follow these steps:

1. **Select a frame in the row of the layer that you want to use.**

   The animation starts in that frame.

2. **Right-click (Windows) or Control+click (Mac) the frame and choose Insert Keyframe from the menu that appears.**

   The first frame on a movie's Timeline is automatically a keyframe, so you don't have to create it.

3. **Create the graphic for the first frame.**

   You can import a graphic, paste a graphic from the Clipboard, or use the Flash drawing tools. (Refer to Chapter 3 for help with creating or importing a graphic.)

4. **Right-click (Windows) or Control+click (Mac) the next frame and choose Insert Keyframe again.**

   The next frame on the Timeline now has the same graphic as the preceding one.

5. **Modify the graphic to create the second frame of the animation.**

6. **Repeat Steps 4 and 5 until you've created all the frames that you need for your animation.**

   While you work, you can continually check your cool animation by pressing Enter (Windows) or Return (Mac) to play it back.

Figure 9-4 shows frames of an animation as the word *New!* is created from a few specks on the page.

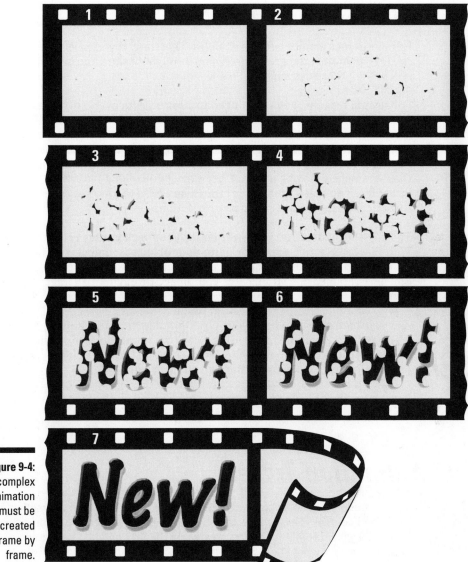

**Figure 9-4:**
A complex animation must be created frame by frame.

## Stillness in the night

Regular frames cannot contain changes. Therefore, if you insert a graphic in the first keyframe, the graphic remains throughout the Timeline until it reaches another keyframe with a new graphic.

For several reasons, you might need to copy objects over a number of frames. Sometimes, you want a still image to sit unmoving for a while on a layer of your animation — as a background image, for example — while your animation moves in front. A background gives context to your animated objects. Even animated objects often need to remain on the Stage after they've finished moving about. A key element of animation is timing, and for example, an animated character is often still for a few moments (even in Disney cartoons) before taking its next action.

To make this happen, add a new layer for your background or other object. With that layer active, create or paste your object (or objects) at the starting frame you choose. Then click your chosen ending frame and choose Insert⇨ Timeline⇨Frame. Flash duplicates your image throughout all intermediate frames.

As a shortcut, after you have your object or objects in the starting frame, Alt+drag (Windows) or Option+drag (Mac) the frame along the Timeline until you reach the last frame that you want to contain the object. Flash copies the contents of the first keyframe through all the frames.

If you copy the objects to a keyframe, they remain on the Stage until the next keyframe.

# The Animation Tween

If your animation follows some simple guidelines, you can save yourself lots of work (and control your file size, too) by using Flash to calculate the in-between frames for you automatically. You create just the first and last keyframes, and Flash figures out what should go in-between. In animation technobabble, that's called *tweening* — a quick, fun way to create great animations.

You can do a lot with Flash's tweening capabilities, including

✔ **Motion tweening:** This is probably the most common type of tweening. Simple motion tweening moves your objects in a straight line from here to there. Flash can, however, easily handle animation along any path that you create, even one with lots of curves.

✔ **Shape tweening:** This type of tweening gradually changes any shape to another shape. You create the first and last shapes. These days, kids call it *morphing*. The results may be a little unpredictable, but always interesting. You can add shape hints to try to tell Flash exactly how you want your shape to morph.

And with both motion tweening and shape tweening, you can

✔ **Change an object's size:** For example, if you make an object smaller as you move it, the object often appears to be moving away from the viewer.

✔ **Rotate an object:** You specify the amount of the rotation. Flash combines the motion or shape tweening with the rotation so that you get both effects at one time.

✔ **Change color and/or transparency:** Flash creates a gradual change in color based on your starting and ending colors.

Animating your graphic's transparency is a particularly cool effect because it lets you fade objects in and out, making them magically appear and disappear at just the right moment.

Of course, you can create several animations, one after another, to mix and match the effects. You can also combine frame-by-frame animation with tweened animation. Let your imagination soar!

## From here to there — motion tweening

In motion tweening, you move an object from one place to another. The movement can be a straight line or any path that you can draw with the Pencil tool. Figure 9-5 shows a few frames from a motion tween that uses a looped path. While the animation progresses, the skateboarder image also scales down to 50 percent of its original size so that it appears to be moving away from you. In this example, the path is made visible so that you can see how the animation works. You usually hide the layer that contains the path.

**Figure 9-5:**
You can
draw any
path and
animate an
object along
the path.

### *Moving symbols, groups, and type*

You can motion tween symbol instances, objects that you've made into a group, or type (text). You can not only move them but also change their size, rotation, and skew. And, in the case of instances, you can also motion tween their color. (To change the color of groups or text during motion tween, you have to convert them into symbols first.) See Chapter 7 to discover all about symbols and instances.

To *skew* an object means to slant it along one or both axes.

To create a simple motion tween animation, follow these steps:

1. **Right-click (Windows) or Control+click (Mac) an empty frame where you want the animation to start and then choose Insert⇨Keyframe.**

   The Timeline's first frame is always a keyframe, so if you're starting from the first frame, just click the frame.

2. **Create a group or text block or drag a symbol instance from the Library.**

   Refer to Chapter 7 for the details on creating symbols and instances. Refer to Chapter 2 for the lowdown on using the Library.

3. **Create another keyframe where you want to end the animation.**

4. **Move the object to a new position.**

5. **If you want to change the object's size, rotation, or color (as we explain in the sections that follow), make the adjustments at this point.**

   See the next two sections of this chapter for details.

6. **Click anywhere in the tween before the last keyframe.**

   The frame just before the last keyframe is a good place to click.

7. **Choose Window⇨Properties⇨Properties to open the Property inspector if it's not already open.**

   If necessary, click the collapse arrow on the Property inspector title bar to expand the inspector to its full size.

8. **From the Tween drop-down list in the Property inspector, select Motion.**

   Flash creates the motion tween. If you want to change the object's size or rotation, specify the settings in the Property inspector, as we explain in the next section.

You're done! Click the first frame and press Enter (Windows) or Return (Mac) to play the animation.

Here's a silly phrase to help you remember the procedure for creating a motion tween:

| | |
|---|---|
| **Funny** | First keyframe |
| **Objects** | Object — place it |
| **Love** | Last keyframe |
| **Moving** | Move object |
| **In** | In the middle — click between the keyframes |
| **Tweens** | Tween — select Motion from the Tween drop-down list |

### Scaling and rotating an animated object

Okay, so you're creative and ambitious and want to do more. Changing other properties of your graphic while you're moving it is easy. In Step 5 of the procedure in the preceding section, you can scale and rotate (including skewing) your object.

Use the Free Transform tool, located on the Tools panel, or any other method of changing size or rotation. (Refer to Chapter 4 for instructions on scaling and rotating objects.)

In Step 7 of the motion tweening procedure in the preceding section, complete the rest of the settings in the Property inspector, as shown in Figure 9-6 (and described in the following text).

**Figure 9-6:**
**The**
**Property**
**inspector.**

After you specify motion tweening, settings appear in the Property inspector, letting you specify how your motion tweening will work:

- **To put into effect any scaling changes you made, select the Scale check box.** Enabling Scale has no effect if you don't change the object's size when you create the motion tween. Clearing the Scale check box disables the scaling.

- **To rotate your graphic, select one of the Rotate options from the drop-down list.** The Auto option automatically rotates the graphic once in the direction that uses the least movement. Or, you can choose to rotate it clockwise (CW) or counterclockwise (CCW) and then type the number of times that you want to rotate your graphic. These options rotate your object even if you didn't rotate it in Step 5 of the motion tweening procedure. If you did rotate the object, however, Flash adds the two rotations to end up with the rotation angle that you specified.

✔ **To control the acceleration or deceleration of the movement, use the Easing slider.** By default, the slider is in the middle, which creates a constant rate of movement throughout all the frames. Move the slider down to start slowly and get faster at the end. Move the slider up to slow down at the end. You can create a sense of anticipation or excitement by using this technique.

✔ **To ensure that your graphic symbol animation loops properly, select the Sync check box.** If your animation is in a graphic symbol and the number of frames it takes up isn't an even multiple of the frames that the symbol occupies on the main Timeline, Flash synchronizes the two timelines so that the graphic symbol loops properly in the main Timeline. (This is a cool feature.)

We cover the Snap and Orient to Path settings later in this chapter, in the section "Tweening along a path." For details on the Sound, Effect, and Sync settings on the right side of the Property Inspector, check out Chapter 11.

### Tweening colors and transparency

To change an object's color, click the keyframe on the Timeline where you want to change its color. Then click the object. Choose Window➪Properties➪ Properties to open the Property inspector if it's not already open. Or if necessary, click the collapse arrow on the Property inspector's title bar to expand the inspector to its full size. If your object is an instance, select one of the options (such as Tint or Alpha) from the Color drop-down list and make the desired adjustments. (Chapter 7 explains how to modify instances of symbols and provides much more detail about using the options on the Color drop-down list.) If your object is a shape rather than an instance, you can simply change its color and opacity in the Color Mixer panel. (See Chapter 3 for more on the Color Mixer.)

You can mix and match motion animation with scaling, rotation, color, and transparency changes to create exciting effects. If an object spins and gets smaller while it moves, it can seem to be rolling away from the viewer. Animating semitransparent objects in front of each other creates interesting mixtures of color and gives a semblance of texture and depth in the 2-D world of the Web. Decreasing alpha (opacity) during a tween makes the object appear to fade as it becomes more transparent. Try out some possibilities and come up with ideas of your own.

Color fades are faster than alpha fades. If you need an object to fade in or out, your movie loads faster if you tween to or from the background color rather than tween to or from transparency.

### Tweening along a path

You can create animation that doesn't move in a straight line by motion tweening along a path that you draw. Suppose that you want to get the skateboarder shown in Figure 9-5 to do some tricks. The following steps show you how to do that.

If you want to follow along with these steps, you can download the skateboarder image (`skateboarder.bmp`) from the Ch09 folder on the companion Web site for this book at www.dummies.com/go/flash8. Then choose File↩Import↩Import To Library and in the File dialog box that appears, navigate to `skateboarder.bmp` and click Import to Library. (We made him in Poser — a cool program for generating 3-D people, in case you're interested. You can find out more about Poser at www.e-frontier.com.)

To tween along a path, follow these steps. (The first steps are the same as the ones we provide earlier in this chapter for motion tweens, in the section "Moving symbols, groups, and type.")

1. **Create the first keyframe (if necessary).**

2. **Place your instance, text block, or group on the Stage.**

   If you're using the skateboarder, drag it from the Library to the left side of the Stage.

3. **Create the ending keyframe.**

   Don't move the object as you usually would when creating a motion tween.

4. **Click anywhere between the two keyframes.**

5. **Choose Window↩Properties↩Properties to open the Property inspector if it's not already open.**

   If necessary, click the collapse arrow in the Property inspector's title bar (Windows and Mac) or bottom-right corner (Mac) to expand the inspector to its full size.

6. **From the Tween drop-down list, select Motion.**

   You now have a motion tween with no motion.

7. **In the Property inspector, select the Snap check box to snap the registration point of the object to the motion path.**

8. **Select the Orient to Path check box if you want to rotate the object with the angle of the motion path.**

9. **Right-click (Windows) or Control+click (Mac) the object's layer and choose Add Motion Guide.**

   A new layer appears on the Timeline. It's labeled Guide and has a motion guide icon. (If you want, you can create this layer before you start the process of creating the animation.)

10. **Draw your path, making a few curves or loop-the-loops, if you want.**

    You can use any of the drawing tools: Pen, Pencil, Line, Circle, Rectangle, or Brush. You can also use the Straighten or Smooth modifiers if you're using the Pencil tool. (The path shown in Figure 9-5 was created by using the Pencil tool with the Smooth modifier.)

     Lock the object's layer while you're drawing the guide path so that you don't move the object by accident. Refer to Chapter 6 for further instructions on hiding and locking layers.

11. **Click the first frame of the animation and drag the object by its registration point (shown by a small circle) to the place on your path where you want your animation to start; let the mouse button go when the registration point snaps to the desired place on the path.**

12. **Click the last keyframe and drag the object by its registration point to the place on the path where you want the animation to end; let go when the registration point snaps to the desired place on the path.**

13. **Press Enter (Windows) or Return (Mac) to play the animation.**

    You should see a few moments of death-defying skateboarding (or whatever animation you've created).

 You can find the completed animation, `skateboarder.fla`, in the Ch09 folder on this book's companion Web site at `www.dummies.com/go/flash8`.

### Getting your tween ready for prime time

The steps listed in the preceding section for tweening along a path provide only the basic process. You often need to make several refinements to motion animation along a path.

Not satisfied with your motion path? No problem. Here's a really great feature that lets you easily modify your path. Select the motion guide layer. Choose the Selection tool and reshape the line by dragging from any point on the line. (Just be sure not to break the line apart!) Press Enter (Windows) or Return (Mac) again, and the skateboarder follows the revised path.

Want to get rid of that unsightly motion guide? That's easy, too. Click the eye column of the motion guide layer to hide it. Press Enter (Windows) or Return (Mac) to play back the animation. (Even if you don't hide the motion guide layer in this way, the motion guide isn't visible when the movie is published.)

 Symbols, groups, text, and bitmap images have registration points that are usually at the center of the graphic. When you tween along a path, you might want another point to follow the path. In the section on groups in Chapter 4, you find out how to change the registration point to get the results that you want.

What if you've already got a motion guide and you want to link it to an object on a different layer? Perhaps you draw an oval and then decide that you want an electron revolving along the oval, so you make the oval's layer a motion guide layer. Here are three ways you can link your motion guide to your object:

✔ **Add a layer:** Create a new layer under the motion guide layer. The new layer appears indented under the motion guide layer, showing that it's linked to the motion guide, as shown in Figure 9-7. Then, any objects that you put on the new layer snap automatically to the motion guide. After putting your objects on the new layer, all you need to do is click the starting keyframe, drag your object to snap to where you want your animation to start on the path, click the ending keyframe, and snap to where you want your animation to end on the path.

**Figure 9-7:**
A guide
layer.

✔ **Drag the layer:** If you already have a layer that you want to attach to your path, drag the layer with your graphics so that it's under the motion guide layer. When the new layer appears indented under the motion guide layer, you know that it's linked.

✔ **Modify Layer Properties:** Select your graphics layer and then choose Modify⇨Timeline⇨Layer Properties. In the Layer Properties dialog box, select Guided and click OK. This links the graphics layer to the nearest motion guide layer above your graphics layer.

## Tweening shapes

In shape tweening, you change an object's shape at one or more points in the animation, and the computer creates the in-between shapes for you. You can get some great animation effects by using shape tweening. This process is often called *morphing*. You can see an example in Figure 9-8.

When shape tweening, you can combine changes in shape with changes in position as well as changes in size, color, and transparency. As with motion tweening, you should work with one shape per layer to avoid problems.

You can shape tween objects that you have created by using the Flash drawing tools.

**Figure 9-8:**
You can
twist and
deform your
objects by
using shape
tweening,
and a circle
becomes
a star!

You can't shape tween a symbol instance, text (type), or a group unless you break them apart into shapes by selecting them and choosing Modify⇨Break Apart. And you have to break apart text blocks twice — once to break the text block into individual letters and again to break the letters into shapes. You can also try to shape tween a bitmap image after breaking it apart, but the results might be unpredictable.

If you break apart a symbol instance, text block, bitmap image, or group by using Modify⇨Break Apart, you might have a number of shapes to animate. Be sure to put each animated object on a separate layer. You can do this easily by selecting the objects and choosing Modify⇨Timeline⇨Distribute to Layers, which we explain in Chapter 6.

To create a simple shape tween, follow these steps:

1. **Right-click (Windows) or Control+click (Mac) an empty frame where you want the animation to start and then choose Insert⇨Timeline⇨ Keyframe.**

2. **Use the drawing tools to create the beginning shape.**

   You can create complex objects by merging objects of the same color or creating cutouts with objects of differing colors. (Refer to Chapter 3 for details.)

3. **Create a new keyframe after the first keyframe wherever you want it on the Timeline by using the same technique that you used in Step 1.**

4. **Create the ending shape.**

   You can erase the old shape and draw a new one; or use the first shape, still on the Stage, and modify it. You can also move the shape and change its color/transparency. You can quickly change the color by using the Color modifiers in the toolbox. Use the Color Mixer panel to change opacity (alpha). Refer to Chapter 3 for more information on colors and transparency.

5. **Click anywhere in the tween between the first and last keyframe.**

   The frame just before the last keyframe is a good place to click.

6. **Choose Window⇨Properties⇨Properties to open the Property inspector if it's not already open.**

   If necessary, click the collapse arrow on the Property inspector's title bar (Windows and Mac) or bottom-right corner (Mac) to expand the inspector to its full size.

7. **Select Shape from the Tween drop-down list.**

8. **Select an Angular Blend or Distributive Blend type.**

   Select the Angular Blend type for blending shapes with sharp corners and straight lines. It preserves corners and straight lines in the in-between shapes of your animation. If your shapes don't have sharp corners, use the Distributive Blend type (the default) for smoother in-between shapes.

   Using the Angular Blend on irregular shapes may cause the animation to vanish!

9. **You're finished! Click the first frame and press Enter (Windows) or Return (Mac) to play the animation.**

Look in the Ch09 folder on this book's companion Web site (www.dummies.com/ go/flash8) for a great example of shape tweening. The file is named opening movie.fla. Here, Jennie Sweo takes two circles and changes them into words using shape tweening. Amazingly, Flash handles this process automatically. To shape tween one circle into a word, start with a circle. When you get to Step 4 of the shape tweening process, delete the circle and create the text wherever you want. Choose any size, color, and font and then break apart the text (choose Modify➪Break Apart). This command breaks the text into letters. Then break apart the text again (choose Modify➪Break Apart) to break the letters into shapes. Finish the shape tween, and you're done! To create the effect that Jennie created, create a second, similar shape tween on another layer. To view the effect, choose Control➪Test Movie. *(The Flash movie is courtesy of Jennie Sweo. You can see this movie on the Web at* `http://sweo.tripod.com`*.)*

### Getting Flash to take a hint — using shape hints

Does the transformation of your shape animation look strange? Flash tries to figure out the simplest and most probable way to change one of your shapes into another, but this solution might not turn out the way that you expect or want.

Never fear. You can use the Flash shape hints feature to fix this problem. A *shape hint* is a marker that you attach to a point on a shape at the beginning and end of a shape change. The shape hints signal to Flash exactly how you want this point and the area around it to move from start to end of the shape tweening process.

You can use up to 26 shape hints per layer. Shape hints are displayed on the Stage as small, colored circles with a letter (a–z) inside. On the starting keyframe, the shape hint is yellow; and on the ending keyframe, it's green. When you first insert a shape hint — before you move it onto your shape — it's red. Figure 9-9 shows an example of beginning and ending shapes with shape hints.

**Figure 9-9:**
Shape hints
guide Flash
as it tweens
your shape.

From this book's companion Web site, at `www.dummies.com/go/flash8`, you can download the Flash movie file shown in Figure 9-9. It's the file `4 to 5 point star with shape hints.fla` in the Ch09 folder.

To use shape hints, follow these steps:

1. **If you haven't already done so, create a shape animation by using shape tweening.**

   Refer to the set of steps in the preceding section if you need help with this task.

2. **Click the keyframe where you want to add your first shape hint.**

3. **With the object selected, choose Modify⇨Shape⇨Add Shape Hint or press Ctrl+Shift+H (Windows) or ⌘+Shift+H (Mac).**

   Your beginning shape hint appears as the letter *a* in a small, red circle somewhere on the Stage.

4. **Click the small, red circle and drag it to the part of your graphic that you want to mark.**

5. **Click the keyframe at the end of the shape animation.**

   The ending shape hint appears somewhere on the Stage, again as the letter *a* in a small, red circle.

6. **Click the small, red circle and drag it to the point on your shape to which you want your beginning point to move.**

   The ending shape hint turns green. If you go back to the first frame of the animation, the beginning shape hint turns yellow.

7. **Press Enter (Windows) or Return (Mac) to play your movie.**

You can drag shape hints off the Stage to remove them. Or choose Modify⇨Shape⇨Remove All Shape Hints to nuke them all — but the layer with shape hints must be selected. (Your animation then reverts to its original tween.) Choose View⇨Show Shape Hints to see all the shape hints in your current layer and keyframe. Choose it again to hide them. (Again, the layer and keyframe with shape hints must be selected.)

### Adjusting shape hints

To tweak your animation, click the keyframe at the start or end of your shape animation and move your shape hint. Then play your animation again to see the new result. The more complicated your shape animation, the more shape hints you need to use. For more complicated shape animations, you can also add more keyframes between your original starting and ending keyframe. This creates intermediate shapes at the new keyframes which you can then tween (using plenty of shape hints, of course). In other words, you can create two or more shape tweens, one immediately following the other.

If you aren't getting the results that you want, make sure that you have placed your shape hints logically. If you have a curve with shape hints a, b, and c — in that order — don't have them tween to a curve with the shape hints in c, b, a order unless you want some unusual effects. Flash does a better job with shape hints when you arrange them in counterclockwise order, starting from the upper-left corner of your object.

# Editing Animation

Of course, nothing is perfect the first time, and Flash is quite forgiving. You can edit keyframes in assorted ways.

You can't edit tweened frames directly — you can view them, but you can edit your objects only in the keyframes, not in the in-between frames. You can overcome this restriction and edit your tweened frames by inserting a new keyframe between your beginning and ending keyframe and then editing the new keyframe. You do this by clicking a frame in the Timeline and then choosing Insert⇨Timeline⇨Keyframe. Don't choose Insert⇨Timeline⇨Blank Keyframe unless you want to nuke your existing tween animation. Of course, you can always edit tweened frames by simply changing the starting or ending keyframe that defines them. When you edit a keyframe of a tweened animation, Flash automatically recalculates the entire tween.

The following sections explain some useful techniques for editing and managing your animations.

## Adding labels and comments

Animation can get complicated after a while. You might find it helpful to add comments to the Timeline to explain what each part of the Timeline is doing. Also, when you start adding interactivity to your movies, you can add labels to frames and then refer to them in your ActionScript. (You can find out more about ActionScript in Chapter 10.)

To add a label or a comment to a frame, follow these steps:

1. **Select a frame.**

   See the next section for information on selecting a frame.

2. **Choose Window⇨Properties⇨Properties to open the Property inspector if it's not already open.**

   If necessary, click the collapse arrow on the Property inspector's title bar to expand the inspector to its full size.

3. **In the Frame Label text box, type the text for the label or comment and press Enter (Windows) or Return (Mac).**

   To make the text function as a comment, type two slashes (//) at the beginning of the comment. (If you get long-winded and go to a new line, type the two slashes at the beginning of the new line as well.)

Adding frame labels can be a really nice way to lay out the timing of a movie, by typing in what you want to happen where on your Timeline, for a kind of brief verbal storyboard. This can be particularly helpful when you're working with others on a project.

## Selecting frames

Flash offers two styles of making selections on the Timeline:

- **Frame-based selection (the default):** In this method, if you click a frame or a keyframe, it's selected. To select a range of frames, you can click and drag over the frames that you want to select, or you can click the first frame, press Shift, and then click the last frame in the range.

- **Span-based selection:** In this method, if you click a frame, it selects the entire sequence containing that frame, from one keyframe to the next. Clicking and dragging moves the entire sequence (between the keyframes) along the Timeline in either direction. To select an individual frame, you need to press Ctrl (Windows) or ⌘ (Mac).

You can change the style of selection by choosing Edit➪Preferences (Windows) or Flash Basic➪Preferences (Mac) or Flash Professional➪Preferences (Mac), clicking the General tab in the Preferences window, and then marking or unmarking the Span Based Selection check box in the Timeline Options section.

In span-based selection, when you click the first or last keyframe of a tween and drag, you change the length of the tween rather than just select frames.

## Copying and pasting frames

You can copy frames that contain contents you want elsewhere. Then you can paste the frames in another location.

To copy and paste frames, follow these steps:

1. **Select one or more frames.**

2. **Choose Edit➪Timeline➪Copy Frames to copy the frames to the Clipboard.**

3. **Select the first frame of your destination or select a sequence of frames that you want to replace.**

4. **Choose Edit⇨Timeline⇨Paste Frames to paste the frames into their new location.**

You can also copy frames by pressing and holding Alt (Windows) or Option (Mac) while you drag the keyframe or range of frames to a new location. You see a small plus sign while you drag.

## Moving frames

You can move frames and their contents. Select the layer and place the cursor over a frame or range of frames. Then drag them to their new home, as shown in Figure 9-10.

**Figure 9-10:**
Move frames by selecting and dragging them.

## Adding frames

You can stretch out your animation by right-clicking (Windows) or Control+ clicking (Mac) and choosing Insert Frame. (Or you can select a frame and then press F5 to insert a frame.) Because you now have more frames between your first and last keyframes, the animation takes longer to complete and therefore appears to be slower. Use this technique to slow down the rate of animation.

## Deleting frames

Delete frames by selecting one or more frames. Then right-click (Windows) or Control+click (Mac) one of the frames and choose Remove Frames from the contextual menu that appears. If you delete frames within a tweened animation, the animation is completed more quickly and appears to be faster.

## Turning keyframes back into regular frames

If you don't like a keyframe, you can change it back to a regular frame by right-clicking (Windows) or Control+clicking (Mac) the offending keyframe and choosing Clear Keyframe. Changing a keyframe into a regular frame removes the change that occurred at that keyframe. You can use this technique to merge two consecutive tweens into one tween — change the keyframe in the middle to a frame.

## Reversing your animation

You can make your animation play backward by selecting the relevant frames in one or more layers and choosing Modify⇨Timeline⇨Reverse Frames. Your selection must start and end with keyframes. (This is a pretty amazing feature, which is worth trying.)

## Changing speed

After you set up your animation, play your movie to check the speed. If one part of your tweened animation is too fast or too slow, you can slide keyframes around on the Timeline to shorten or lengthen the time between keyframes. You can do this simply by clicking a keyframe and dragging it to another point on the Timeline. This technique gives you lots of control over the timing of your animation.

If you have difficulty dragging an ending keyframe, create a new keyframe somewhere to the keyframe's right and then drag the obstinate keyframe.

Figure 9-11 shows two possible versions of the Timeline for the shape tween shown in Figure 9-9. The black dots on the Timeline are the keyframes. To create the version on the bottom, we dragged the last keyframe to the right, thereby lengthening the tween. Because the same change in shape now occurs over a longer period, the tween appears slower.

**Figure 9-11:**
You can change the length of a tween.

The effect is even more noticeable when an object is moving across the stage during a tween. For example, if a symbol (or shape) moves from the left of the Stage to the right and you shorten the tween, the symbol (or shape) appears to move across the Stage more quickly because it must get from the left to the right in fewer frames.

## Changing the animation settings

You can always go back and change some of the settings in the Property inspector. For example, you can add *easing* (acceleration or deceleration of movement) or change the blend type (angular or distributive) of a shape tween in the Property inspector. We explain these settings earlier in this chapter, in the sections "Scaling and rotating an animated object" and "Tweening shapes."

## Using onion skins

To help you visualize the flow of your animation, you can turn on the onion-skinning feature. Onion skinning lets you see a "ghost image" of some or all of the frames in your animation. (Normally, you see only the current frame on the Stage.) Figure 9-12 shows an example of both regular and outlined onion skinning. Onion skinning displays frames as transparent layers, like the transparent layers of an onion skin.

**Figure 9-12:** Onion skinning helps you to see where your animation is going.

To display onion skinning, click the Onion Skin button at the bottom of the Timeline.

To display onion skinning with outlines, click the Onion Skin Outlines button. Sometimes this makes it easier to see how your objects are animating.

When you display onion skinning, Flash places markers at the top of the Timeline around the frames that are displayed as onion skins. (See Figure 9-13.) Usually, these markers advance automatically when the current frame pointer advances. You can manually adjust the beginning and ending of the onion-skinning effect by clicking and dragging either the left or right marker to a new location on the Timeline.

**Figure 9-13:**
When you display onion skinning, markers are placed on the Timeline.

Onion skin markers

 To edit any of the frames on the Timeline no matter where your current frame pointer is, click the Edit Multiple Frames button. If you also have onion skinning turned on, you can then edit any frame while viewing all the other onion-skinned frames.

 Click Modify Onion Markers to display a menu to help you adjust the way that your onion markers work:

- ✔ **Always Show Markers:** Shows onion markers even when you've turned off onion skinning.

- ✔ **Anchor Onions:** Locks the onion markers in their current position and prevents them from moving along with the current frame pointer, as they normally do.

- ✔ **Onion 2:** Applies onion skinning to the two frames before and the two frames after the *playhead* (the current frame pointer).

- ✔ **Onion 5:** Applies onion skinning to the five frames before and the five frames after the playhead.

- ✔ **Onion All:** Applies onion skinning to all the frames on your Timeline.

Hidden or locked layers never show as onion-skinned. Hide or lock layers to isolate them from the layers that you really want to change and to keep your onion skinning from getting out of control. Chapter 6 explains how to hide and lock layers.

## Moving everything around the Stage at once

If you move a complete animation on the Stage without moving the graphics in all frames and all layers at one time, you might quickly go nuts when you discover that every little thing must be realigned. Instead, retain your sanity and move everything at one time.

To move a complete animation, follow these steps:

1. **Unlock all layers that contain the animation you want to move and then lock or hide any layers that you don't want to move.**

   To lock (or unlock) a layer, click beneath the lock icon on that layer's row. To hide (or unhide) a layer, click beneath the eye icon on that layer's row. See Chapter 6 for more information on working with layers.

2. **Click the Edit Multiple Frames button at the bottom of the Timeline.**

   If you ever need to resize a project, this button is your new best friend.

3. **Drag the onion-skin markers to the beginning and ending frames of your animation.**

   Alternatively, if you want to select all frames, click the Modify Onion Markers button at the bottom of the Timeline and choose Onion All.

4. **Choose Edit⇨Select All.**

5. **Drag your animation to its new place on the Stage.**

# Making the Scene

Animations can get complicated fast, and one way to manage that complexity is by organizing them in layers and layer folders. (Refer to Chapter 6 for the lowdown on layers and layer folders.) Another great way to manage the complexity of your animations is to break them into chunks of time — into scenes. You can then use scenes as the modular building blocks of your movies, which you can then rearrange in any way that you want.

When is a good time to break up your movie into scenes? If your movie is simple, one scene might be all that you need. But if the movie gets more complex, you might want to break it up into a loading message, an introduction, the main act, the ending, and the credits.

Or, if your Timeline becomes longer than one screen will hold at a time, you might want to find logical places to separate segments of your animation into scenes. If your cast of graphics characters changes at a particular time, that might be a good place to break into a new scene. And if a section of your movie can conceivably be reused elsewhere in other movies, you might have an excellent reason to break it out into its own scene.

## Breaking your movie into scenes

When you create a new Flash movie file (by running Flash for the first time or by choosing File➪New and selecting a Flash Document under the General tab), by default the file contains one empty scene, cleverly titled *Scene 1*. Any animations that you create then become part of Scene 1.

If you want to add a scene, choose Insert➪Scene. The Stage clears, and the Timeline is labeled *Scene 2*.

## Manipulating that scene

To keep track of your scenes, open the Scene panel by choosing Window➪Other Panels➪Scene, as shown in Figure 9-14. The Scene panel lists all the scenes in your movie. When you choose Control➪Test Movie, the scenes play in order from the top of the list down.

**Figure 9-14:**
The Scene panel lets you make a big scene.

Here's how to use the Scene panel to control your scenes:

- ✔ **To change the order in which scenes play,** drag a scene's name on the Scene panel to a new place in the list.

- ✔ **To rename a scene,** double-click the scene's name in the Scene panel, type the new name, and then press Enter (Windows) or Return (Mac).

To delete a scene, select that scene and click the Delete Scene button at the bottom of the Scene panel.

 To duplicate a scene, click the Duplicate Scene button at the bottom of the Scene panel.

To view a particular scene, click its name on the Scene panel. Or, choose View↪ Go To and choose the name of the scene that you want from the submenu.

 Look in the Ch09 folder on this book's companion Web site (at www.dummies. com/go/flash8) for picturetour.fla, which is a nice example of a Flash movie divided into scenes. This movie is part of The Raj's Web site, at www. theraj.com. *(Thanks to Lindsay Oliver, of The Raj, and Jesse Spaulding, the movie's creator, for this Flash movie.)*

# Chapter 10

# Getting Interactive

. . . . . . . . . . . . . . . . . . . . . . . . . . . . . . . . . . . . . . . . . .

. . . . . . . . . . . . . . . . . . . . . . . . . . . . . . . . . . . . . . . . . .

*T*he real fun with Flash begins when you start to make your art and animations interactive. *Interactivity* means that a computer user's input triggers immediate changes on the computer screen, which the user can then respond to further, as if a conversation is taking place between the user and the computer. Examples include clicking a button to go to another Web page and choosing to stop the music.

Flash uses actions to specify how the interactivity works. *Actions* are simply short instructions that tell Flash what to do next. By combining actions, you can create very complex sets of instructions to give your Flash movies sophisticated capabilities. You can use actions to control your animation without interactivity, if you want. Flash actions offer a great deal of flexibility, and only your imagination limits what you can do.

## Understanding Actions

Flash lets you put actions in only two places:

✔ A keyframe on the Timeline

✔ An instance of a symbol (that is, an instance of a button, a movie clip, a graphic symbol, or a font symbol)

When you create an action, you first specify what has to occur for the action to be executed. This is the *when* part of the process. For example, if you add an action to a button instance, you can specify that the action will happen *when* the user releases the mouse button after clicking it.

Next you specify the action itself — *what* will happen. The action must come from the list of actions in Flash. Many actions have parameters that you must add. For example, to get a button to bring your viewer to another Web page, you use the `getURL` action and add the exact Uniform Resource Locator (URL; Web page address) as a parameter.

## Using Behaviors

You can easily add ActionScript to your movies by inserting behaviors with a click of the mouse. *Behaviors* are prewritten collections of ActionScript code that you add from the Behaviors panel. You can add them to frames, buttons, and movie clips in your Flash movies.

To add a behavior, follow these steps:

1. **Click a frame if you want to add an action to a frame. Create a symbol and place an instance of the symbol on the Stage if you want to add an action to a symbol.**

   For example, to create a button that links to a Web site, select the button instance. Check out Chapter 8 if you need help with creating buttons.

2. **With the frame or instance selected, choose Window⇨Behaviors to open the Behaviors panel, as shown in Figure 10-1.**

   If necessary, click the Behaviors panel's title bar to expand the panel.

**Figure 10-1:** The Behaviors panel lets you instantly add ActionScript to your movie.

3. **Click the plus button in the upper-left corner of the Behaviors panel and choose a category; then choose one of the behaviors listed in that category.**

   In our example, choose Web⇨Go To Web Page from the pop-up menu.

   We list the categories and the behaviors that they contain after these steps. The behaviors that are available depend on the type of object that you choose. In our example, the Go To URL dialog box appears. Other behaviors prompt you for the appropriate information.

4. **Enter the required information in the dialog box that appears.**

   In our example, type a URL in the URL text box, such as **http://www.infinityeverywhere.net**.

5. **Click OK.**

   You see the behavior listed in the Behaviors panel. If you chose a button or a movie clip, an event might be listed as well. An *event* describes under what circumstances the behavior occurs, such as releasing the mouse button or pressing a key. In our example, you would see the On Release event.

6. **If you chose a button or a movie clip and want to change the event, click the event to display a down arrow. Select a new event from the drop-down list.**

   See Table 10-2 for events available for buttons and Table 10-3 for events for movie clips (both later in this chapter).

7. **To see your brand new ActionScript code, choose Window⇨Actions to open the Actions panel if it isn't already open (see Figure 10-2).**

**Figure 10-2:**
The Actions panel is your key to adding actions to your frames. Here the window is shown with Script Assist enabled.

Flash's behaviors allow you to add interactivity for controlling graphics, movie clips, sound, video, and more. Table 10-1 lists the available behaviors.

| Table 10-1 | ActionScript Behaviors | |
|---|---|---|
| *Category* | *Behavior* | *Description* |
| Data | Trigger Data Source | Loads and manipulates information from data sources. |
| Embedded Video | Fast Forward | Fast forwards embedded video by the number of frames that you specify. For more information, see Chapter 11. |
| Embedded Video | Hide | Hides the video. |
| Embedded Video | Pause | Pauses the video. |
| Embedded Video | Play | Plays the video. |
| Embedded Video | Rewind | Rewinds the video by the number of frames that you specify. |
| Embedded Video | Show | Displays the video. |
| Embedded Video | Stop | Stops playing the video. |
| Movie Clip | Bring Forward | Brings the movie clip one level higher in the stacking order. |
| Movie Clip | Bring to Front | Brings the movie clip to the top of the stack, so it's on top of all other movie clips. |
| Movie Clip | Send Backward | Sends the movie clip one level lower in the stacking order. |
| Movie Clip | Send to Back | Sends the target movie clip to the bottom of the stack. |
| Movie Clip | Load External Movieclip | Loads an external SWF file into a movie clip. |
| Movie Clip | Load Graphic | Loads a JPEG graphic file that is external to the movie (FLA) file. |
| Movie Clip | Unload Movieclip | Removes a movie loaded with the Load Movie behavior or action. |
| Movie Clip | Duplicate Movieclip | Duplicates a movie clip. You can offset the new movie clip by a specified x and y distance. |

| Category | Behavior | Description |
|----------|----------|-------------|
| Movie Clip | Goto and Play at frame or label | Plays a movie clip. You can specify the frame number or label. |
| Movie Clip | Goto and Stop at frame or label | Stops a movie clip. You can specify the frame number or label. |
| Movie Clip | Start Dragging Movieclip | Starts dragging a movie clip. For more information about dragging movie clips, see Chapter 14. |
| Movie Clip | Stop Dragging Movieclip | Stops the current drag. |
| Projector | Toggle Full Screen Mode | Toggles full-screen mode on and off when you play a movie with a projector (a self-playing movie). For more information on projectors, see Chapter 13. |
| Sound | Load Sound from Library | Loads a sound from a runtime shared library. For more information, see Chapter 12. |
| Sound | Load Streaming MP3 File | Loads an MP3 sound file. |
| Sound | Play Sound | Plays a sound. |
| Sound | Stop All Sounds | Stops all sounds. |
| Sound | Stop Sound | Stops a specific sound. |
| Web | Go to Web Page | Displays the Web page found at the URL you specify. |

# Adding Actions to Frames

You add an action to a frame to control what happens when the movie reaches that frame. *Frame actions* are often used to play a movie clip or to loop a movie so that a certain section of the animation is repeated. Another use for frame actions is to stop a movie or to automatically link to another URL (such as a Web page address). You can also use frame actions for more complex programming of Flash.

You can add many actions to frames. Later in this chapter, we list the major actions and how to use them.

## Adding a basic action to a frame

To add a basic action to a frame, follow these steps:

1. **Create a new layer for your actions (if you haven't already done so).**

   Chapter 6 explains how to add a new layer.

2. **Click a keyframe.**

   If the frame that you want to use is not a keyframe, right-click it (Windows) or Control+click it (Mac) and choose Insert Keyframe.

3. **Choose Window➪Actions to open the Actions panel (refer to Figure 10-2) if it isn't already open.**

   If necessary, click the Actions panel title bar to expand the panel. And if the left pane of the Actions panel is not visible, click the tiny triangle in the middle of the left side of the Actions panel to make the left pane appear.

4. **Click the Script Assist button on the right side of the Actions window if it isn't already enabled.**

   In Script Assist mode, the right-hand side of the Actions window is split in half into two horizontal sections, so that the upper-right pane of the Actions window can display any parameters you need to type in to write your actions.

   Using Script Assist makes creating actions much easier for you. We love it, and leave it on all the time, and suggest that you do, too.

5. **Click a category and subcategory in the left pane of the Actions panel and either double-click an action or drag the action to the right side.**

   You can also click the plus sign, choose a category, and then choose an action from the submenu.

6. **If the action requires parameters, type the required information at the top of the Actions panel.**

   We list the details of specific actions and their parameters later in this chapter. You can continue to add actions by repeating Steps 4 through 6.

If you want to get the Actions panel out of the way, click the panel's title bar.

## Stopping the movie before it starts

A simple example of using a frame action is to place a `Stop` action at the beginning of the movie. You might provide a button that starts the movie so that viewers can choose whether they want to see it. (They might want to get down to business right away and purchase something. Who are you to make them wait?) In this example, the movie loads, but the first thing that it encounters is a command to stop. Nothing happens until someone clicks a button to start the movie. Of course, the Web page should contain other buttons and information that viewers can use to navigate through your Web site.

To add the Stop action to your movie, follow these steps:

1. **Create your animation.**

2. **Choose Control⇨Test Movie and watch your animation run.**

3. **Create a layer for your action and name it *Actions*.**

    Chapter 6 explains how to create and name layers.

4. **Click the keyframe where you want to add the action.**

5. **Choose Window⇨Actions to open the Actions panel if it isn't already open.**

    If necessary, click the Actions panel's title bar to expand the panel.

6. **In the left pane, click Global Functions, click Timeline Control, and then double-click Stop in the list of actions.**

7. **Choose Control⇨Test Movie again.**

    This time, the movie doesn't run; the Stop action halts it.

# Adding Actions to Buttons

A common way to add interactivity is to create a button. The viewer clicks the button and something happens (or stops happening). Usually, you add text near or on the button so that your viewers know what the button is for.

If you already work on a Web site, you're familiar with the concept of hyperlinks. If you know HyperText Markup Language (HTML) — the language behind Web pages — you know that you can create hyperlinks by using the <a> tag and its href attribute. This tag links text or an image to another URL. When people click the text or the image, they are teleported to that URL. You can create Flash buttons that accomplish the same purpose but with much greater flair. (Check out the end of Chapter 8 for an example of a button that links to a different Web page.)

Buttons can do more! They can start or stop animation, jump to different parts of a movie, and stop sounds, among other things.

The process of adding an action to a button is simple. The difficult part is deciding which actions to use. Later in this chapter, we review all the possible actions and discuss how to use them. You can also add an action to a button by using behaviors, as we explain earlier in this chapter.

To create a button with actions, follow these steps:

1. **Create the button and place an instance of the button on the Stage.**

   Chapter 8 tells you about creating buttons.

2. **With the instance selected, choose Window⇨Actions to open the Actions panel.**

   If necessary, click the Actions panel's title bar to expand the panel. And if the left pane of the Actions panel is not visible, click the tiny triangle in the middle of the left side of the Actions panel to make the left pane appear.

3. **Click the Script Assist button on the right side of the Actions window if it isn't already enabled.**

   In Script Assist mode, the right-hand side of the Actions window is split in half into two horizontal sections so that the upper-right pane of the Actions window can display any parameters you need to type in to write your actions.

4. **In the left pane of the Actions panel, click a category (such as Global Functions) and a subcategory (such as Timeline Control), and then double-click an action (such as the `goto` action).**

   In the Script pane on the right of the Actions panel, the `on` statement appears with the default event set to `release`, followed by the action you choose (such as `gotoAndPlay`). If the action you choose requires parameters, they appear in the Parameters area at the top of the Actions panel, as shown in Figure 10-3.

   The `on` action can respond to the mouse button, the motion of the mouse, and key-presses.

   In the example earlier in this chapter in the section "Stopping the movie before it starts," we explain how to put a stop action on a frame so that Flash stops and waits for the user to press a button. Now here, if you, for example, choose the `gotoAndPlay` action, you can make your movie advance to a new frame on the Timeline when the user clicks the button.

5. **If the action requires parameters, type the required information in the Parameters area in the upper-right pane of the Actions panel.**

   We list some of the most common actions and their parameters later in this chapter, in the "Using Actions" section. You can continue to add actions by repeating Steps 4 and 5.

**Figure 10-3:**
In this example, a gotoAndPlay action has been added to the button.

6. **If you want to change the default `on (release)` statement, click to select `release` in the lower-right pane of the Actions panel, and then select a different option in the Parameters area in the upper-right pane of the Actions panel.**

   See Table 10-2 for more information on the events you can use to define when a button action goes into effect.

7. **When you've had enough action, click the Actions panel title bar to collapse the panel.**

| Table 10-2 | Mouse Events |
|---|---|
| *Event* | *When the Action Occurs* |
| `Press` | When the user clicks the mouse button |
| `Release` | When the user releases the mouse button |
| `Release Outside` | When the user moves the mouse outside the hit area and releases the mouse button |
| `Key Press` | When a key that you specify is pressed (for example, `keyPress "<Left>"` specifies the left-arrow key) |
| `Roll Over` | When the mouse cursor moves over the button's hit area without clicking |
| `Roll Out` | When the mouse cursor moves out of the button's hit area without clicking |

*(continued)*

**Table 10-2 (continued)**

| Event | When the Action Occurs |
|---|---|
| Drag Over | When the mouse cursor moves over the button's hit area with the mouse button held down |
| Drag Out | When the mouse cursor moves out of the button's hit area with the mouse button held down |

The hit area of a button is the button's *active area* — the area that responds to mouse clicks and other user interactions. Turn to Chapter 8 to find out all about buttons.

# Adding an Action to a Movie Clip

You add an action to a movie clip in the same way you add one to a button; both are objects to which you can add an action. Actions in movie clips work within the Timeline of the movie clip, not on the main Timeline of the entire movie. Therefore, you can create movie clips that are interactive within themselves.

You can use actions in movie clips to do all kinds of things. You can use ActionScript within one movie clip to control a second movie clip — the ActionScript could set the second movie's properties, for instance, and change its size, visibility, and so on. You can use ActionScript to start or stop a movie clip from playing and to replace one movie clip with another. For example, you might make a movie clip that contains a cartoon of a TV set, and add actions to the movie clip so that each time you click it, the TV shows a different cartoon.

You can also add actions to movie clips by using behaviors, as we explain earlier in this chapter.

To add an action to a movie clip, follow these steps:

1. **Create the movie clip and place an instance of the movie clip on the Stage.**

   Chapter 7 explains how to create movie clips.

2. **With the instance selected, choose Window➪Actions to open the Actions panel.**

   If necessary, click the Actions panel title bar to expand the panel. And if the left pane of the Actions panel is not visible, click the tiny triangle in the middle of the left side of the Actions panel to make the left pane appear.

3. **Click the Script Assist button on the right side of the Actions window if it isn't already enabled.**

In Script Assist mode, the right-hand side of the Actions window is split in half into two horizontal sections so that the upper-right pane of the Actions window can display any parameters you need to type in to write your actions.

You can attach many kinds of actions to movie clips. A typical example might be that you want something to happen when the movie clip loads.

4. **Find the action that you want in the left pane of the Actions panel and double-click it.**

In the Script pane on the right of the Actions panel, the action appears. Flash also automatically inserts an `onClipEvent` statement, using the default `load` event.

If the action you choose requires parameters, they appear in the Parameters area at the top of the Actions panel.

5. **If the action requires parameters, type the required information in the Parameters area at the top of the Actions panel.**

We list several common actions and their parameters later in this chapter, in the "Using Actions" section. You can continue to add actions by repeating Steps 4 and 5.

6. **If you want to change the default `onClipEvent (load)` statement, click to select `load` in the lower-right pane of the Actions panel (as shown in Figure 10-4), and then choose a different option in the Parameters area in the upper-right pane of the Actions panel.**

See Table 10-3 for a list of the events available for `onClipEvent`.

7. **Click the Actions panel title bar to collapse the panel.**

**Figure 10-4:** In this example, a gotoAndPlay action has been added to the movie clip.

| Table 10-3 | Movie Clip Events |
|---|---|
| *Event* | *When the Action Occurs* |
| Load | As soon as the movie clip loads into memory (that is, when the movie clip first appears on the Timeline) |
| EnterFrame | When the movie clip enters each frame |
| Unload | In the first frame after the movie clip is removed from the Timeline |
| Mouse Down | When the mouse button (Mac) or left mouse button (Windows) is clicked |
| Mouse Up | When the mouse button (Mac) or left mouse button (Windows) is released |
| Mouse Move | When the mouse is moved (anywhere on the screen) |
| Key Down | When a key is pressed |
| Key Up | When a key is released |
| Data | When data is received in a loadVariables or a loadMovie action |

# Using Actions

Before you can create actions, you need to know which actions are available. In this chapter, we explain only the basic actions. For more information about advanced actions and programming in ActionScript, choose Help⇨Flash Help, and in the Help window that appears, browse through Learning ActionScript 2.0 in Flash or ActionScript 2.0 Language Reference. Then refer to the preceding sections for instructions on inserting actions into frames, movie clips, and buttons.

The following sections describe the most common actions.

## Timeline Control actions

The Timeline Control category of the Actions panel contains actions you can use to control which frames play in your movie at what time. (To see this category list, choose Window⇨Actions to open the Actions panel and, if necessary, click the title bar to expand the panel. And if the left pane of the Actions panel is not visible, click the tiny triangle in the middle of the left side of the

Actions panel to make the left pane appear. Click Global Functions and then Timeline Control in the left pane of the Actions panel.)

In the following descriptions, we assume you have Script Assist mode on, so be sure to turn it on by clicking the Script Assist button on the right side of the Actions window if it isn't already enabled.

### Go To

Go To tells your movie to go to a different frame. To define the frame, insert the action, click the Type drop-down list at the top of the Actions panel, and select one of the options. You can define the frame in several ways:

- **Frame Number:** Defines the frame by its number on the Timeline. In the Frame text box, type the number of the frame.

- **Frame Label:** Defines the frame by a label you have given it. In the Frame text box, type the frame label. Using a label is preferable if you might move frames to a different location on the Timeline, thereby changing their numbers. If you move a frame with a label, the label follows the frame. (Create a label by typing it in the Frame Label text box of the Property inspector.)

- **Expression:** Defines the frame number by some ActionScript code you write. (ActionScript code that produces a number as a result of a calculation is called an *expression.*) This code might be a combination of ActionScript code, for example, that calculates a frame number based on the current location of the mouse. In the Frame text box, type in the ActionScript code that defines the frame number.

- **Next Frame:** Goes to the next frame.

- **Previous Frame:** Goes to the previous frame.

What do you want to happen after your movie goes to the desired frame? Go To has two variations:

- **Go To and Stop:** The movie goes to the specified frame and stops playing. You might choose this option if you want to wait for the user to press one of several buttons at that frame's location. For example, if you're creating a Flash movie for an art gallery, you might put introductory information and buttons on frame one of your Timeline, with a stop action on frame one as described earlier in this chapter in the section "Stopping the movie before it starts." When the user chooses a category of artist by pressing one of the buttons, the Flash movie can then Go To and Stop at a new frame. This new frame can contain new information and new buttons that Go To and Stop to more new frames about individual artists in that category.

   To create a Go To and Stop action, choose Global Functions⇨Timeline Control⇨goto in the left pane of the Actions panel, and then click the Go

To and Stop radio button that appears in the upper-right pane of the Actions panel.

✔ **Go To and Play (default):** The movie goes to the specified frame and plays. Use this option when you want to jump to a new area of the movie and play the animation there. This option is commonly used to loop a movie. On the last frame, you insert an action that goes to the first frame and plays the movie over again. `gotoAndPlay` is also used in *preloaders,* short scenes that encourage the viewer to wait while a bigger movie is loading. (See Chapter 12 for more information on preloaders.)

### On (mouse event)

You use the `On` (*mouse event*) action to respond to mouse clicks, the motion of the mouse, and pressing a key on the keyboard.

The default mouse event is "release," but you can choose other mouse events as we describe earlier in this chapter in the section "Adding Actions to Buttons." See Table 10-2 for a list of mouse events.

When you add an action to a button in Script Assist mode, Flash automatically adds the `On` (*mouse event*) action so that you can specify when the action will occur — for example, passing the mouse cursor over it or clicking it. We explain the procedure for adding an action to a button earlier in this chapter as well as in Chapter 8.

You can, however, manually add the `On` (*mouse event*) action. You would do this if you were writing your own ActionScript and not choosing an action from the list of actions (which you can do if you turn off the Script Assist button in the Actions panel).

You can also add the `On` (*mouse event*) action to a movie clip, by selecting a movie clip and then in the Actions pane choosing Global Functions⇨Movie Clip Control⇨On.

### Play

The `Play` action tells a movie to start playing.

### Stop

`Stop` stops a movie from playing. (Did you guess?) One important use is at the end of a movie clip because, otherwise, movie clips automatically loop. You can also put a `Stop` action on a button so that users can stop an introduction and get to the rest of your site. For a tidy ending to a movie, Flash users often place a `Stop` action at the end.

### stopAllSounds

The `stopAllSounds` action simply stops all sounds from playing.

# Browser/Network actions

Next, we look at some actions that you find in the Browse/Network category of the Actions panel. (To see this list, choose Window⇨Actions to open the Actions panel and, if necessary, click the title bar to expand the panel. In the left pane of the panel, click Global Functions to expand that category, and then click Browser/Network to expand that subcategory.)

In the following instructions, we assume you have Script Assist mode on, so be sure to turn it on by clicking the Script Assist button on the right side of the Actions window, if it isn't already enabled

## fscommand

You can use the fscommand to control the Flash Player or other applications, like browsers. For example, the fscommand lets you execute JavaScript that you have written on the Web page. To use this action, select the Script Assist button in the Actions panel, and then choose Global Functions⇨ Browser/Network⇨fscommand in the list in the left pane of the Actions panel. Then double-click fscommand in the lower-right pane of the Actions panel. The parameters required then appear in the upper-right pane of the Actions panel. In the Command text box in the upper-right pane, type the name of the JavaScript command that you've created. In the Arguments text box in the upper-right pane, add any arguments that your command requires or takes.

You need to add some code to the HTML page. For more information, see the fscommand in the ActionScript Language Reference. (You can get there fast by selecting fscommand on the left side of the Actions panel and then clicking the Help button on the right side of the panel.)

## getURL

As you may remember from Chapter 8, the getURL action is the Flash equivalent to a hyperlink in HTML, which is the language used to code Web pages. You often use getURL on buttons, so when you click the button, you jump to another Web page. You need to supply the URL so that Flash knows where to send your viewers.

To use this action, double-click getURL in the list in the Actions panel. Then in the URL text box in the Actions panel, type in the URL (such as **http://www. infinityeverywhere.net**). From the Windows drop-down list, select from the following options:

- ✔ _self: Opens the new Web page in the current window. Viewers can return to the previous window by using the Back button of their browsers.

- ✔ _blank: Opens a new window.

✔ `_parent`: If you have a movie within a nested frame, this option puts the new Web page in the parent of the nested frame (that is, one level above the nested frame).

✔ `_top`: If your movie is in a frame within a window, this option blows away all the frames and replaces them with the new Web page.

You can leave the Variables setting at its default of Don't Send. (The reason why is beyond the scope of this book.)

### loadMovie

The `loadMovie` command lets you load any Flash Player movie (an `.swf` file) or PNG, JPEG, or GIF image file that Flash can find. It can be another movie or image residing in the same folder or somewhere else on the Web. You can use `loadMovie` to let users choose what they want to see next. This type of transition is smoother than using `getURL` to load new Web pages. (What's cool about PNG is that if you use an image containing transparency, the transparency works, and you see the PNG superimposed over any image behind it.)

To use this action, double-click `loadMovie` in the list in the Actions panel. Then you need to set the following parameters:

✔ **URL:** Type the URL. If the movie or image that you're loading is in the same folder as the current movie, you can just type its name. If it's in a subfolder, for example, type just the path to the file, such as `movies/mymovie.swf`. But if the movie or image is elsewhere on the Web, type the entire URL (for instance, **http://www.mum.edu/multimedia/arts/digital-media.swf**).

While you're testing your movie, you must place the SWF, PNG, GIF, or JPEG file in the same folder as the open movie and simply list the filename. Therefore, if you plan to use a different arrangement on the Web, be sure to change the reference to the file as necessary. If you don't, the SWF, PNG, GIF, or JPEG file won't appear for your viewers.

✔ **Location:** Select Level and specify a level number if you want to maintain more than one open movie or image at a time.

• To replace the main (original) open movie or image (and any other loaded movies or images) with the new one, specify level 0. This is like switching movies or switching images in a slideshow.

• To load a new movie or image without replacing the original (or any other loaded movie or image), specify a level number not used by any other movie or image. You can continue to load movies and images on different levels above the one in level 0. The frame rate, background color, and movie size are determined by the movie on the lowest level.

- To replace a movie or image that is already loaded, use the level number of that movie or image. You can select Target rather than Level if you want to replace a particular movie clip. Type the name of a movie clip that you want to replace. Specifying the URL and the target lets you replace a movie clip (the target) with an external movie or image (the URL). Note that the new movie or image will be placed in the same location as the original movie clip, with the same rotation and scale.

You can leave the Variables setting at its default of Don't Send. (The reason why is beyond the scope of this book.)

### unloadMovie

unloadMovie unloads Flash Player movies that you've loaded with the loadMovie command. To use this action, double-click unloadMovie in the list in the Actions panel. Then specify either Level or Target as well as the parameters we explain in the preceding section. Using this command helps to make sure that transitions are smooth, and it frees up your computer's memory sooner rather than later.

# Making Objects Work for You

In ActionScript, information is organized into classes that share similar properties and capabilities. (The capabilities are called *methods*.) You can create multiple instances of a class in ActionScript to use in your scripts. These instances are called *objects*.

ActionScript comes with many objects already built-in and ready to use. Buttons, for example, are one kind of object in ActionScript, and sounds are another.

Objects such as buttons, text, movie clips, and sounds have properties and methods built into them in ActionScript, and this makes it easy to use ActionScript to control them.

## Method acting

You can make an object work for you by calling on one of its built-in methods. Doing this is easy: You specify the object by name, followed by the dot (.) operator, followed by the method and the parameters that you want to pass to it.

For example, if you have a movie clip with an instance named owl, you can set up to change its color by creating a variable named `my_color`, like this:

```
var my_color:Color = new Color(owl);
```

Then you can change owl's color by specifying the color object by name, followed by the dot (.) operator, followed by the `setRGB` method (to set its red, green, and blue intensity), followed by a number for the new color you want, like this:

```
my_color.setRGB(0x445566)
```

As usual, Flash makes it easy for you to control objects and their built-in methods — you can just click methods in the list of actions on the Actions panel, and Flash shows you the parameters you need to fill in. The following sections look at some examples of how this process works with two examples: animated masks and drag-and-drop movie clips.

## Creating animated masks with movie clips

Flash has loads of useful methods built into its objects. One is the movie clip's `setMask` method, which you can use to create an animated mask. When a mask is animated, the mask reveals the background beneath while it moves. (For more on masks, refer to Chapter 6.)

To use the `setMask` method to make a movie clip into a mask, follow these steps:

1. **Create a movie clip and place an instance of it on the Stage.**

   This instance will be the background movie clip behind the mask. If you need to know how to create movie clips, check out Chapter 8.

2. **With the instance selected, choose Window⇨Properties⇨Properties to open the Property inspector.**

   If necessary, click the Property inspector title bar to expand the inspector.

3. **Enter an instance name for the movie clip (such as *Background*) in the text field near the upper-left corner of the Property inspector.**

4. **Create another movie clip and place an instance of it on a new layer on the Stage. Enter an instance name (such as *Binoculars*) for the second movie clip in the Property inspector.**

   This instance will be the mask movie clip. Check out Chapter 6 for information on creating new layers. See Chapter 9 for information on creating animation.

5. Create some animation for this movie clip so that it moves over the background movie clip.

6. Click Frame 1 of the new layer on the Timeline.

7. With the frame selected, choose Window➪Actions to open the Actions panel.

   If necessary, click the Actions panel title bar to expand the panel.

8. In the left pane of the Actions panel, choose ActionScript 2.0 Classes➪Movie➪MovieClip➪Methods, and then double-click `setMask`.

   The code `not_set_yet.setMask();` appears in the Script pane of the Actions panel.

9. Enter the first movie clip's instance name (such as *Background*) in the Object text field at the upper-right pane of the Actions panel.

10. Enter the mask movie clip's instance name (such as *Binoculars*) in the Mask Movieclip text field in the Actions panel. Deselect the Expression check box.

    You deselect the Expression check box because you're typing in the actual name of the instance, not a mathematical expression that when computed will result in the name.

    If your mask movie clip's instance name is `Binoculars` and your other movie clip instance is named `Background`, the code in the Actions panel should now look like this:

    ```
    Background.setMask("Binoculars");
    ```

11. Choose Control➪Test Movie and enjoy the new animation.

# Exploring Advanced ActionScript

Flash contains approximately one zillion more actions than the basic actions that we cover in this chapter. For more information, choose Help➪Flash Help, and in the Help window that appears, browse through Learning ActionScript 2.0 in Flash or ActionScript 2.0 Language Reference. In the following sections, we briefly explain a few of the more advanced aspects of ActionScript programming to give you an idea of some of the possibilities.

## Programming constructs

If you're familiar with programming, you will recognize several familiar commands, such as `For` and `While`, which let you process certain actions repeatedly while certain conditions that you specify are true. The `If` and `Else` statements create conditional expressions.

## Start-and-stop drag

Flash lets you create objects that your audience can drag around the screen. Draggable objects are used for games, slider bars, and other fun purposes.

You can create draggable movie clips to use for games, drag-'n'-drop interfaces, or slider bars. Although creating draggable movie clips is an advanced function, it's too much fun to leave out of this book. To create a draggable movie clip, follow these steps:

1. **Choose Insert⇨New Symbol to create a new symbol.**

2. **In the Create New Symbol dialog box that appears, name your new symbol, select the radio button for the Movie Clip behavior, and click OK.**

3. **On the Stage, create an object that you want the viewer to be able to drag.**

4. **Choose Edit⇨Edit Document to return to the main Timeline.**

5. **Drag the movie clip that you created from the Library to the Stage.**

   An instance of the movie clip appears on the stage.

   To open the Library, choose Window⇨Library.

6. **Choose Window⇨Properties⇨Properties to open the Property inspector if it's not already open.**

7. **In the Property inspector, type in a name in the Instance Name text box.**

   Your instance now has a name.

8. **Select the first frame in a layer in your movie.**

9. **Choose Window⇨Actions to open the Actions panel if it's not already open.**

   If necessary, click the collapse arrow on the Actions panel title bar to expand it.

10. **Click the Script Assist button to turn it off if it is selected.**

11. **Type in this code in the right pane of the Actions panel:**

```
horse.onPress=function(){
    this.startDrag();}
horse.onRelease=stopDrag;
```

   If your instance isn't named `horse`, substitute the name you gave to your instance instead.

This code tells Flash to start dragging your movie clip instance when you click on it, and to stop dragging it when you release the mouse button.

**12. Choose Control⇨Test Movie and then click and drag your movie clip.**

The movie clip follows your mouse!

You can constrain the movement of the movie clip to certain areas. For example, on a slider bar, you don't want the movie clip going all over the page — only along the bar. You can constrain the movement by specifying a constraint rectangle for the movie clip. See `startDrag` in the ActionScript 2.0 Language Reference for more details. (In the Actions window, select `startDrag` and click the Help button next to the Script Assist button to view the discussion of `startDrag` in the Help section.)

For another example of drag-and-drop techniques, look for `drag_and_drop.fla` in the Ch14 folder of the companion Web site (`www.dummies.com/go/flash8`). Open the movie and choose Control⇨Test Movie. Drag the red circle to see it snap to the source or target. To understand how it works, close the Text Movie window, and then choose Window⇨Actions to check out the ActionScript. *(Thanks to Keith Peters of The BIT-101 Lab, at `www.bit-101.com`, for this file.)*

## Making comments

To help make your ActionScript clear when you look back at it a few months from now, you should add comments that explain the purpose of the ActionScript. To do this, if you have Script Assist on, first temporarily turn off Script Assist in the Actions panel by clicking the Script Assist button. Then in the Script pane you can type two slashes (//) and then your comments. Anything on the line after the two slashes is ignored when running the animation. If you need more than one line for comments, you can type the two slashes at the beginning of each comment line.

If you're like we are, you'll love Script Assist and will want to turn it on again (by clicking the Script Assist button again) after typing your comments.

## ActionScript 2.0

ActionScript 2.0 is a major new version of ActionScript that became available in Flash MX 2004 — the predecessor of Flash 8. The new version adds new commands to ActionScript that are mostly of interest to intermediate or advanced programmers who are building applications in Flash which implement new classes and subclasses of objects. These new commands provide even more ways to use Flash to build extremely sophisticated applications that easily support rich media formats.

## External scripting

You can keep your actions in separate text files that your Flash movie can load when needed. This makes it easier to reuse your beautiful ActionScript code in multiple movies. You can create your ActionScript files with any text editor that you like.

Macromedia recommends that rather than attaching actions or behaviors to your buttons, movie clips, and other symbols, you instead put all the ActionScript code for your symbols in a single place, making it easier to find and debug all your code. You can do this by giving instance names to your symbols and then using each object's built-in methods, as we explain in the earlier section "Making Objects Work for You." You can then put all this code anywhere you like — in the first frame of the Timeline, for example, or in a separate text file. When starting to use Flash, though, it's probably easier to stick with putting your actions in frames, buttons, graphics, and movie clips.

To create a separate new ActionScript file within Flash, choose File⇨New and then choose ActionScript File from the General tab of the New Document dialog box. You can type in your ActionScript code in this file and save it.

You can create separate ActionScript files by using Dreamweaver or a separate text editor, such as Notepad (Windows) or TextEdit (Mac). (In TextEdit, choose TextEdit⇨Preferences, and when the Preferences window appears, in the New Document Attributes section, select Plain Text rather Rich Text.) Be sure to save the file with the .as suffix, which stands for ActionScript, of course.

To include the code from a separate ActionScript file in any part of your movie, simply add this ActionScript into the relevant frame, button, or movie clip:

```
#include "your-filename-goes-here.as"
```

This specifies an ActionScript file in the same directory as your .fla or .swf file.

## Discovering more about ActionScript

ActionScript gives you tremendous power over your Flash movies. If you enjoy using ActionScript, you might want to check out some of the great resources we list in Chapter 15. Another great reference is the *Macromedia Flash 8 ActionScript Bible,* by Robert Reinhardt and Snow Dowd, due out in early 2006 (Wiley Publishing, Inc).

# Chapter 11

# Extravagant Audio, High-Velocity Video

S ilent movies have been gone for a long time now. Why should your Flash movies be silent? You can create music and sound effects that play continuously or are controlled by your animation Timeline. You can also add sounds to buttons to liven things up a little. You can edit sounds and control when they start and stop. But be careful: Sound adds overhead to a movie, slowing down loading on a Web site, and some audiences might not be in the mood to hear any sound. If you're careful about how you use sounds, however, you can get great results.

You can also easily include video clips in your Flash animations. You can import video clips in a variety of file formats and then scale them, rotate them, tween them, stack them up in layers, animate their transparency level, and do all the other creative things that you're used to doing in Flash, just as though the video clips were regular Flash animations. And you can stream your video clips in Flash, so your audience may view the clips while they're downloading.

## Acquiring Amazing Audio

To add some great sound to your Flash movie, you must first import the sound. You can import AIFF, WAV, and MP3 sounds. Flash places these sounds in your Library. (See Chapter 2 for more information about the Library.)

Sounds vary in *sample rate, bit rate,* and *channels.* These statistics are important because they affect both the quality and the size of the sound file. Of course, the length of the sound also affects its size. Here's what you need to know:

- ✔ **Sample rate:** The number of times the recorder samples an audio signal when it's recorded in digital form. Measured in kilohertz (kHz). Try not to use more than 22 kHz unless you want CD-quality music.

- ✔ **Bit rate:** The number of bits used for each audio sample. Sometimes called *bit resolution.* Sixteen-bit sound files are clearer with less background noise, but if you need to reduce file size, use 8-bit sound.

- ✔ **Channels:** Typically one channel of sound (monophonic) or two channels (stereophonic). In most cases, mono is fine for Flash files and uses half the amount of data that stereo uses.

Often, you need to take a sound as you find it unless you have software that can manipulate sounds. Luckily, you can set the specs of sounds when you publish your movie to an .swf file. You generally get best results by starting with high-quality sounds and compressing during publishing. (Turn to Chapter 13 for details on settings for publishing Flash files.)

You can check a sound's stats after you've imported the sound into Flash. The next section explains how to import a sound.

## Importing sounds

Importing a sound is easy. To import a sound, follow these steps:

1. **Choose File⇨Import⇨Import To Library to open the Import dialog box.**

2. **Locate the sound that you want to import.**

3. **Click Open.**

Nothing seems to happen, but Flash has placed your sound in the Library. Choose Window⇨Library to check it out. To see the sound's stats, click the name of the sound in the Library window. Then click the Properties button (with the little "i" symbol) at the bottom of the Library window.

## Placing sounds into a movie

After you import a sound into your movie, you need to place it and set its parameters. To place sounds in a movie, follow these steps:

1. **Create and name a new layer for the sound.**

Click the Add Layer icon in the lower-left corner of the layer list to add a new layer. Each sound should have its own layer. Sounds are combined (mixed) when the movie is played.

2. **With the keyframe in the new layer selected, open the Library and drag the sound to the Stage.**

   Flash places the sound on the active layer. Flash extends the sound until the next keyframe, if there is one. (If there isn't a next keyframe, you need to add one to see the sound.) The image of the sound waves appears in the Timeline between the keyframes.

3. **Choose Window➪Properties➪Properties to open the Property inspector, if it isn't already open.**

   If necessary, click the collapse arrow at the lower-right corner of the Property inspector title bar to expand the inspector to its full size.

4. **From the Sound drop-down list, select the sound that you want to place in your movie.**

   If necessary, click the keyframe where the sound starts. The Sound drop-down list shows all sounds that you've imported. Below the name of the sound, at the bottom of the Property inspector, the sound's stats are listed (sample rate, channels, bit rate, duration, and file size), as shown in Figure 11-1.

**Figure 11-1:**
You can set sound parameters in the Property inspector.

5. **If desired, select an effect from the Effect drop-down list.**

   These effects are fairly self-explanatory. For example, Left Channel plays the sound from only the left speaker. Fade In starts the sound softly and gradually brings it up to full volume. The default setting is None.

6. **Select one of the following synchronization options from the Sync drop-down list:**

   • **Event:** Plays the sound when its first keyframe plays and continues to play the sound until it's finished, even if the movie stops. If Flash plays the keyframe again before the sound is finished, Flash starts the sound again. Use this setting for button sounds when you want the sound to play each time that the button is passed over or clicked. (Check out Chapter 8 for more information on adding sounds to buttons.) This setting is the default.

- **Start:** Plays the sound when its first keyframe plays and continues to play the sound until it's finished, even if the movie stops. If the keyframe is played again before the sound is finished, Flash doesn't start the sound again.

- **Stop:** Stops the sound. (See Chapter 10 for details on the Stop All Sounds action.)

- **Stream:** Synchronizes the sound to the Timeline. Flash skips animation frames if it can't draw them fast enough to keep up with the sound. The sound stops when Flash plays the last frame containing the sound wave. Use this option when you want to match the sound with a portion of the animation in your movie. You can insert an ending keyframe before placing the sound to control when the sound ends.

7. **In the Loop text box, type the number of loops if you want to repeat the sound.**

   You can figure how many loops you need to play a sound throughout an animation by knowing how many seconds the sound is, how many frames your animation is, and what the frame rate is. If your animation is 48 frames and the rate is 12 frames per second (12 fps; the default), your animation is 4 seconds. If your sound is 2 seconds long, loop it twice to play it throughout your animation. Use a high number of loops if you don't want to do the math, just to make sure.

If you want, you can manually edit the sound, as we discuss in the "Editing Sounds" section, later in this chapter.

After you place the sound, press Enter (Windows) or Return (Mac) or use the Controller to play your movie and hear the results.

Sounds can add significantly to file size and download time. You can place sounds in a shared library to reduce file size. See Chapter 12 for information on creating and accessing shared libraries.

# Editing Sounds

After you place a sound, you can edit the sound to fine-tune its settings. You should delete unused or unwanted portions of a sound to reduce file size. You can also change the volume while the sound plays.

To edit a sound, follow these steps:

1. **Click a frame that contains a sound (or import a sound, as we describe in the preceding section, "Placing sounds into a movie").**

2. **Choose Window⇨Properties⇨Properties to open the Property inspector, if it isn't already open.**

   If necessary, click the collapse arrow on the Property inspector title bar (Windows) or in the Property inspector's lower-right corner (Mac) to expand the inspector to its full size.

3. **Click the Edit button to open the Edit Envelope dialog box (see Figure 11-2).**

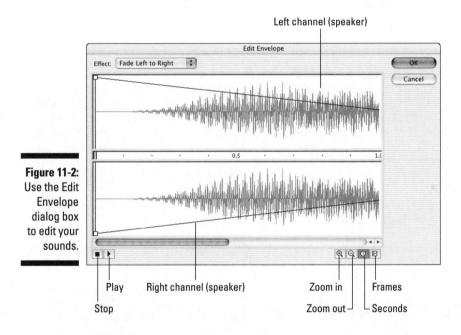

Left channel (speaker)

Play

Stop

Right channel (speaker)

Zoom in

Zoom out ⎤  ⎣ Seconds

Frames

**Figure 11-2:**
Use the Edit
Envelope
dialog box
to edit your
sounds.

 To see a specific section of a sound in more detail, click the Zoom In button. Zoom in when you want to edit small details of a sound.

 To see more of a sound's timeframe, click the Zoom Out button. Zoom out to edit the sound as a whole.

 You can display sounds in terms of seconds or frames. Click the Seconds button to show sounds in seconds. Click the Frames button to display sounds by frames.

## Deleting parts of a sound

Between the left (top) and right (bottom) channel display is a narrow strip that controls the starting and ending points of a sound. By deleting the beginning and end of a sound, you can eliminate unused portions of the sound. Along this strip are two vertical bars: one at the beginning of the sound and another at the end. These bars control when the sound starts and ends. Use them to edit the sound as follows:

- **Time In control:** This bar, on the left edge of the sound, specifies the start of the sound. Drag the bar to the right to delete the beginning of the sound.

- **Time Out control:** This bar, on the right edge of the sound, specifies the end of the sound. Drag the bar to the left to delete the end of the sound.

## Changing the volume

On both the left and right channel displays, Flash shows an envelope line to indicate the approximate direction of the sound's volume (refer to Figure 11-2). Where the volume changes, Flash places small squares, called *envelope handles*. To change the sound's volume, drag an envelope handle up (to increase volume) or down (to decrease volume).

You can click an envelope line to add a new envelope handle. This new handle enables you to create a new direction for the sound's volume at the handle's location.

When you finish editing a sound, click OK to close the Edit Envelope dialog box.

# Managing Sound

Sound can increase the size of your movie by such a great extent that you need to be very careful how you use it. You should make every effort to compress the sound. You can also lower the sampling rate; however, your sound's quality is then reduced. Nevertheless, you should try out all the possibilities until you get the best results.

The *sampling rate* is the rate at which the computer measures sound and converts it into numerical data. The computer makes these sample measurements many thousands of times per second. A higher sampling rate provides more information about the sound and, therefore, better audio quality. But all those extra measurements make for a much bigger data file.

Flash offers two ways to control the properties of a sound:

- ✔ **Use the Publish Settings dialog box to specify properties for all the sounds in a movie.** If you have only one sound or a couple similar sounds, specifying settings this way is easy.

- ✔ **Use the Sound Properties dialog box to specify properties of specific sounds.** As long as you don't specifically override these properties when you publish, these settings stick. Use the Sound Properties dialog box when you want to specify different properties for each sound.

Because you specify the publish settings when you publish a movie, we discuss those settings in Chapter 13. In this section, we explain how to fine-tune sound properties in the Sound Properties dialog box.

To open the Sound Properties dialog box, open the Library (choose Window⇨ Library) and double-click the icon of the sound that you want to work with. Figure 11-3 shows the Sound Properties dialog box.

**Figure 11-3:** Use the Sound Properties dialog box to set the properties of individual sounds, including their compression and quality.

| Sound Properties | |
|---|---|
| Crowd Applause | OK |
| /Users/professorgurdyleete/Desktop/Crowd Applause | Cancel |
| | Update |
| Tuesday, August 28, 2001 2:00 PM | Import... |
| 44 kHz Mono 16 Bit 6.4 s 563.5 kB | Test |
| | Stop |

Export settings

Device sound:

Compression: Default

Will use default settings on export          Advanced

At the top of the dialog box, Flash displays statistics for the sound — its location, date, sample rate, channels, bit rate, duration, and file size. Use the Export Settings section to specify how you want to export the file. For each compression type, Flash displays the settings available for that type. When you choose settings, look at the bottom of the dialog box, where Flash displays the new file size in kilobytes and in percentage of original size. The file size reduction can be pretty amazing. Here are the options available in the Compression drop-down list box:

- ✔ **Default:** This option uses the compression settings specified in the Flash tab of the Publish Settings dialog box when you publish your `.swf` file. (Chapter 13 gives you more information on publishing to `.swf` files.)

- ✔ **ADPCM:** You can convert stereo to mono to cut down file size. Available sampling rates are 5, 11, 22, and 44 kHz. You can choose from 2, 3, 4, or 5 bits. Five bits results in the best sound; the default is 4 bits. ADPCM is short for *Adaptive Differential Pulse Code Modulation.* This compression method produces files that take up less storage space than CD-quality audio. In case you're wondering what the heck this compression is, it's used to store music on Sony Mini Discs.

- ✔ **MP3:** MP3 has been available since Flash 4 and is a popular and efficient compression method. (To change the settings of an imported MP3 file, be sure to deselect the Use Imported MP3 Quality check box.) You can convert stereo to mono and choose a bit rate, measured in kilobits per second. You can choose from 8 Kbps (poor quality) to 160 Kbps (near-CD quality). Generally, you want something between these two extremes. Try a bit rate between 20 and 84 Kbps for a good balance of file size and quality. You can also choose the quality — Fast, Medium, or Best. The Fast option optimizes the sound for faster download from your Web site but with some quality compromise.

    For music, MP3 provides the best compression, letting you keep your quality as high as possible.

- ✔ **Raw:** This option exports the sound with no sound compression. You can convert stereo to mono and select the same sampling rates as for ADPCM.

- ✔ **Speech:** This option exports the sound with compression techniques specially designed for speech. You can select the same sampling rates as for ADPCM. A good choice for speech is 11 kHz.

After you specify a group of settings, click the Test button. This handy button lets you hear how your sound file sounds with each setting.

The Sound Properties dialog box also lets you update the original sound after you modify it with sound-editing software — just click the Update button. You can also click Import to import a sound file. The Stop button stops playing a sound that you're previewing.

When you're done, click OK to finalize your settings and close the dialog box.

# Video Magic

The Flash Player has achieved more universal adoption than any other Web video technology, so Flash can be a great way to deliver video over the Web. Flash Player version 6 and later can play video, and (at this writing)

Macromedia claims that more than 96 percent of U.S. Web surfers have Flash Player 6 or higher, and 97.6 of all Web surfers have some version of Flash, compared with 84.3 percent for Windows Media Player, 64.1 percent for Apple's QuickTime Player, and 58.9 percent for Real Player. The Macromedia Web site provides more details — you can check it out at `www.macromedia.com/software/player_census/flashplayer/tech_breakdown.html`.

Flash 8 includes important new video features, including support for the powerful new VP6 *codec* (video signal coder and decoder) for greatly improved video quality on the Web. Some experts think the greatly improved video capabilities make Flash a significant competitor for Windows Media technology, RealNetworks' Real video format, and Apple Computer's QuickTime video format.

Flash can use a variety of video formats. You can use Flash to create or import Macromedia Flash Video (FLV) files. (*FLV* is a file format developed by Macromedia for video on the Web.) If you have QuickTime 7 installed on your Mac or QuickTime 6.5 for Windows on your PC, you can import files in the AVI, MPG/MPEG, MOV, and DV formats. If you have DirectX 9 or higher installed on your Windows PC, you can import files in the AVI, MPG/MPEG, and Windows Media File (WMV and ASF) formats.

## Four cool ways to use video in Flash

You may include video in your Flash movie in various ways. For starters, you may embed video in your SWF file and play it in the Timeline. This lets you play your video from within your `.swf` file. This can work well for short video clips (perhaps 10 seconds or less), but longer video clips might make your Flash file take a loooooooong time to download, and these clips might have problems with audio/video synchronization. For more information, see the next sections in this chapter, "Preparing to embed video in Flash" and "Embedding and editing a video."

And using Flash Professional 8, you may also

✔ **Stream video from your Web server.** You can connect to an `.flv` video file from within your `.swf` file and play the video while it downloads from a plain old Web server. This is a really cool feature and definitely a good idea if you have a video longer than around 10 seconds. Your audience can start to watch the video while it's still downloading, and the audio and video won't get out of sync. For more information, see the section "Streaming a video," later in this chapter.

✔ **Stream video from a Flash Video Streaming Service.** You can play your video from a Web hosting service provider that specializes in Flash video. This can give you good performance if you want to do fancy things like host video-on-demand applications, webcam chats, live-event broadcasts, and real-time collaboration applications. But it's not cheap.

✔ **Stream video from a Flash Communication Server.** You can play your video from a Flash Communication Server that you host. This can give you good performance for heavy-duty deployment of multiple Web video streams, as if you are your own Flash Video Streaming Service, but the Flash Communication Server software is complex, and again it's not cheap, with prices ranging from $499 to $7,500.

## Preparing to embed video in Flash

Before you embed video into your Flash file, you need to find out the frame rate of your video and make sure your Flash document has the same frame rate to avoid erratic playback. On the Mac, you can do this by following these steps:

1. **Click the Finder in the Dock. In a Finder window, open your Applications folder and double-click the QuickTime Player.**

   The QuickTime Player starts, and the QuickTime Player menus appear.

2. **In the QuickTime Player menus, choose File⇨Open File, and in the file dialog box that appears, locate and select your video, and then click the Open button.**

   Your video appears.

3. **Choose Window⇨Show Movie Info.**

   The Movie Info window appears.

4. **Make a note of the video's frame rate (shown in the Movie Info window as FPS — frames per second).**

   You might also want to note the Normal Size of the video. (A typical size is 720 x 480 pixels.)

5. **Choose File⇨Quit.**

   The QuickTime Player closes.

6. **Return to Flash (perhaps by clicking the Flash icon in the Dock) and choose Modify⇨Document.**

   The Document Properties dialog box appears, showing the document's dimensions, frame rate, and other properties.

7. **To avoid unstable video playback, change the number in the Frame Rate text box to match your video's frame rate.**

In Windows, you can match your Flash movie's frame rate to your video's frame rate by following these steps:

1. **If you don't have the QuickTime Player installed on your Windows PC, point your Web browser to www.apple.com/quicktime/download and follow the instructions there to download and install QuickTime.**

2. **From Windows, choose Start➪QuickTime➪QuickTime Player.**

   The QuickTime Player appears.

3. **In the QuickTime Player, choose File➪Open Movie in New Player.**

   The Open dialog box appears.

4. **Locate and select your video, and then click the Open button.**

   Your video appears.

5. **Choose Window➪Show Movie Info.**

   The Movie Info window appears.

6. **If necessary, click the More Info disclosure triangle to see the detailed information about the movie. Make a note of the video's frame rate (shown in the Movie Info window as Movie FPS — frames per second).**

   You might also want to note the Normal Size of the video. (A typical size is 720 x 480 pixels.)

7. **In the video window, choose File➪Exit.**

   The QuickTime Player closes.

8. **Return to Flash and choose Modify➪Document.**

   The Document Properties dialog box appears, showing the document's dimensions, frame rate, and other properties.

9. **To avoid unstable video playback, change the number in the Frame Rate text box to match your video's frame rate.**

## Embedding and editing a video

You can easily import video directly into your Flash animations. Flash's Import Video wizard walks you through the complexities of compressing and embedding your video. The wizard even lets you split up your video clips before importing them so that after they're in Flash, it's easy to rearrange different sections of them.

Embedding video in your Flash movie is convenient if your video is short — perhaps 10 seconds or less. If the video is longer, downloading your video while the Flash movie plays is probably a better approach. To do that, you need Flash Professional 8, as we describe in the section "Streaming a video," later in this chapter.

Before you embed video into Flash, first you should make sure that the frame rate of your video and your Flash movie match, which we show you how to do in the preceding section, "Preparing to embed video in Flash." After you've done that, you can make video clips part of your Flash movie by following these steps:

1. **Click a keyframe (or create one by clicking a frame and choosing Insert⇨Timeline⇨Keyframe).**

2. **Choose File⇨Import⇨Import Video.**

   The Video Import Wizard appears.

3. **If you're using Flash Basic 8, skip to Step 4. If you're using Flash Professional 8, select the On Your Computer radio button to import a video from your computer.**

4. **Click the Choose button.**

   The Open File dialog box appears

5. **Find and choose a movie file in the Open File dialog box and then click the Open button. Then in the Import Video dialog box, click the Next (Windows) or Continue (Mac) button.**

   The Import Video dialog box now gives you choices for deploying your video, including Embed Video in SWF and Play in Timeline.

6. **Select the Embed Video in SWF and Play in Timeline radio button, and then click Next (Windows) or Continue (Mac).**

   The Video Import Wizard now gives you a choice of symbol type for your embedded video. You can also decide whether to import your audio track integrated with the video or as a separate track. Embedding your video as a movie clip symbol, and with the audio track integrated, are usually good choices.

   You have a choice of importing the entire video or editing it first. If your movie's codec doesn't support editing, the edit option is not available. (The *codec* is the software that encodes the movie's images and sound into a computer file and then decodes it for playback. Many codecs exist, and they use different techniques with varying advantages and disadvantages.)

7. **You probably want to select Movie Clip from the Symbol Type drop-down list, and you probably want to select Integrated from the Audio Track drop-down list. Select the Edit the Video First radio button if you want to do that; otherwise, select the Embed the Entire Video radio button and skip to Step 20.**

8. **Click Next (Windows) or Continue (Mac).**

   The Split Video pane in the Video Import Wizard appears, as shown in Figure 11-4.

   To view your video in the preview pane, click the Play button or drag the playhead (the triangle above the scrubber bar). Click the Stop button to stop playing the video. To zero in on a particular frame of video, you might want to move backward or forward a frame at a time by clicking the Backward or Forward button.

**Figure 11-4:**
In the Video
Import
Wizard, you
can split
your video
clip into
sections
while
bringing
them into
Flash.

9. **To change the beginning frame of a video clip, drag the leftmost triangle below the scrubber bar, or move the playhead to the desired frame and click the In button to set the new beginning frame. To change the ending frame of a video clip, drag the rightmost triangle below the scrubber bar, or move the playhead to the desired frame and click the Out button, to set the new ending frame.**

The beginning and ending frames are *In* and *Out* points, respectively.

10. **To see your video with the new In and Out points, click the Preview Clip button.**

The video plays in the preview pane, starting at the new In point and ending at the new Out point.

11. **When you're happy with the In and Out points that you've set, click the + (Plus) button to create a video clip with the current In and Out points.**

The name of the clip appears in the scroll pane on the left side of the Video Import Wizard.

12. **To rename the clip, click the name in the scroll pane and type a new name.**

The new name appears in the scroll pane.

13. **Repeat Steps 9 through 12 to extract additional clips with new In and Out points from the same file.**

14. **To change the In and Out points in one of the new clips in the scroll pane, click the clip's name in the scroll pane, move the In and Out points as we describe in Step 9, and then click the Update Clip button.**

15. **To delete a clip from the scroll pane, click the name of the clip in the scroll pane, and then click the – (minus) button at the top of the scroll pane.**

    The selected clip disappears from the list.

16. **Click Next (Windows) or Continue (Mac).**

    The Encoding pane in the Video Import Wizard appears, as shown in Figure 11-5. This pane lets you select an encoding profile and advanced settings.

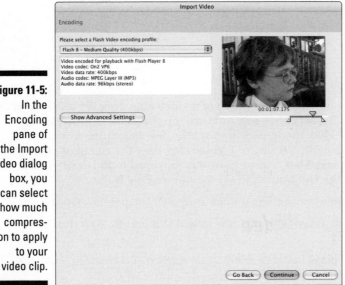

**Figure 11-5:**
In the Encoding pane of the Import Video dialog box, you can select how much compression to apply to your video clip.

17. **Click the Flash Video encoding profile drop-down list and select a suitable profile.**

    You can select profiles for users with modems or with the different speeds (150–700 Kbps) of local area networks, digital subscriber lines (DSLs), or cable modems.

    Higher-speed connections make it practical to use higher-quality video that requires less compression.

18. **You may grab and drag the In point and Out point markers (the triangles below the scrubber bar, below your video image in the Encoding**

pane of the Video Import Wizard) to give the video clip displayed there a new starting and ending point, if you want.

This is convenient because sometimes you want to import only part of a video clip.

To facilitate this, grab and drag the playhead pointer (the triangle above the scrubber bar, below your video image in the Video Import Wizard window) to preview different locations in your video clip.

19. **Click Next (Windows) or Continue (Mac).**

The Finish Video Import pane appears in the Video Import Wizard, summarizing your choices.

20. **If you want to change any of your choices, click Go Back. Otherwise, click Finish.**

The Flash Video Encoding Progress window appears. When Flash finishes encoding your video, the window disappears, and the movie clip or clips (or embedded video symbol or symbols) containing your video appear in your library (which you can view by choosing Window⇨ Library, if it isn't visible).

Now your video segments are inside movie clips (if you choose that in Step 7), and as with any other movie clips, you can drag them around on the Timeline, rearrange them, rotate them, motion tween them, paint on top of them in other layers, and tween their brightness and transparency — you can mangle them, destroy them, and bring them to life in all the usual Flash ways. This is pretty amazing. (See Chapter 9 for lots more animation ideas.)

## *Streaming a video*

If you have Flash Professional 8, you can set your movie up to stream a video while the video appears inside your Flash movie. That means that viewers can see the video play fairly smoothly even while it's still downloading from the Web — without having to wait until the entire video has downloaded. This is a fantastic feature. You'll certainly want to do this rather than embed your video in Flash if your video is more than a few seconds long.

In Flash Professional 8, to make an .flv video file to put online and then stream, follow these steps:

1. **Click a keyframe (or create one by clicking a frame and choosing Insert⇨Timeline⇨Keyframe).**

2. **Choose File⇨Import⇨Import Video.**

The Video Import Wizard appears.

3. **Select the radio button labeled "On Your Computer" if you want to import a video from your computer. If you want to import an .flv video file from the Web, select the radio button labeled "Already deployed to a Web server, Flash Video Streaming Service, or Flash Communication Server," type the Web address of the video file into the URL text box, and skip to Step 11.**

   Importing a video file from the Web works only for video files that are already in the .flv format.

4. **Click the Choose button.**

   The Open File dialog box appears.

5. **Find and choose a movie file in the file dialog box, and then click the Open button.**

6. **In the Import Video dialog box, click the Next (Windows) or Continue (Mac) button.**

   The Import Video dialog box now gives you choices for deploying your video.

7. **Select one of the three radio buttons: Progressive Download from a Web Server, Stream from Flash Video Streaming Service, or Stream from Flash Communication Server.**

   Using a Flash Video Streaming Service or the Flash Communication Server isn't cheap, so if you're just getting started, you probably want to choose "Progressively download from a Web server." This lets you convert your video into an .flv file and play it within your .swf file while it downloads from any Web server.

   This is a really cool feature — you are about to find out how to make an .flv file that you can put on any Web server to stream video that you've made.

8. **Click Next (Windows) or Continue (Mac).**

   The Encoding pane in the Video Import Wizard appears. This pane lets you select an encoding profile and advanced settings.

9. **Click the Flash Video encoding profile drop-down list and select a suitable profile.**

   You may choose between profiles for users with modems or with the different speeds (150–700 Kbps) of local area networks, digital subscriber lines (DSLs), or cable modems.

   Higher-quality video is less compressed and therefore requires a larger file size and higher bandwidth for speedy delivery.

10. **You may grab and drag the In point and Out point markers (the triangles below the scrubber bar, below your video image in the Video**

**Import Wizard) to give the video clip displayed there a new starting and ending point, if you want.**

This is convenient because sometimes you want to import only part of a video clip.

To facilitate this, you can grab and drag the playhead pointer (the triangle above the scrubber bar) to preview different locations in your video clip.

11. **Click Next (Windows) or Continue (Mac).**

   The Skinning pane of the Import Video dialog box appears.

12. **Select the style of play controls you want for your video from the Skin drop-down list.**

   The *skin* is the graphic design of the video play controls. You can infer the characteristics of some skins from their names. For example, the skin named `ArcticOverPlaySeekMute.swf` has an Arctic color scheme (in someone's mind, at least), and the play controls are placed Over the video and include Play, Seek, and Mute buttons. And the skin named `ClearExternalNoVol.swf` has a Clear color scheme, and the play controls are placed External to the Video and include No Volume control.

   You are probably going to love fooling around choosing your skin — it's so easy.

   The skin you select in the drop-down list appears as a preview in the pane above the drop-down list.

13. **Click Next (Windows) or Continue (Mac).**

   The Finish Video Import pane appears in the Import Video dialog box, summarizing what happens next, and you may want to make notes on that, because unfortunately this information disappears when you click Finish in Step 14. Among other things, this pane tells you where your new `.flv` file will be located relative to your `.swf` file.

14. **If you want to change any of your choices, click Go Back. Otherwise, click Finish.**

   The Flash Video Encoding Progress window appears. When Flash finishes encoding your video, the window disappears, and the encoded video and the player controls appear on the Stage.

15. **Choose Window⇨Component Inspector.**

   The Component inspector appears. If necessary, click the collapse arrow at the upper-right corner of the title bar to expand the inspector to its full size.

16. **Click the Parameters tab in the Component inspector, and click the row labeled contentPath.**

   The name of the `.flv` file is highlighted.

17. **Click the magnifying glass next to the contentPath text box, and the Content Path dialog box appears. Here you can enter the Web address of the final location for your `.flv` file on your Web server or Flash Communication Server.**

    For example, you might type **http://www.helpexamples.com/flash/video/clouds.flv.**

18. **Upload your new `.flv` file to your Web server, your Flash Communication Server, or your Flash Video Streaming Service. Also, upload the video skin you chose in Step 12 — you can find a copy of it on your computer in the same folder as your `.fla` file.**

    For instance, if you choose `MojaveExternalPlaySeekMute` in Step 12, you see a file there called `MojaveExternalPlaySeekMute.swf`, which you need to upload to your Web server in the same directory as your `.fla` file.

19. **Choose Control⇨Test Movie.**

    A new window appears showing your Flash movie, and your video appears with the play controls in the style of the skin you chose in Step 12.

20. **Use the play controls to play your streaming video.**

    Your video `.flv` file plays from within your·Flash movie while it downloads from your Web server, your Flash Communication Server, or your Flash Video Streaming Service.

    It probably looks great. This is pretty amazing.

# Part V
# The Movie and
# the Web

"See? I created a little felon figure that runs around our Web site hiding behind banner ads. On the last page, our logo puts him in a non lethal choke hold and brings him back to the home page."

# In this part . . .

The not-so-secret desire of every Flash movie animation is to appear under the bright lights on the Web. In this part, we show you how to make that happen. We explain how to put all the pieces together to create a way-cool Flash-only site. You see how to build a Web site that contains a complete navigational system so that viewers can quickly get the information they need. We cover three techniques for creating a complete site.

We also discuss the nitty-gritty details of publishing your Flash movie to a Flash Player file, the only kind of Flash file a Web browser can display. Besides the Flash Player file, Flash can create the HTML code you need and the alternative images you might want to use in case a viewer doesn't have the Flash Player. Flash makes it easy: Just specify your settings and click Publish.

# Chapter 12

# Putting It All Together

*W*hen creating your Flash animation, you need to consider how you will integrate it with your entire Web site. Are you creating a small animation to insert into an existing HyperText Markup Language (HTML) site, or do you want your entire site to be *Flashed?* In this chapter, we cover techniques for creating entire presentations, Web pages, and sites by using Flash.

## Using Named Anchors

One complaint that people have about earlier versions of Flash is that their browsers' Forward and Back buttons don't allow them to navigate through Flash movies. If Flash takes over your entire Web page, suddenly your Forward and Back buttons can seem dead.

Flash fixed that problem by letting you insert *named anchors* into your movies. Your Web browser sees these anchors as though they're delineating separate Web pages within your Flash file. This makes it easy for a Web browser's Forward and Back buttons to work in movies. When someone watching your Flash movie clicks the Web browser's Back button, the browser simply moves to your movie's nearest previous frame that contains a named anchor. If the previous named anchor is in an earlier scene, the

browser moves to the named anchor point in that scene. Clicking the
Forward button undoes the results of pressing the Back button.

Named anchors work only when you save your work as Flash Player 6, 7, or 8
movies and when they're viewed with Flash Player 6 or above.

To use named anchors in your movie, follow these steps:

1. **Create a new Flash document by choosing File⇨New and then choosing Flash document in the General tab of the New Document dialog
   box that appears. Or use an existing document that you want to add
   named anchors to.**

2. **Choose Window⇨Properties⇨Properties to open the Property inspector if it's not already open. If necessary, click the collapse arrow on
   the Property inspector title bar to expand it.**

3. **Click the keyframe where you want to add a named anchor.**

4. **In the upper-left corner of the Property inspector, type a name in the
   Frame Label text box.**

5. **Choose Anchor in the Type pop-up menu near the Frame Label text box.**

   An anchor icon appears in the keyframe that you clicked in Step 3.

To publish your Flash movie with named anchors, follow these steps:

1. **Add named anchors to your Flash document as described in the preceding step list.**

2. **Choose File⇨Publish Settings.**

   The Publish Settings dialog box appears.

3. **In the Formats tab of the Publish Settings dialog box, select the Flash
   check box and the HTML check box.**

4. **Choose the Flash tab of the Publish Settings dialog box and adjust the
   settings as desired.**

   See Chapter 13 for information on all the settings in the Flash tab.

5. **Choose the HTML tab of the Publish Settings dialog box, and in the
   HTML tab, choose Flash with Named Anchors in the Template drop-
   down list.**

   For details on other settings, see the section in Chapter 13 on specifying
   HTML settings in the Publish Settings dialog box.

6. **Click Publish.**

Flash saves an `.swf` file and an HTML file, both of which contain code supporting named anchors.

At this writing, named anchors don't work properly in all Web browsers, unless you add a bunch of complex code to your Web pages to patch things up.

# Adding the Power of Components

*Components* in Flash are built-in, pre-coded wonders that simplify the creation of interactive Flash movies. Components can be used to add interaction and navigation elements to your Flash movies, allowing you to use Flash to create surveys, forms, interactive art galleries, or even complete graphical user interfaces for your Flash movies. Among other things, you can also use components (with the help of some fairly sophisticated ActionScript) to access and manipulate data from the Web and other sources.

Flash 8 ships with more than a dozen components, and you can download more components built by Flash community members by choosing Help➪ Flash Exchange. Some of the components that ship with Flash 8 are

- **Radio buttons:** These let you make one choice from several buttons.
- **Check boxes:** You can mark or clear each check box.
- **Push buttons:** Clicking one of these makes something happen in your movie.
- **Combo boxes:** These are drop-down lists.
- **List boxes:** These are scrolling lists of choices.
- **Scroll panes:** These are scrollable (but not draggable) windows for your movie clips, JPEG images, and Flash Player files.
- **Windows:** These are draggable windows within your Flash movie that can display a movie clip, JPEG image, or Flash Player file. They also include a title bar, a border, and a Close button.

To add a component to your Flash movie, drag it from the Components panel (see Figure 12-1) onto the Stage.

In the following sections, we look at how you use several types of components. We skip push buttons because button symbols (which we describe in Chapter 8) are easier to use and do almost everything that you need.

**▼ Components**

**FLV Playback Custom UI**
- BackButton
- BufferingBar
- ForwardButton
- MuteButton
- PauseButton
- PlayButton
- PlayPauseButton
- SeekBar
- StopButton
- VolumeBar

**User Interface**
- Button
- CheckBox
- ComboBox
- Label
- List
- Loader
- NumericStepper
- ProgressBar
- RadioButton
- ScrollPane
- TextArea
- TextInput
- UIScrollBar
- Window

**Figure 12-1:**
The
Components
panel
contains
pre-built
user
interface
elements
that you can
use in your
Flash
movies.

# Using radio buttons in a Flash movie

Radio buttons are groups of buttons that permit you to choose one item from the group, like the buttons on a car radio. To use a set of radio buttons in your Flash movie, follow these steps:

1. **If the Components panel is not already visible, choose Window⇨Components. If necessary, click the collapse arrow on the Components panel title bar to expand it.**

2. **If necessary, click the plus sign (Windows) or the right-pointing arrow (Mac) to the left of the User Interface category in the Components panel to display all the components in the category.**

3. **Drag two or more radio buttons from the Components panel onto the Stage.**

   You need at least two radio buttons in every set of radio buttons because one must always be on. In a Flash movie, when you enable a radio button in a set, that button is turned on, and all the others in the set are turned off.

4. **Choose Window⇨Properties⇨Properties to open the Property inspector if it's not already open. If necessary, click the collapse arrow on the Property inspector title bar to expand it and click the Parameters tab.**

The Property inspector appears with the Parameters tab on top. The Property inspector lists five parameters.

5. **Select the radio button whose parameters you want to set.**

6. **To change the radio button's label, click in the label field on the Property inspector, type a new name for the radio button, and press Enter (Windows) or Return (Mac).**

   The radio button's label changes on the Stage.

7. **To change the radio button's initial state, click the Selected drop-down list on the Property inspector and select True or False, depending on what you want.**

   If you select True, the radio button is initially selected. If you select False, the radio button is initially clear.

8. **To change the group to which the radio button belongs, type a new name in the Group Name text field on the Property inspector.**

   For example, type **myRadioGroup** into the Group Name text field.

   All the radio buttons with the same group name act as one group. Selecting one radio button in the group deselects all the other radio buttons with the same group name.

9. **To change the radio button's label placement, click the Label Placement drop-down list on the Property inspector and select the right, left, top, or bottom option to place the label to the right, left, top, or bottom of its radio button.**

   If you choose top or bottom, you undoubtedly want to type in a larger value in the Height text box in the Property inspector to increase the height of the radio button box.

10. **To associate additional information with the radio button, enter the information in the Data text field on the Property inspector.**

    Step 13 shows you how to use this data.

11. **Repeat Steps 5 to 10 for each radio button.**

12. **Decide which elements of your Flash movie will change when a radio button is selected; then add those elements to the Flash movie if you haven't already done so.**

    If for example, you decide that the contents of a dynamic text box will change when a radio button is selected, create a dynamic text box on the Stage and give it an instance name, such as myInfo. (See Chapter 5 to discover how to create dynamic text.)

13. **Choose Window⇨Actions to open the Actions panel if it isn't open already, and in the Actions panel click the Script Assist button to deselect it (if it's selected).**

14. **Select Frame 1 in the Timeline and enter the following code in the Script pane of the Actions panel:**

```
myEvent = new Object();
myForm = new Object();
myForm.click = function(myEvent){
    myInfo.text = myEvent.target.selection.data;
}
myRadioGroup.addEventListener("click",myForm);
```

You can replace `myForm`, `myEvent`, `myInfo`, and `myRadioGroup` with any names that you like. `myInfo` in this example is the name of the dynamic text field that we mention in Step 12, and `myRadioGroup` is the group name of your radio buttons.

Lines 1 and 2 of the preceding code create new little bundles of methods and properties named `myEvent` and `myForm`. Line 6 adds an event listener to `myForm` so that when you select one of the radio buttons in `myRadioGroup`, the code in Lines 3, 4, and 5 sets the text of the dynamic text field to whatever is in the data parameter of the radio button that you click.

The second line of code shows an example of how to change the contents of the dynamic text box that we describe in Step 11, but you can replace this line with other ActionScript code to do something else in your movie to respond to changes in which radio button is selected.

For example, if you want to set the text of the dynamic text field to be the label of the radio button that you click, replace this line:

```
myInfo.text = myEvent.target.selection.data;
```

with this line:

```
myInfo.text = myEvent.target.selection.label;
```

For radio buttons, the Property inspector has two tabs in the upper-right corner — one tab for properties and one tab for parameters. If you have a radio button selected but its parameters don't show on the Property inspector, you probably clicked the Properties tab by accident. Click to select the Parameters tab in the upper-right corner of the Property inspector; now it should display the radio button parameters.

When you look at the preceding code, on some deep level you may be thinking, "Huh?" But it's possible to do a lot of coding in Flash without getting a PhD in ActionScriptology first. You can accomplish a lot by copying existing code, playing with it, and observing the effect.

## Using check boxes in a Flash movie

Check boxes are square boxes that you can check or uncheck to indicate that an option is selected or deselected. To use check boxes in your Flash movie, follow these steps:

1. **Choose Window⇨Components to view the Components panel if it isn't already open.**

2. **Drag a check box from the Components panel onto the Stage.**

3. **Choose Window⇨Properties⇨Properties to open the Property inspector if it isn't already open. If necessary, click the collapse arrow on the Property inspector title bar to expand it, and click the Parameters tab.**

   The Property inspector appears with the Parameters tab on top. The Property inspector lists three parameters: Label, Label Placement, and Selected.

4. **To change the check box's label, click the Label field on the Parameters tab of the Property inspector, type a new name for the check box, and press Enter (Windows) or Return (Mac).**

   The check box's label changes on the Stage.

5. **To change the check box's initial state, click the Selected drop-down list on the Property inspector and select True or False.**

   If you choose True, the check box is initially marked. If you choose False, the check box is initially cleared.

6. **To change the check box's label placement, click the Label Placement drop-down list on the Property inspector and select Right, Left, Top, or Bottom.**

7. **To give the check box an instance name, type a name in the Instance Name field on the Property inspector.**

   For instance, you can enter **myCheckBox**.

8. **Decide which elements of your Flash movie will change when a check box is selected; then add those elements to the Flash movie if you haven't already done so.**

   For example, if you decide the movie will go to and play Frame 20 when a check box is marked, create a keyframe at Frame 20. (See Chapter 9 to discover how to create keyframes.)

9. **Choose Window⇨Actions to open the Actions panel if it isn't open already, and in the Actions panel click the Script Assist button to deselect it (if it's selected).**

**10. Select Frame 1 in the Timeline and enter the following code in the Script pane of the Actions panel:**

```
myEvent2 = new Object();
myForm2 = new Object();
myForm2.click = function(myEvent2){
    if (myEvent2.target.selected){
    gotoAndPlay(20);
    }
}
myCheckBox.addEventListener("click",myForm2);
stop();
```

You can replace myForm2, myEvent2, and myCheckBox with any names that you like. myCheckBox in this example is the instance name of your check box.

You might not need the stop() action in the last line of the code, depending on what you want your movie to do. We assume in this example that you want the movie to wait in Frame 1 for the user to press a button or mark the check box, so for that you would want to stop the action in Frame 1.

Lines 1 and 2 of the preceding code create new little bundles of methods and properties named myEvent2 and myForm2. Line 8 adds an event listener to myForm so that when you mark the check box named myCheckBox, the code in Lines 3, 4, 5, 6 and 7 causes Flash to go to Frame 20 and start playing there.

An *event listener* is a little bit of software that checks for events generated by one object and notifies a second object when they occur.

So the code in Line 8 sets up an event listener that notifies a function named myForm2 whenever myCheckbox has been clicked. In the code in Lines 3, 4, and 5, whenever myForm2 receives a message that myCheckbox has been clicked, myForm2 checks to see if myCheckbox was selected or deselected, and if myCheckbox was selected, then Flash goes to frame 20 and starts playing there.

Lines 4 and 5 of the code show an example of how to set the Flash playhead to move to another section of the movie if the viewer selects the check box. You can replace this line with other ActionScript code to make the movie do something else when the viewer selects the check box.

## Using combo boxes in a Flash movie

A *combo box* is text box that shows the current selection, combined with a drop-down list of possible selections. To use combo boxes in your Flash movie, follow these steps:

1. **Choose Window⇨Components to view the Components panel if it isn't already open.**

   Refer to Figure 12-1 to see the Components panel in all its splendor.

2. **Drag a combo box from the Components panel onto the Stage.**

3. **Choose Window⇨Properties⇨Properties to open the Property inspector if it isn't already open. If necessary, click the collapse arrow on the Property inspector title bar to expand it and click the Parameters tab.**

   The Property inspector appears with the Parameters tab on top. The Property inspector lists four parameters: Data, Editable, Labels, and Row Count.

4. **Type a name in the Instance Name text field in the upper-left corner of the Property inspector.**

5. **To control whether the user can edit the items on the combo box's menu list, select True or False from the drop-down list for the Editable parameter.**

   Selecting True allows the user to rename each item on the menu list. Selecting False prevents that from happening.

6. **To create items on the menu list, click the magnifying glass next to the Labels text field in the Parameters tab of the Property inspector.**

   The Values dialog box appears.

7. **In the Values dialog box, click the plus sign to add a menu item or click the minus sign to delete a menu item. Click the upward-pointing triangle to move an item up on the list and click the downward-pointing triangle to move a menu item down on the list.**

   When you add an item to the list, it is excitingly named `defaultValue`.

8. **To change a menu item's name from `defaultValue` to something more interesting and meaningful, click the menu item in the Values dialog box and type a more useful name there.**

9. **Click OK.**

   The Values dialog box closes.

10. **To change the number of items that can be displayed in the combo box without a scroll bar, click the Row Count field on the Property inspector and type a new number.**

    The default number is 5.

11. **If you want to make the combo box wider so that longer menu items are more readable, choose Modify⇨Transform⇨Scale and change the size of the combo box by pulling the handles that appear on its borders.**

**12. Decide which elements of your Flash movie will change when a menu item in the combo box is selected. Add those elements to the Flash movie if you haven't already done so.**

If, for example, you decide that the contents of a dynamic text box will change when a menu item in the combo box is selected, create a dynamic text box on the Stage and give it an instance name, such as `myInfo3`. (See Chapter 5 to discover how to create dynamic text.)

**13. Choose Window➪Actions to open the Actions panel if it isn't open already, and in the Actions panel click the Script Assist button to deselect it, if it's selected.**

**14. Select Frame 1 in the Timeline and enter the following code in the Script pane of the Actions panel:**

```
myEvent3 = new Object();
myForm3 = new Object();
myForm3.change = function(myEvent3){
    myInfo3.text = myComboBox.selectedItem.label;
}
myComboBox.addEventListener("change",myForm3);
```

You can replace `myForm3`, `myEvent3`, `myInfo3`, and `myComboBox` with any names that you like. `myInfo3` in this example is the name of the dynamic text field that we mention in Step 12, and `myComboBox` is the instance name of your combo box.

When you play your Flash movie, note the sleek, subtle animation when you click the combo box, which is impossible with a plain old HTML Web page.

Lines 1 and 2 of the preceding code create new little bundles of methods and properties named `myEvent3` and `myForm3`. Line 6 adds an event listener to `myForm3` so that when you select one of the menu items in `myComboBox`, the code in lines 3, 4, and 5 sets the text of the dynamic text field to whatever is the label of the combo box menu item that the viewer selects.

The third, fourth, and fifth lines of code show an example of how to change the contents of the dynamic text box that we describe in Step 12, but you can replace this line with other ActionScript code to do something else. For example, here you might instead put some ActionScript code that sets the Flash playhead to move to different sections of the movie depending on which menu item in the combo box is selected.

If things aren't working when you test your combo box, there may be typos or other errors in the ActionScript code that you typed in. Flash often reports these errors in the Output panel when you choose Control➪Test Movie. The error messages in the Output window may seem obscure, but they can give you an idea of where your problem may be.

# Using list boxes in a Flash movie

A *list box* is a scrollable list of selectable items. To use list boxes in your Flash movie, follow these steps:

1. **Choose Window⇨Components to view the Components panel if it's not already open.**

2. **Drag a list box from the Components panel onto the Stage.**

3. **Choose Window⇨Properties⇨Properties to open the Property inspector if it isn't already open. If necessary, click the collapse arrow on the Property inspector title bar to expand it and click the Parameters tab.**

   The Property inspector appears with the Parameters tab on top. The Property inspector lists four parameters: Data, Labels, Multiple Selection, and Row Height.

4. **Type a name in the Instance Name text field in the left corner of the Property inspector.**

   For example, you might name the instance `myListBox`.

5. **To create items in the list box, click the magnifying glass next to the Labels text field on the Parameters tab of the Property inspector.**

   The Values dialog box appears.

6. **In the Values dialog box, click the plus sign to add a list item or click the minus sign to delete a list item. Click the upward-pointing triangle to move an item up on the list and click the downward-pointing triangle to move an item down on the list.**

   When you add an item to the list, it is cleverly named `defaultValue`.

7. **To change a list item's name from `defaultValue` to something more useful, click the menu item in the Values dialog box and type a more descriptive name there.**

8. **Click OK.**

   The Values dialog box closes.

9. **To set whether the user can select multiple items on the list, select True or False from the drop-down list for the Multiple Selection parameter.**

   Selecting True allows the user to select multiple items on the list. Selecting False allows the user to select only one item on the list.

10. **To change the height (in pixels) of each item in the list, click the Row Height field on the Property inspector and type a new number.**

    The default height is 20 pixels.

11. **Choose Modify⇨Transform⇨Scale and change the size of the list box if you want to make the list box wider in order to make the menu items more legible.**

12. **Decide which elements of your Flash movie will change when a viewer selects a menu item in the list box. Add those elements to the Flash movie if you haven't already done so.**

    If, for example, you decide that the contents of a dynamic text box will change when a list item is selected, create a dynamic text box on the Stage and give it an instance name, such as myInfo4. (See Chapter 5 to discover how to create dynamic text.)

13. **Choose Window⇨Actions to open the Actions panel if it isn't open already, and in the Actions panel click the Script Assist button to deselect it (if it's selected).**

14. **Select Frame 1 in the Timeline and enter this code in the Script pane of the Actions panel:**

    ```
    myEvent4 = new Object();
    myForm4 = new Object();
    myForm4.change = function(myEvent4){
        myInfo4.text = myListBox.selectedItem.label;
    }
    myListBox.addEventListener("change",myForm4);
    ```

    You can replace myForm4, myEvent4, myInfo4, and myListBox with any names that you like. myInfo4 in this example is the name of the dynamic text field that we mention in Step 12, and myListBox is the instance name of your list box.

In Lines 1 and 2 of the preceding code, we create new objects named myEvent4 and myForm4. Line 6 adds an event listener to myForm4 that "listens" for whenever the viewer selects one of the menu items in myListBox. When the viewer selects one of the menu items, myListBox broadcasts to Flash that it has changed. myForm4 "hears" that and, using the code in lines 4, sets the text of the dynamic text field to whatever is the label of the list box menu item that the viewer selects.

You can replace Line 4 with other ActionScript code to do something else. For example, Line 4 might instead set the value of some variable depending on which menu item in the list box is selected. The new value of that variable might then be used to, for example, change the size of a graphic on the Stage.

## Using scroll panes in a Flash movie

*Scroll panes* allow you to put a movie clip, a JPEG image, or an .swf file inside a pane with scroll bars. This feature is useful if you want to display big movies or images without taking up lots of space on the Stage.

To add a scroll pane to your Flash movie, follow these steps:

1. **Choose Window⇨Components to view the Components panel if it isn't already open.**

2. **Drag a scroll pane from the Components panel onto the Stage.**

3. **Choose Window⇨Properties⇨Properties to open the Property inspector if it isn't already open. If necessary, click the collapse arrow on the Property inspector title bar to expand it and click the Parameters tab.**

   The Property inspector appears with the Parameters tab on top. The Property inspector lists these parameters: Content Path, Horizontal Line Scroll Size, Horizontal Line Page Size, Horizontal Scroll Policy, Scroll Drag, Vertical Line Scroll Size, Vertical Page Scroll Size, and Vertical Scroll Policy.

4. **To set the content of the scroll pane, click the Content Path field on the Property inspector and type the symbol linkage ID of the movie clip that you want to display. Alternatively, you can type the relative or absolute path to a JPEG image file or an `.swf` file.**

   For information on creating a symbol linkage ID, see the section "Sharing Libraries on the Run," later in this chapter.

5. **To specify whether horizontal or vertical scroll bars are displayed, click the Horizontal Scroll Policy drop-down list or the Vertical Scroll Policy drop-down list and select Auto, True, or False.**

   True means that the scroll bar will be displayed. False means that it won't. Auto means that the scroll bar will be displayed only if necessary. Therefore, Auto is usually a good choice.

6. **To specify whether the user must scroll in the window by grabbing and dragging the image or by grabbing and dragging the scroll bar(s), select True or False from the Scroll Drag drop-down list.**

   True means that the user must drag the image. False means that the user must drag the scroll bars. False is the default.

7. **To change the number of pixels that a scroll bar moves horizontally or vertically each time that the viewer pushes one of the scroll bar's arrow buttons, click the Horizontal Line Scroll Size or Vertical Line Scroll Size field on the Property inspector and type the number that you want.**

   The default value is 5 pixels.

8. **To change the number of pixels that a scroll bar moves horizontally or vertically each time that the user pushes the scroll bar track (above or below one of the scroll bar arrow buttons), click the Horizontal Page Scroll Size or Vertical Page Scroll Size field on the Property inspector and type the number that you want.**

   The default value is 20 pixels.

## Using windows in a Flash movie

*Windows* allow you to put a movie clip, a JPEG image, or an SWF file inside a movable window with a title bar, a border, and an optional Close button. The window appears inside your Flash movie. You can't drag the window outside the movie.

To add a window to your Flash movie, follow these steps:

1. **Choose Window➪Components to view the Components panel if it's not already open.**

2. **Drag a window component from the Components panel onto the Stage.**

3. **Choose Window➪Properties➪Properties to open the Property inspector if it isn't already open. If necessary, click the collapse arrow on the Property inspector title bar to expand it and click the Parameters tab.**

   The Property inspector appears with the Parameters tab on top. The Property inspector lists three parameters: Close Button, Content Path, and Title.

4. **To set the content of the window, click the Content Path field on the Property inspector and type the symbol linkage ID of the movie clip that you want to display. Alternatively, type the relative or absolute path to a JPEG image file or an SWF file.**

   For information on creating a symbol linkage ID, see the section "Sharing Libraries on the Run," later in this chapter.

5. **To specify whether the window has a close button, click the Close Button drop-down list and select True or False.**

   True means that the Close button will be displayed. False means that it won't. Some tricky ActionScript code is needed to make the window close when you click the Close button, so for now, choose False.

6. **To specify the name of the window that will appear in the title bar, click the Title field on the Property inspector and type a name.**

## Creating a Preloader

If you're very ambitious and create a huge Flash file, downloading it to a viewer's browser might take a long time. Your audience won't wait forever. To solve this problem, you can create a *preloader,* which is a tiny movie that loads quickly and tells your viewers to wait. Often, it simply says `loading`, followed by a percentage loaded.

Flash 8 comes with a Loader component and a ProgressBar component that you can use to build preloaders, but they require more lines of fancy ActionScript code than you may want to deal with if you're new to Flash. For now, you might want to start out with a simple preloader using a few lines of more old-fashioned ActionScript code, which you can create by following these steps:

1. **Create two scenes — the second for your main movie and the first for the preloader. Or if your movie already has multiple scenes, add another scene for the preloader and make it the first scene.**

   The scenes must be within the same movie. See Chapter 9 for the low-down on creating and changing the order of scenes.

2. **In the first scene (the preloader), create whatever you want your audience to see while the rest of your movie loads. Keep this scene simple so that it loads quickly.**

3. **Click the first frame of your preloader scene. Then choose Window⇨ Actions to open the Actions panel if it isn't already open, and if necessary, click the collapse arrow on the title bar to expand it. In the Actions panel, click the Script Assist button to deselect it (if it's selected).**

4. **In the Script pane on the right side of the Actions panel, type in the following ActionScript code:**

   ```
   if (_root._framesloaded >= _root._totalframes) {
   gotoAndPlay("Scene 2",1);
   }
   ```

   The ActionScript specifies that if the number of frames loaded is greater than or equal to the total number of frames in your movie (in other words, if the last frame of the main movie is loaded), the playhead of the Timeline should go to the first frame of the scene named Scene 2 and play it. Turn to Chapter 10 to find out about ActionScript.

5. **Click the last frame of your preloader scene.**

6. **From the list of action types on the left side of the Actions panel, click the Global Functions category and then the Timeline Control subcategory; then double-click the `gotoAndPlay` action.**

   `gotoAndPlay();` appears in the Script pane on the right side of the Actions panel.

7. **Type 1 in the Script pane.**

   Now your code should look like this:

   ```
   gotoAndPlay(1);
   ```

   This ActionScript loops your preloader so that it plays over and over until your main movie is loaded.

You can test your preloader by choosing Control⇨Test Movie, but your main movie might load so quickly that you don't even see the preloader. Choose View⇨Simulate Download to see how your preloader works while your main movie loads. (See Chapter 13 for more information on testing a movie and analyzing its download performance). You can also upload your file to a test page on your Web site to see how the preloader works. Make sure that your preloader is long enough for the human eye to see. Remember that one frame is displayed for only a fraction of a second.

# Adding Web Search Information to Your Flash Movie

You can easily add information to your `.swf` file to help Web search sites (such as Google, Clusty, and so on) find your Flash movie. The information you add is called *search metadata*. (It's called metadata because it's *information about the information* in your document.)

This is a good thing if you want to be noticed because search engines typically ignore the contents of Flash movies, which are more difficult to decipher than the contents of regular HTML Web pages.

To add metadata for Web search sites to your Flash movie, follow these steps:

1. **Choose Modify⇨Document.**

    The Document Properties window appears.

2. **Enter a meaningful title for the document in the Title text box and enter additional descriptive information in the Description text box.**

    The descriptive information may include searchable keywords, copyright and author information, and other brief information about the content of the document.

3. **Click OK.**

# Creating an Entire Web Site with Flash

You can use Flash to create the complete user interface, along with all the graphics and text, on your site. Some Web sites are almost 100 percent Flash (for example, www.funonmars.com, the Web site of this book's Technical Editor, Sally Cruikshank). But most Flash Web sites (including www.macromedia.com) are a hybrid of Flash and HTML. So, typically, a Flash Web site has the following structure:

   ✔ An HTML home page that contains these items:

      • A user interface (and perhaps other graphics) built in Flash

      • Tests that detect the Flash Player and Player version

- Automatic or user-controlled download of the Flash Player from Macromedia

- JavaScript that automatically redirects viewers to an HTML site if they don't have Flash, or a button that viewers can use to surf to an HTML site if they have a slow connection or don't want to download the Flash Player.

- A Flash Player movie (perhaps requiring the latest Flash Player) including a preloader (if needed) and all the visual content of the page, with all text, graphics, and navigation created in Flash

✔ Additional HTML pages that, like the home page, utilize a user interface (and other graphics) built in Flash, for all the remaining pages in the Web site. You might want each of these pages to also test for Flash in case your viewers don't enter the site via your home page.

✔ An HTML page for viewers without the required version of Flash, suggesting that they download and install it.

✔ HTML pages that contain a non-Flash version of the Web site (if you want the site to be available to those who don't have and don't want to install the required version of Flash).

For information on creating an HTML page that tests for the Flash Player, see the "Testing for the Flash Player" section, later in this chapter.

The opening HTML page is (usually) the first thing that your viewers see. On the World Wide Web, first impressions are important if you want to your audience to stick around, so be sure to think carefully about what your goals are for this page.

To match a Flash movie in a Web page to the rest of the page, match the background colors of the movie (by choosing Modify➪Document) and the HTML page. (This technique doesn't work if your Web page uses an image for a background.) To set the background of the HTML page to a different color, edit the HTML file that Flash creates when you publish your movie. After determining the background color in hexadecimal code (by looking at the HTML code for the existing Web page), change the BGCOLOR tag in the HTML code in three places:

✔ In the background color where you see `<BODY bgcolor="#99CCFF">` (for example)

✔ In the OBJECT tag where you see `<PARAM NAME=bgcolor VALUE= #99CCFF>`

✔ In the EMBED code where you see `BGCOLOR=#99CCFF`

After people get to your Flash page, you can do whatever you want. Some sites using Flash start with an intro, which is a preliminary movie that either briefly explains what your site is for or just wows your viewers. Intros were a hot thing in Flash a few years ago, when people were more captivated by the novelty of vector animation on the Web. But now intros tend to simply irritate the viewer, so in this century an intro is probably a really bad idea. You want people to get to the main content of your site immediately. If the information in your intro is valuable, put that information in the main content of your site instead, where people won't feel annoyed that they're forced to view it.

Your site probably contains buttons that people can use to navigate through your site, get more information, or contact you.

You can create the navigation structure in three main ways:

✔ Attach `On (mouse event)` or `Load Movie` actions to the buttons to display the content of movie clips or Flash Player movies (`.swf` files).

✔ Attach `getURL` actions to the buttons to link to other HTML pages or movies on your site. You can, of course, create the HTML pages with Flash.

✔ Use the buttons to display information or graphics located on other parts of your Timeline by using the `gotoAndPlay` or `gotoAndStop` action.

We describe the `On (mouse event)` and `Load Movie` actions in Chapter 10. We explain the `getURL` action in Chapters 8 (with regard to buttons) and 10. You can use combinations of these methods. For example, you can use `On (mouse event)` to display information when the mouse cursor is over a button, and you can use `getURL` to link to another page when the user clicks the button.

## Creating navigation with getURL

When you attach a `getURL` action to a button, the button links to another HTML page in the same way that a button on a regular, non-Flash, HTML Web page does. For more information on the `getURL` action, see Chapter 10. Also, Chapter 8 explains how to add an action to a button.

## Using the Timeline to store Web content

In most cases, you use the Timeline to display frames in sequence — in other words, animation. But the Timeline can also store static frames. You can create anything on the Stage in those frames, and you can display what is in those frames whenever you want. So different frames on the Timeline can become the equivalent of separate Web pages.

Suppose that you have several buttons on the left side of your page. You want viewers to see different graphics and animation on the right side of the page when they click each button. Perhaps clicking one button displays information about a product. Clicking another button might display information about a second product.

To create a set of buttons that move the playhead to different sections of the Timeline, follow these steps:

1. **Place instances of your buttons in separate layers on the first frame of the Timeline of your movie.**

2. **On each layer, about 20 or so frames after the first frame, add a keyframe.**

   These 20 or so frames leave room to store static display frames or movie clips on the Timeline. The buttons continue to be displayed throughout the movie until the ending keyframe. If you have a lot of buttons, you might need to choose a keyframe that's more than 20 frames after the first frame. The more buttons you want to provide descriptions for, the further out your ending keyframe needs to be.

3. **Create a new layer to display the right side of the page and give it a name, such as Product Views.**

4. **A few frames out (on Frame 10, for example) on the Product Views layer, create a keyframe.**

   This step starts a Timeline section for the product displayed when the user clicks your first button.

5. **Open the Property inspector if it isn't already open (choose Window⇨ Properties⇨Properties). If necessary, click the collapse arrow on the Property inspector title bar to expand it and click the Properties tab.**

6. **In the Frame Label text box on the left side of the Property inspector, type a label name.**

7. **On the Stage, create the graphics and words that you want to be displayed when a user clicks the first button. If you want to display animation when a user clicks the first button, drag a movie clip from the Library. (Check out Chapter 7 for the scoop on creating movie clips.)**

   Place the graphics so that they don't cover the buttons when they appear.

8. **Repeat Steps 4 through 7 to create labels and displays on the Product Views layer for all your buttons, using later sections of the Timeline each time until you reach the ending keyframe.**

9. **Select a button.**

10. **Choose Window⇨Actions to open the Actions panel if it's not already open, and in the Actions panel click the Script Assist button to select it, if it's not selected.**

11. **In the list on the left side of the Actions panel, choose the Global Functions category, then the Timeline Control subcategory, and then double-click goto.**

12. **Click the first line of ActionScript, which by default says** on
    (Release) {.

13. **From the list of mouse events at the top of the Actions panel, deselect
    Release and select Roll Over.**

    The Roll Over event causes the action to occur when your viewer passes
    the mouse cursor over the button.

14. **Click the second line of ActionScript.**

15. **At the top of the Actions panel, select the Go To and Stop radio button.**

16. **For the Type drop-down list, select Frame Label.**

17. **From the Frame drop-down list, select the first label that you created
    on your Timeline in Step 6.**

    Your ActionScript should now be the same as the code shown in
    Figure 12-2.

**Figure 12-2:**
ActionScript
that displays
a section of
the Timeline
when the
viewer
presses a
button.

18. **Repeat Steps 9 through 17 for the rest of your buttons and their
    respective frame labels.**

19. **Create a new layer and name it** *Actions*.

20. **Place a** stop **action on the first frame.**

    Turn to Chapter 10 for instructions on how to add an action to a frame.

    If you don't do this final step, your movie simply plays through all the
    frames, displaying your descriptions one after another. You want view-
    ers to see those frames only when they click a button.

Choose Control⇨Test Movie to try it out! When you roll over a button, the graphics, text, and movie clip animation on the appropriate frames appear.

Figure 12-3 shows a Timeline with frames that are displayed when the mouse cursor passes over buttons.

If you choose `Release` instead of `Roll Over` in Step 13, you can display different information when the mouse clicks each button.

**Figure 12-3:**
You can use the Timeline to display different graphics and text when the cursor passes over each button.

Look for `HelpDesk-Timeline.fla` in the Ch12 folder on the companion Web site (`www.dummies.com/go/flash8`) for an example of buttons that use the Timeline to display information about the purpose of the buttons. To test the move, choose Control⇨Test Movie. To see the ActionScript, click a frame with an *a* in it and choose Window⇨Actions to open the Actions panel.

# Testing for the Flash Player

Although most people have the Flash Player installed, some viewers might still have totally out-of-date browsers. For viewers who don't have the Flash Player, it often downloads automatically (as a result of the code that Flash places in the HTML file when you publish your `.swf` and HTML files, as we describe in Chapter 13). If Flash doesn't download automatically, those viewers simply might not be able to view your site. You can test for the presence of the Flash Player and, even more, you can test to see which version of the Flash Player they have. If you're using features that exist only in Flash 8, make sure that viewers have Flash Player 8 because many people might still have Flash Player 7 (or an even earlier version) installed.

You can test for the Flash Player in several ways; we describe two possibilities in the following sections.

## Letting the user decide

Some sites let the viewer simply choose between a Flash site and a non-Flash site. The problem with this method is that many users have no idea what Flash is, let alone whether they have the Flash Player.

A better method to let users determine whether they have the Flash Player is to place a small Flash animation that is also a button on an initial HTML Web page. Instructions tell them to click the button if they can see the animation, which links them to the main portion of your Flash site. If they cannot see the animation, you can offer an image with a link (or linked text) to the Macromedia Flash Player download site and another link to an alternative HTML site. (See Chapter 8 for instructions on creating a Flash button.)

At the very least, you should offer users the opportunity to download the Flash Player. Do this with a link that connects them to the following URL:

```
www.macromedia.com/go/getflashplayer
```

## Detecting the Flash Player version

A more sophisticated method is to automatically test for a particular version of the Flash Player. Then you might have one site for Flash Player 5 or later, for example, and a second HTML site for viewers that don't have Flash Player 5 or later.

You may detect a particular Flash Player version simply by marking the Detect Flash Version check box in the HTML tab in Flash's Publish Settings before you publish your movie. (See Chapter 13 for the scoop on specifying Publish Settings.) This does a great job of detecting a particular Flash Player version but generates a lot of fairly fancy JavaScript code. This works really well if you don't need to customize the code, but the code isn't easy for beginners to customize.

Suppose you do enable the Detect Flash Version check box (as we describe in Chapter 13). Then when you publish your Flash file, the resulting HTML code displays `Alternate HTML content should be placed here` on your Web page if the Flash Player of the specified version can't be found or if the Web browser doesn't have scripting enabled.

You can edit the HTML to replace the sentence `Alternate HTML content should be placed here` with whatever alternative content you want to display to the viewer if the Flash Player version can't be found.

You can even paste in the HTML here from another page you publish that checks for an earlier version of the Flash Player.

So you could check first for Flash Player 8, for example, and then if that isn't detected, the HTML code for the alternative HTML content might check for Flash Player 6. And if even that isn't detected, the alternative HTML content could consist of HTML code for a page in a series of HTML-only, non-Flash pages.

## Creating alternative sites

Some Flash sites include a complete set of non-Flash (HTML) pages for view-ers who don't have the Flash Player and don't want to bother downloading it.

If you use features unique to Flash 8, you can also create a Flash 6 site that uses only features available in Flash 6. The overwhelming majority of Web surfers have Flash Player 6 or later. But don't forget how much time you spend updating your Web site now. Imagine updating two or three sites! Make sure that you think through the consequences of having so many alternatives.

For detailed information on how many computer users have which versions of the Flash player, check out the latest Macromedia statistics at www.macromedia.com/software/player_census/flashplayer/version_penetration.html. You may be surprised by the statistics there.

# Using the Movie Explorer

The Movie Explorer is a great tool for analyzing an entire movie. When you start creating complex relationships among several Timelines, you might have trouble remembering what you've done. The Movie Explorer lays out the entire structure of your movie for you to see. The Movie Explorer is also a great tool for troubleshooting problems that might arise. By visually display-ing your movie's components, you can more easily find where the trouble lies.

Another use for the Movie Explorer is to analyze other people's FLA files. When you open someone else's movie, you might wonder where the movie is. It might all be hidden in movie clips and actions that call other movies and movie clips. The Movie Explorer can help you ferret out the magic behind the animation.

To open the Movie Explorer, choose Window➪Movie Explorer. The Movie Explorer is shown in Figure 12-4.

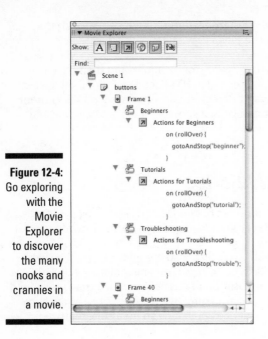

**Figure 12-4:**
Go exploring
with the
Movie
Explorer
to discover
the many
nooks and
crannies in
a movie.

You usually know what you're looking for when you open the Movie Explorer. For example, you might be looking for ActionScript or movie clips. Use the buttons at the top of the Movie Explorer to specify which movie elements are shown in the main window:

- ✔ **Show Text:** Displays all text objects in the movie.

- ✔ **Show Buttons, Movie Clips, and Graphics:** Displays a list of those objects.

- ✔ **Show Action Scripts:** Lists all ActionScript in the movie.

- ✔ **Show Video, Sounds, and Bitmaps:** Lists those objects.

- ✔ **Show Frames and Layers:** Shows each frame and each layer that contains objects.

- ✔ **Customize Which Items to Show:** Opens the Movie Explorer Settings dialog box, where you can indicate which items you want to show by marking or clearing them in a list of check boxes. You can also choose to display Movie Elements (scenes), Symbol Definitions (a separate listing by symbol), or both. Click OK to close this dialog box.

Movie elements are shown in a hierarchical manner in the Movie Explorer. For example, if a button has an action attached to it, you see a plus sign (Windows) or a right-pointing triangle (Mac) next to the button. Click any plus sign or right-pointing triangle to expand the display — in this case, to reveal the ActionScript for that button. Click any minus sign (Windows) or downward-pointing triangle (Mac) to collapse the display.

In the Find text box, you can type any expression to search the entire movie. Suppose that you want to know whether a movie contains the getURL action. Just type **getURL** in the Find text box, and the Movie Explorer displays every instance containing that word.

The Find feature is not case-sensitive, which is handy if you can't remember how things are capitalized. But the Find feature is sensitive to spaces, so if the movie contains *getURL* and you type **get URL**, you don't get any result. Also, be sure to clear your search when it's done, or the Movie Explorer will seem to stop working.

You can use the Movie Explorer to select objects on the Stage or frames. Just click the item in the Movie Explorer, and Flash selects the object or frame. (If you select a frame, Flash also includes the frames up to the next keyframe.) If you select a scene, Flash selects the first frame of the scene.

The Movie Explorer contains an extensive menu that you can access by either clicking in the upper-right corner of the Movie Explorer panel, or right-clicking (Windows) or Control+clicking (Mac) inside the Movie Explorer panel.

Some of the more useful features of this menu are

- ✔ **Find in Library:** Opens the Library (if it isn't already open) and highlights the object that you previously selected in the Movie Explorer.
- ✔ **Rename:** Lets you rename the selected object, such as a button instance.
- ✔ **Copy All Text to Clipboard:** Copies all the text in the Movie Explorer to the Clipboard (of course) so that you can paste it into another application.
- ✔ **Print:** Prints the entire contents of the Movie Explorer. All items, whether collapsed or expanded, are printed.

If you have difficulty understanding one of the more advanced Flash movies on our companion Web site, try opening the Movie Explorer in the movie. Look for actions and movie clips. You might be surprised at what you can discover by using this tool.

# Making Your Site More Accessible

Flash includes capabilities that make it possible for you to make Flash more accessible to people with disabilities.

Most of the components in Flash 8 are designed to be accessible to the visually impaired through the use of screen readers, which generate a spoken description of the contents of your Flash screen. Screen reader software is widely available from a variety of companies.

Users can also navigate around most of Flash's components by using the keyboard rather than the mouse — this is automatically built into the components. And ActionScript has features that can enhance the accessibility of Flash documents.

One of the easiest ways to make your Flash movie more accessible to people with disabilities is to use the Accessibility panel. When you add buttons, movie clips, text, Input Text fields, or components to your movie, you can use the Accessibility panel to make them accessible to screen readers. (Not all components can be made accessible, but most can.) To make a button, movie clip, text, Input Text field, or component accessible, follow these steps:

1. **Choose Window➪Other Panels➪Accessibility to open the Accessibility panel if it isn't already open. If necessary, click the collapse arrow on the Accessibility panel title bar to expand it.**

2. **Select the button, movie clip, text, Input Text field, or component on the Stage.**

3. **In the Accessibility panel, select Make Object Accessible.**

4. **If you selected a movie clip in Step 2, select the Make Child Objects Accessible check box in the Accessibility panel if you want objects embedded within the movie clip to also be accessible.**

   For example, select the Make Child Objects Accessible check box if you want to allow text objects in the movie clip to be read by the screen reader software.

5. **In the Accessibility panel's Name text field, type in a name for the symbol or component.**

   The screen reader can read this name aloud.

6. **In the Accessibility panel's Description text field, type in a description of the symbol or component.**

   The screen reader can read this description aloud.

7. **In the Accessibility panel's Shortcut text field, type in a keyboard shortcut that viewers can use to select the object, if appropriate.**

   If, for instance, the object is a radio button that needs to be selected to receive input, follow this step.

   The screen reader can then use this information to read aloud something like, "The shortcut for this text field is Ctrl+K." (Not all screen readers support this feature.) Typing in information in the Shortcut text field doesn't actually implement keyboard shortcut functionality. You need to use ActionScript to detect and respond to any shortcut key-presses.

8. **In Flash Professional 8 only, in the Accessibility panel's Tab Index field, you may enter the number corresponding to the object's tab index value, if appropriate.**

The *tab index* determines how users can use the Tab key to navigate through and select one of the buttons, check boxes, and other controls in your movie. For example, suppose that you have three buttons with a tab index of 1, 2, and 3, respectively. When the movie starts, if the user presses the Tab key three times, the button with the tab index of 3 would be selected for input.

If you have the Accessibility panel open when nothing in your movie is selected, the panel offers you the option to Make Movie Accessible, which is selected by default. This allows screen readers to read the different objects in the Flash movie. You definitely want this option selected if you want to make your movie accessible to screen readers and other hardware and software for people with disabilities. Of course, you also have to name each object by using the Accessibility panel, as we describe in the preceding steps, for this to be useful.

# Sharing Libraries on the Run

A *runtime shared library* is a library in a movie that has been posted to a Web site and is used by another Flash Player file (`.swf`). The movie using the shared library object doesn't contain the object but just uses it from the shared library. Shared libraries can help make it easier to manage and revise the elements in your movies. For example, you can use a single shared library for multiple Flash movies to access a sound; when you update the sound in the shared library, the sound is updated for all the movies that share it.

## Creating a shared library

A runtime shared library can be a movie clip, a button, a graphic symbol, a sound, a bitmap, or a font symbol. (See Chapter 7 for the lowdown on symbols.)

You create a runtime shared library when you want to make an element in your movie available to other SWF player files. You do this by defining linked objects in a movie's library. To create a runtime shared library, follow these steps:

1. **With the Library panel open, select a symbol, sound, or bitmap from the Library panel. Then right-click (Windows) or Control+click (Mac) and choose Linkage from the contextual menu that appears.**

   You can select any kind of symbol: a graphic symbol, button, movie clip symbol, or font symbol.

   The Linkage Properties dialog box appears.

2. **In the Linkage Properties dialog box, select the Export for Runtime Sharing check box.**

3. **Type a name (no spaces allowed) for the symbol in the Identifier text box.**

4. **In the URL text box, enter the planned URL (location on the Web) of the .swf file containing the shared resource.**

5. **Click OK.**

   The Linkage Properties dialog box closes.

6. **Save the file.**

7. **Publish the file as an .swf file.**

   See Chapter 13 for instructions on publishing files.

8. **Upload the file to your Web site — to the location that you specified in Step 4.**

   In Step 3, you give the shared Library a name; and in Step 4, you give the shared library an address. The next section describes how you can use this name and address to link to the shared library from within a different movie.

To share a font, you first have to create a font symbol, but that's easy. To create a font symbol, follow these steps:

1. **Choose Window➪Library to open the Library panel.**

2. **Click the Options menu in the upper-right corner of the Library panel and then choose New Font.**

   The Font Symbol Properties dialog box appears.

3. **Select a font from the Font menu in the dialog box. Alternatively, type in the name of the font in the Font text box.**

4. **Type in a name for the font symbol in the Name text box.**

5. **Select bold or italic text (if you like) and then type in the font size that you desire in the Size box.**

6. **Click OK.**

   The dialog box disappears, and the name that you gave the font symbol appears in the Library panel.

## Using a shared library

After you create a shared Library, you can use it from within a different movie by specifying its name and URL, or by dragging it into the destination movie. To use a shared Library by specifying its name and URL, follow these steps:

1. **In the destination movie, choose Window⇨Library.**

   The Library panel appears.

2. **Select an object on the Library panel, right-click (Windows) or Control+click (Mac), and choose Linkage from the contextual menu that appears.**

   The Linkage Properties dialog box appears.

3. **In the Linkage Properties dialog box, select the Import for Runtime Sharing check box.**

4. **Type the name of the shared resource that you want into the Identifier text box (no spaces allowed).**

   This name should be identical to the Identifier you assigned to the shared library you want to use.

   If the Identifier text box already has a name in it, ignore that name and type in the name of the shared library you want to use.

5. **Enter the URL of the shared resource you want.**

6. **Click OK.**

   The Linkage Properties dialog box closes.

To use a runtime shared Library by dragging it into your destination movie, follow these steps:

1. **Open your source movie.**

   The *source* movie is the `.swf` file whose runtime shared Library you want to use.

2. **Choose File⇨Open.**

   The Open dialog box appears.

3. **In the dialog box, navigate to your destination movie, select it, and click Open.**

   The destination movie file opens.

4. **If the Library panel isn't open, choose Window⇨Library. If necessary, click the collapse arrow on the Library panel title bar to expand it.**

   The Library panel shows the library of the destination movie.

5. **Choose the name of the source file from the drop-down list beneath the title bar of the Library panel.**

   The Library panel now shows the contents of the library of the source movie.

6. **Drag the linked object from its Library panel onto the Stage of your destination movie.**

Working with shared libraries requires that all the pieces be in the proper place at the same time. We suggest checking a movie that contains an object from a shared library to verify that the object is displayed properly. You can do so by going online and viewing it in your browser.

# Chapter 13

# Publishing Your Flash Files

*Y*our Flash movie is done. Now you need to publish it in its final form — most likely an .swf file that you can post on your Web site. In this chapter, we explain how to prepare a Flash movie for publishing and help you determine the ideal publish settings for your needs. We also discuss how to publish to other graphic file formats such as PNG, in case you want to create a non-Flash site or use your material in another program. We cover all the bases so that you can get your animation up and running.

The filenames of Flash-published movies end with the .swf suffix. The letters *SWF* originally stood for *Shockwave Flash*, but Macromedia no longer uses that term for Flash-published movies, even though the letters remain the same. So, to follow the Macromedia usage, we refer to SWF files as Flash Player files, not Shockwave Flash files. Flash converts your movie data into a highly compact and efficient form in an SWF file so that your SWF file contains only the information needed for playback of your movies. In contrast, when you save your movies by choosing File⇨Save (or File⇨Save As), they are saved with the .fla suffix. They are saved in a format that can be read by the Flash 8 application, but not the Flash Player. The .fla file contains lots of information about layers, Library items, your video source files, and so on, which you need when you are creating your movies and which the Flash Player doesn't need.

# Optimizing Your Movies for Fast Download

Throughout this book, we offer suggestions for designing a Flash movie with speedy downloading in mind. In this section, we put the suggestions together so that you can review your movie as a whole before you publish it.

Reducing your Flash Player file sizes is no longer so important because many people now have high-speed Internet connections. But not everyone does. So it still isn't a bad idea to spend a little time thinking about shrinking the size of your Flash movies.

## Simplifying artwork

By simplifying the artwork in your movie, you can greatly reduce the size of a Flash movie, thereby increasing its speed. Here are the most important techniques:

- **Use symbols for every object that appears more than once.** You can turn any object or group of objects into a symbol. Nest your symbols — for example, turn an object into a symbol and then use it in a movie clip or button. Remember that you can change the color of symbol instances — you don't need to create a new symbol. (Chapter 7 covers symbols in detail.)

- **Group objects whenever possible.** Groups are almost as efficient as symbols. (Chapter 4 explains how to create groups.)

- **Avoid bitmaps as much as possible.** If you must use bitmaps, use them only for still elements — don't animate them. (Chapter 3 explains how to import a bitmap and how to turn it into a vector graphic by tracing the bitmap.)

- **Optimize curves (choose Modify➪Shape➪Optimize).** Whenever possible, optimize curves to reduce the number of lines used to create a shape. (Check out Chapter 4 for further explanation.)

- **Use solid lines rather than dashed, dotted, and other line types when possible.** Try to avoid custom line widths. (We explain line types in Chapter 3.)

- **Use the Pencil tool rather than the Brush tool whenever possible.** The Pencil tool uses fewer bytes in your movie.

- **Use the Web-safe color palette.** Avoid custom colors. (Check out Chapter 3 for the lowdown on colors.) Custom color definitions are kept with the Flash Player file.

✔ **Avoid using transparency when you don't need it.** Using transparency doesn't make your Flash file bigger, but it can slow down playback because of extra calculation required. (On the other hand, sometimes transparency effects make your movie look really great.) See Chapter 7 to find out about changing the transparency of the elements in your movie.

✔ **Use solid fills rather than gradients.** Gradients are more complex and make the Flash Player file bigger.

## Optimizing text

Text can consume lots of bytes. Here's what you can do to reduce the byte bite:

✔ **Reduce the number of fonts and font styles (bold, italic) as much as possible.** Use simpler sans serif fonts if you can. You get the best results file-size-wise with the device fonts (sans, serif, and typewriter), although you might find these device fonts boring. Flash doesn't need to store the outlines of device fonts in the .swf file, so these take up fewer bytes. (See Chapter 5 for more information on fonts.)

✔ **If you create text fields, limit the text and specify any restrictions that you can in the Character Options dialog box.** (Choose Window⇨ Property⇨Properties to open the Property inspector if it's not already open, and then click Character in the Property inspector to open the Character Options dialog box.) For example, exclude unnecessary character outlines, such as numbers.

## Using shared libraries

If you're using some of the same elements in more than one movie, you can put them into a shared library, and then your audience will need to download them only once. This can be especially useful for items that can be large, like music and fonts. Check out Chapter 12 for the details on shared libraries.

## Compressing sound

You can compress sounds to reduce file size. When you compress individual sounds in the Sound Properties dialog box, you can fine-tune settings for each individual sound in your movie. Later in this chapter, we review how to compress sound when you publish a Flash movie. Use the MP3 format whenever possible because it compresses well. If you need more information on compressing sounds, check out Chapter 11.

Here are some other ways that you can reduce the size of your sound files:

- ✔ Adjust the sound's Time In and Time Out points to prevent silent areas from being stored in your `.swf` file.
- ✔ Reuse sounds by using different In and Out points and by looping different parts of the same sound.
- ✔ Don't loop streaming sound.

See Chapter 11 for more information on editing, looping, and streaming sound.

### Animating efficiently

One of the most effective ways to reduce file size is to use tweens (see Chapter 9) whenever possible. Frame-by-frame animation creates larger files. Keeping animation localized in one area also helps. Small animations (animations where the objects don't move much) use less space than wide-area animations. Finally, place non-animated objects on different layers from animated objects.

## Testing Movies

Before publishing your movie, you should test it. The first step is to simply play your animation, as we explain in Chapter 9. But playing the animation on the Stage doesn't provide you with enough information to determine the file size. Movie clips and certain actions that interface with other movies (such as `Load Movie`) don't function from within your `.fla` file. To find those kinds of bugs, you have to use the Test Movie command or test your movie in a browser. The following sections tell you how to test both ways.

Flash 8 is optimized for the tasks (such as drawing, adding keyframes, showing and hiding layers, typing in ActionScript code, and so on) that you perform when creating a Flash movie. It's not optimized for playing back your animation — the Flash Player is optimized for that. Your `.fla` file contains lots of information that you need when you're creating your movies and which the Flash Player doesn't need. The Flash Player plays only `.swf` files, which you can create when you choose File⇨Publish.

### Using the Test Movie command

After playing your animation, you want to use the `Test Movie` (or `Test Scene`) command. These commands provide estimates of downloading speed, so you can find bottlenecks that pause your animation. You can also see the results of movie clips and all actions.

To test a movie or scene, follow these steps:

1. **Choose Control⇨Test Movie (or Test Scene).**

   Flash publishes your movie to an .swf file by using the current settings in the Publish Settings dialog box (see the section "Publishing Flash Movies," later in this chapter) and opens a new window. You see your animation run. You can change the settings in the Publish Settings dialog box (choose File⇨Publish Settings) before using this command.

2. **Choose View⇨Download Settings and choose a downloading speed between 14.4 Kbps and 131.2 Kbps.**

   If you repeatedly change the download settings, you get a better sense of their effect.

   To specify your own settings, choose Customize, and in the Custom Modem Settings dialog box, enter the menu text that you want to appear on the menu and the bit rate in bytes per second. Click OK. Then open the Download Settings menu again and choose your customized setting, which now appears on the menu.

3. **Choose View⇨Bandwidth Profiler to see the graph that shows the downloading performance.**

   The bandwidth profiler (as shown in Figure 13-1) displays the byte size of each individual frame. Frames whose bars rise above the lower red horizontal line cause loading delays.

**Figure 13-1:**
When you test a movie, Flash helps you analyze the downloading performance of your movie.

Frames with bars above this line cause loading delays.

4. **To see settings for any one frame, stop the movie by clicking the frame's bar.**

   To the left of the bandwidth profiler, Flash displays the movie's statistics — dimensions, frame rate, file size, movie duration, and the amount of animation to preload in frames and seconds. You also see the size of each individual frame.

5. **Choose View⇨Streaming Graph to see how the Flash movie streams into a browser.**

6. **Choose View⇨Frame by Frame Graph to see which frames contribute to delays. A frame whose bar extends above the red line may cause a bottleneck.**

   By default, Flash opens the SWF window in Streaming Graph mode.

7. **Choose View⇨Simulate Download if you want to see the Flash movie play as if loading at the speed you choose in Download Settings in Step 2.**

8. **To close the SWF window, click its Close button.**

After you analyze your movie, you can go back and optimize it to eliminate delays. A short delay in the first frame is usually acceptable, but significant delays during the movie result in jerky animation or pauses.

If you have a long movie divided into scenes, you can save time by using the `Test Scene` command instead of the `Test Movie` command.

## *Testing a movie in a Web browser*

The final steps of testing a movie are publishing it and viewing it in a Web browser. For a quick view, you can use the `Publish Preview` command. Flash publishes your movie to an `.swf` file, creates the appropriate HTML file, and opens the HTML file in your default browser. Viewing your Flash Player file in a browser reveals how the browser will display the movie when you upload it to a Web site.

Flash uses the current settings in the Publish Settings dialog box to create the preview, including the types of file formats that you have selected.

To preview your movie in a browser, follow these steps:

1. **Choose File⇨Publish Settings to open the Publish Settings dialog box and choose the desired file formats and publish settings. Then click OK.**

   See the "Publishing Flash Movies" section, later in this chapter, for more information on the Publish Settings dialog box.

2. **Choose File⇨Publish Preview and choose the desired format from the submenu.**

   Generally, you can use the first (default) HTML option, but if you have specified HTML settings, choose the second HTML option. Flash opens your browser and runs your movie.

3. **Close your browser to end the preview.**

As with any Web page material, you need to consider the following when testing a Flash Player file:

- ✔ **The browser that your audience is using:** Preview your Flash Player file in the current version of both Internet Explorer (IE) and Mozilla Firefox, if possible. Ideally, you should try out at least one earlier version of Internet Explorer, too. And you should test it in Safari on a Mac. Okay, so you probably won't do all this, but don't say that we didn't tell you.

- ✔ **The resolution of viewers' screens:** Test at least the following most common settings: 800 x 600 and 1024 x 768. Remember that the amount of material that appears on the screen changes with the resolution. If you preview at 640 x 480, you can be sure that people with higher resolutions can see your entire movie.

- ✔ **The color settings of viewers' screens:** Color settings might range from 256 colors to 16 million. If you aren't using Web-safe colors, some viewers might not see them accurately. But the vast majority of viewers now have thousands or millions of colors, which means that it's not so important to test that your movie looks good with fewer colors.

Professional Web site developers take this testing phase seriously. No matter how good an animation looks on your screen, if it doesn't translate well to your target number of viewers' screens, it's not a good animation.

# Saving Your Work in Flash MX 2004 Format

If you're collaborating on a Flash project with a group of friends or coworkers and they're still using Flash MX 2004 (the predecessor of Flash 8), there is still hope for them. You can save your work in Flash MX 2004 format.

To save your work in Flash MX 2004 format, follow these steps:

1. **Choose File⇨Save As.**

   The Save As dialog box appears.

2. **Choose where you want to save your file and type the filename that you want.**

3. **Click the Format drop-down list and select Flash MX 2004.**

4. **Click Save.**

   If you're using features new to Flash 8, a window appears, listing the new features that won't be saved in the Flash MX 2004 file and asking whether you want to continue. Click the Save as Flash MX 2004 button if you want to continue. If you do so, some of the data in your file will be lost.

# Publishing Flash Movies

So you're finally ready to publish your Flash masterpiece. It's time to choose File➪Publish Settings. This brings you to the Publish Settings dialog box. Don't be overwhelmed by all the options. Usually, you use only a few of them. Start by specifying the settings. Then publish the movie to create the .swf file viewed on a Web page.

After you specify the settings, you can click OK rather than Publish if you want to go back to your Flash movie file and choose Control➪Test Movie to see the results of your settings. You can try various settings until you're satisfied. Then click Publish to create the final SWF (Flash Player) file. Published files are in the same folder as your FLA movie file by default; you can specify another location if you want. Of course, you can also move the files afterward.

The Publish Settings dialog box lets you easily specify all your settings in one place. Then you click the Publish button, and Flash creates the SWF (Flash Player) file according to your settings. Choose File➪Publish Settings to open the Publish Settings dialog box, as shown in Figure 13-2, with the Formats tab on top.

**Figure 13-2:**
The Publish Settings dialog box is your one-stop place for starting the publishing process of your Flash movie.

Publish Settings

Current profile: Bounce Publish Profile

Formats  Flash  HTML

Type:

☑ Flash (.swf)            bounce.swf
☑ HTML (.html)            bounce.html
☐ GIF Image (.gif)        bounce.gif
☐ JPEG Image (.jpg)       bounce.jpg
☐ PNG Image (.png)        bounce.png
☐ Windows Projector (.exe)  bounce.exe
☐ Macintosh Projector     bounce Projector
☐ QuickTime (.mov)        bounce.mov

Use Default Names

Publish    Cancel    OK

Flash automatically names the files that it creates for you, using the Flash movie's name and adding the appropriate file extension, such as `.html` and `.swf`. You can see the names in the Publish Settings dialog box when you have the Formats tab on top. To specify your own name for a file, click in the File text box and type the name that you want. To revert back to the default filenames, click the Use Default Names button.

Most of the time, you need only the Flash (SWF) and HTML formats. But if you want other formats, select them on the Formats tab. When you mark an additional format, the dialog box adds a new tab for that format (except for the projector formats, which don't need one).

After you mark the formats that you want, click each tab to specify the settings for that format. The next few sections of this chapter explain each format, why you might want to use it, and how to specify the settings.

After you finish specifying all your settings, click the Publish button, and Flash does your bidding, creating the files that you need to put your great creation on the Web.

# Publishing to SWF

The second tab in the Publish Settings dialog box (choose File➪Publish Settings) is the Flash tab, which creates the Flash Player file, also called an `.swf` file. On this tab, as shown in Figure 13-3, you specify settings that affect the `.swf` file.

Flash gives you the following options:

- **Version:** Allows you to save in previous version formats for backward compatibility (or in the Flash Lite format for playing Flash movies on mobile phones, but that's a subject for another book). If you use new features but choose an old Flash Player version, Flash warns you of potential problems when you publish your movie.

- **Load Order:** Specifies how Flash displays the first frame of the Flash movie. Bottom Up (the default) loads layers from the lowest layer upward. Top Down loads layers starting from the top layer and moving downward. Your viewers will see the difference between these two settings only if the Flash movie is loading slowly (because of a slow Internet connection, for instance).

- **ActionScript Version (for Flash Player 6, 7, and 8 only):** Specifies whether your movie is using ActionScript 1.0 or ActionScript 2.0. ActionScript 2.0 was introduced in Flash MX 2004, the predecessor to Flash 8. ActionScript 2.0 adds new commands to ActionScript that are mostly of interest to intermediate or advanced programmers who are building applications in Flash which implement new classes and sub-classes of objects.

*ActionScript 2.0* is ActionScript 1.0 with powerful new programming constructs added to it. If you don't implement new classes and subclasses of objects (and you certainly didn't if you're not sure what this means), you can safely choose ActionScript version 1.0 in the ActionScript Version drop-down list. Throughout this book, all the ActionScript features that we describe are part of both ActionScript version 1.0 and 2.0, and so we simply refer to ActionScript rather than the version number.

✔ **Generate Size Report:** Creates a `.txt` file that you can use to troubleshoot problem areas. The report relates the various parts of your movie to the number of bytes that they require in the `.swf` file.

The size report can be more useful than the bandwidth profiler in pinpointing where the giant-size parts of a movie are. It's worth reviewing, and it's interesting (and often surprising) to see the size of the various elements of the `.swf` file.

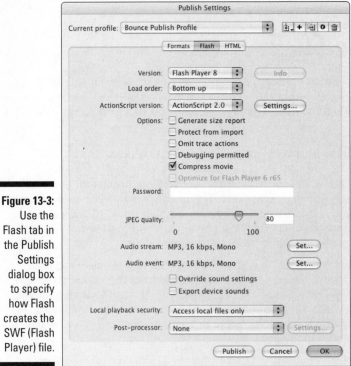

**Figure 13-3:**
Use the Flash tab in the Publish Settings dialog box to specify how Flash creates the SWF (Flash Player) file.

✔ **Protect from Import:** Prevents the .swf files from being downloaded from the Web site and imported back into Flash. This feature doesn't provide 100-percent-guaranteed protection, but it helps keep your work from being "borrowed."

✔ **Omit Trace Actions:** Omits special codes used by programmers. *Trace actions* insert into Flash movies the codes used to record and display technical information about a Flash movie's progress in a special window, named the Flash Debugger. Programmers use this information to *debug* (remove errors from) their ActionScript programming. If you added Trace actions to your Flash movie, select the Omit Trace Actions check box to omit these codes from the .swf file, and your file will be smaller.

✔ **Debugging Permitted:** Lets you use the Debugger to debug a Flash movie from another computer. If you permit debugging, you can add a password to protect the movie file. Although this option is useful for ActionScript programmers, discussing it is beyond the scope of this book.

✔ **Compress Movie:** Compresses your Flash Player file, especially text and ActionScript, so that it can download faster. This option is great except that your compressed file does not play in Flash Player versions earlier than Flash Player 6.

Your Flash movie probably uses some feature that's been added to Flash after Flash Player 5 anyway, so you might as well go for it and compress your movie.

✔ **Optimize for Flash Player 6 r65:** This option appears if you choose Flash Player 6 when you choose the Flash Player version at the top of the dialog box. Flash Player 6 r65 was an updated version of Flash Player with significant bug fixes and performance enhancements.

✔ **Password:** Allows you to select a password for debugging, if you enable the Debugging Permitted (or Protect from Import) check box. This option prevents viewers from debugging (or importing) the movie unless they have the password.

✔ **JPEG Quality:** Sets the compression (size) versus quality of bitmaps, if you have any in your movie. You can set the quality anywhere from 0 (the lowest quality and highest compression) to 100 (the highest quality and lowest compression).

✔ **Audio Stream:** Displays and sets the audio compression for *stream sounds* (sounds that use the Stream Sync setting in the Property inspector when a frame with the sound is selected). This setting applies if you haven't set the compression for individual sounds in the Sound Properties dialog box. Also, if you enable the Override Sound Settings check box in the Publish Settings dialog box, this setting overrides the setting in the Sound Properties dialog box. To change the current setting, click Set. The options are the same as in the Sound Properties dialog box. (Turn to Chapter 11 for details on setting sound properties.)

✔ **Audio Event:** Displays and sets the audio compression for event sounds (as set in the Property inspector when a frame with the sound is selected). Otherwise, it's the same as Audio Stream.

✔ **Override Sound Settings:** Select this check box to override settings in the Sound Properties dialog box. Then the settings here apply to all sounds in your movie.

✔ **Export Device Sounds (Flash 8 Professional only):** This gives you the option of exporting sounds in formats suitable for playback on mobile devices, such as certain mobile phones and personal digital assistants (PDAs). To do this, you use proxy sound files, which are beyond the scope of this book.

✔ **Local Playback Security:** If you select Local Access Only, your Flash movie can interact only with files and resources on the computer it's playing on. If you select Access Network Only, your movie can interact only with files and resources on the network, and not with those on the computer it's playing on. (This separation of local and network access helps make it more difficult for a malicious programmer to create a Flash file that collects data from your computer and transmits it over a network such as the Internet.)

✔ **Post-Processor (Flash 8 Professional only):** Here you can choose a post-processor from the drop-down list. A *post-processor* is software you might install to automatically make changes to your SWF file when you publish it. Macromedia says that they mainly envision this as a way to prepare SWF files for various future new versions of mobile devices, which is beyond the scope of this book.

If all these settings seems like a bit much, you can always just use the default settings, roll with the flow, and see how it goes.

# Publishing to HTML

Many people create Web pages by using HTML. If you work on a Web site, you can write the HTML code from scratch or use an HTML editor. However, many people use a Web authoring program, such as Dreamweaver by Macromedia or FrontPage by Microsoft.

To place a Flash Player file on a Web page, you need the proper HTML code. Luckily, Flash creates this code for you, in formats suitable for both Internet Explorer and Mozilla Firefox browsers. The HTML code simply tells the browser to look for and display your Flash Player file. Of course, you can write the HTML code yourself, but this method is easier.

# Understanding the HTML code for a movie

Figure 13-4 shows the default HTML code created for a Flash movie, displayed in TextEdit on a Mac. (In TextEdit, before opening your HTML file, be sure to choose TextEdit⇨Preferences and then select the Plain Text radio button in the New Document Attributes section of the Preferences dialog box.) Windows users can use Notepad to view HTML code created by the Publish command.

**Figure 13-4:**
Flash
creates
HTML code
that looks
like this
when you
publish a
movie to a
player file.

```
● ● ●                        ⊜ movie of the year.html
<html xmlns="http://www.w3.org/1999/xhtml" xml:lang="en" lang="en">
<head>
<meta http-equiv="Content-Type" content="text/html; charset=iso-8859-1" />
<title>movie of the year</title>
</head>
<body bgcolor="#ffffff">
<!--url's used in the movie-->
<!--text used in the movie-->
<!-- saved from url=(0013)about:internet -->
<object classid="clsid:d27cdb6e-ae6d-11cf-96b8-444553540000" codebase="http://
fpdownload.macromedia.com/pub/shockwave/cabs/flash/
swflash.cab#version=8,0,0,0" width="550" height="400" id="movie of the year"
align="middle">
<param name="allowScriptAccess" value="sameDomain" />
<param name="movie" value="movie of the year.swf" />
<param name="loop" value="false" />
<param name="quality" value="high" />
<param name="bgcolor" value="#ffffff" />
<embed src="movie of the year.swf" loop="false" quality="high"
bgcolor="#ffffff" width="550" height="400" name="movie of the year"
align="middle" allowScriptAccess="sameDomain" type="application/x-shockwave-
flash" pluginspage="http://www.macromedia.com/go/getflashplayer" />
</object>
</body>
</html>
```

If you know some HTML, this page will look familiar to you. (And if you don't, you might want to check out *HTML 4 For Dummies,* 5th Edition, by Ed Tittel and Mary Burmeister, from Wiley Publishing, Inc.) It starts with the *tags* (codes) that all HTML documents contain, namely <html>, <head>, <title>, and <body>. Here's how to understand the code in Figure 13-4:

- ✔ After <body, you see bgcolor="#ffffff">. This is the background color of the entire HTML page.

  By default, Flash makes the background color of the HTML page the same color as the background of your Flash movie, but you might prefer to change it to a different color to help visually define the Flash movie.

- ✔ After the comments (which start with !--), you see the object code. Microsoft Internet Explorer requires this tag in order to display your Flash Player files. The object code includes the following:

- Detailed codes (which are required to tell Internet Explorer how to display your player file).

- The specification of the version of the Flash viewer to look for and where to download it if necessary.

- The width and height of the display in the browser.

- The name of the file (`value="movie of the year.swf"`).

- Parameter settings for local or network access, looping, quality, and background color. You set the background color by choosing Modify⇨Document in Flash and choosing a background color in the Document Properties dialog box. (See Chapter 2 for details on using this dialog box.)

- The `embed` code is for Netscape Navigator, Mozilla, and Mozilla Firefox browsers, and accomplishes the same thing as the `object` code.

✔ Finally, you see the closing `</object>` tag as well as the tags that end every HTML document: `</body>` AND `</html>`.

If you want to use the HTML document as is, you can. But if you want to place your Flash Player file in an existing HTML file, as you would for a Flash button, for example, you need to insert the `<embed>` and `<object>` codes into the desired location of your existing file. To do this, copy the HTML code starting from `<object` through `</object>`. Then paste this code into your existing HTML document, perhaps within the code for a table cell or wherever you want your Flash Player file to be displayed on your page.

If you didn't change your default folder locations in the Formats section of the Publish Settings dialog box, your `.swf` file will be in the same folder as the HTML file that Flash creates when you publish your movie. In that case, the HTML `<object>` and `<embed>` tags created by the Flash publishing process reference the `.swf` file by simply mentioning the filename. For that to work, the `.swf` file must be in the same folder on your Web site's server as your Web page's HTML file.

If you usually keep images in a subfolder and want to place your `.swf` file in that subfolder, you can specify them in the Formats tab of the Publish Settings dialog box. Or you can edit the HTML code in a text editor to change the references for *both* the `<object>` and `<embed>` tags to add the path to the subfolder. If you already do this for other images, the process is the same for the `.swf` file. For example, if you keep your images in a subfolder named `images` and the current code refers to `tulip.swf`, change the reference for both the `<object>` and `<embed>` tags to `"images/tulip.swf"`.

# Specifying Flash Player detection and other HTML settings

To create the HTML file, you need to specify the HTML settings from the HTML tab of the Publish Settings dialog box, as shown in Figure 13-5.

**Publish Settings**

Current profile: Bounce Publish Profile

Formats | Flash | HTML

Template: Flash Only | Info

☑ Detect Flash Version

Version: 8 . 0 . 0

Dimensions: Match Movie

Width: 550 X Height: 400 pixels

Playback: ☐ Paused at start ☑ Display menu ☑ Loop ☐ Device font

Quality: High

Window Mode: Window

HTML alignment: Default

Scale: Default (Show all)

Flash alignment: Horizontal: Center Vertical: Center

☑ Show warning messages

Publish | Cancel | OK

## Templates

The first setting lets you select a template. The *template* determines the format and contents of the HTML file. To keep matters simple, select the default, Flash Only. Table 13-1 explains the other template options. For more information, see Chapter 12.

| Table 13-1 | HTML Template Options |
|---|---|
| *Option* | *Comments* |
| Flash for Pocket PC 2003 | Creates an HTML file with `<object>` and `<embed>` tags and with Pocket PC–specific alignment. Can be used with Pocket IE and with desktop Internet Explorer and Netscape browsers. |
| Flash HTTPS | Creates an HTML file with `<object>` and `<embed>` tags, using the HTTPS protocol to specify where to go to download the Flash Player if that's necessary. *HTTPS* is a method that is designed to send data over the Web more securely than the standard method (HTTP). |
| Flash Only (Default) | Creates an HTML file, as we describe in the earlier section "Understanding the HTML code for a movie," with `<object>` and `<embed>` tags. |
| Flash with AICC Tracking | Includes support for AICC (Aviation Industry Computer-Based-Training Committee) tracking when using Macromedia Learning Interactions. |
| Flash with FSCommand | Used when you have added an `FSCommand` action to your movie to interface with JavaScript. The HTML file also includes the `<object>` and `<embed>` commands. |
| Flash with Named Anchors | Adds browser scripting and HTML anchors so that viewers can bookmark Flash content in Flash Player 6 and later, and thus use the Web browser's Back button effectively while navigating within a Flash movie. |
| Flash with SCORM 1.2 Tracking | Includes support for SCORM (Sharable Content Object Reference Model) version 1.2 tracking when using Macromedia Learning Interactions. |
| Flash with SCORM 2004 Tracking | Includes support for SCORM 2004 tracking when using Macromedia Learning Interactions. |

| Option | Comments |
|--------|----------|
| Image Map | (If you don't know what an image map is, don't worry about this option.) Rather than display an SWF player file, uses a GIF, JPEG, or PNG image (which you need to choose from the Formats tab) as a client-side image map coded in your HTML page. |
| QuickTime | Creates `<embed>` and `<object>` tags in an HTML page to display a QuickTime Flash movie based on your Flash movie. You need to select the QuickTime check box on the Formats tab. A QuickTime Flash movie plays with only QuickTime 4 or later. QuickTime 4 can recognize only Flash 3 features. QuickTime 5 can recognize Flash 4 features. (QuickTime 4 and 5 are pretty old, so this isn't a very interesting way to publish your Flash movies.) |

Beneath the Template drop-down list is the Detect Flash Version check box. (This option is available only if you choose Flash Player 4 or later in the Flash tab of the Publish Settings dialog box, and you choose the Flash HTTPS or Flash Only template.) Select this check box to add browser scripting to detect the Flash Player for the version of Flash you specify on the Flash tab. When this check box is enabled, the Version Number text boxes below it are also enabled. If you want to more exactly specify the minimum version required, type revision numbers in the Major Revision and Minor Revision text fields there.

If you enable the Detect Flash Version check box, when you publish your Flash file, the resulting HTML code prints "Alternate HTML content should be placed here" in your Web page if the Flash Player of the specified version can't be found or if the Web browser doesn't have scripting enabled. (Scripting must be enabled by the Web browser for the Flash Player version detection to work.) You can edit the HTML to replace the sentence "Alternate HTML content should be placed here" with whatever alternative content you want to display to the viewer in case the Flash Player version can't be found.

If you enable the Detect Flash Version check box, viewers who have the Flash Player but who have disabled scripting in their Web browser will see only your alternative content — not your Flash Web pages.

## Dimensions

The Dimensions options control the size allotted to your Flash Player movie on your Web page. You have three options:

- ✔ **Match Movie** matches the width and height that you set in the Movie Properties dialog box (choose Modify⇨Document).

- ✔ **Pixels** lets you specify, in pixels, the Width and Height. Type the desired values in the text boxes.

- ✔ **Percent** lets you specify the area used by the Flash Player movie as a percentage of the browser window size. The 100% setting is ideal for pages that are designed to take up the entire page. Type the desired values in the text boxes.

## Playback

The Playback section determines the values of parameters in the HTML code. You have four options:

- ✔ **Paused at Start** creates a PLAY parameter whose value is FALSE. The viewer must start the movie by clicking a button in the movie — the button's instance needs to have a Play action in it. Alternatively, viewers can right-click (Windows) or Control+click (Mac) the movie and choose Play from the shortcut menu, but they might not be aware of this. By default, this check box is deselected, so movies start to play automatically.

- ✔ **Loop** creates a LOOP parameter whose value is TRUE. The movie repeats over and over. By default, this check box is selected, so make sure to clear it if you don't want to loop your movie!

- ✔ **Display Menu** creates a MENU parameter set to TRUE. This option enables viewers to right-click (Windows) or Control+click (Mac) the movie and choose from a menu. The menu options in Flash Player 8 are Zoom In/Out, Show All, Quality (High, Medium, or Low), Play, Loop, Rewind/Forward/Back, Settings, Print, Show Redraw Regions, Debugger, and About Macromedia Flash Player. Without this option, Settings, Show Redraw Regions, Debugger, and About Flash Player are the only items on the shortcut menu. By default, Display Menu is selected.

  In case you're wondering, Show Redraw Regions shows you the outlines of which regions of your movie Flash refreshes every frame.

- ✔ **Device Font** applies to Windows playback only. When this check box is enabled, the HTML file includes a DEVICE FONT parameter set to TRUE, and Flash substitutes *anti-aliased* (smoothly curved) system fonts for fonts not available on the viewer's system. This applies only to static text you create in Flash. By default, this item is deselected.

## *Quality*

The Quality section determines the `quality` parameter in the `<object>` and `<embed>` tags of the HTML code. Quality refers to the level of *anti-aliasing*, which means the smoothing of the artwork so that it doesn't have jagged edges. Of course, the lower the quality, the faster the playback. Usually, you want to find a middle ground between quality and speed. You have six options:

- ✔ **Low** doesn't use any anti-aliasing.

- ✔ **Auto Low** starts at low quality but switches to high quality if the viewer's computer, as detected by the Flash Player, can handle it.

- ✔ **Auto High** starts at high quality but switches to low quality if the viewer's computer can't handle the playback demand. This option should provide good results on all computers.

- ✔ **Medium** applies some anti-aliasing but doesn't smooth bitmaps. This option is a good middle ground between low and high.

- ✔ **High** always uses anti-aliasing for vector art. Bitmaps are smoothed only if the file doesn't contain tweens. This setting is the default. (See Chapter 9 for the scoop on tweens.)

- ✔ **Best** always uses anti-aliasing, including for bitmaps.

## *Window Mode*

Window Mode specifies how the player movie's window interacts with the rest of the page. Here are your options:

- ✔ **The Window setting** plays your movie as an opaque rectangle within your Web page and does not allow your HTML to render other content in that rectangle.

- ✔ **The Opaque Windowless setting** creates an opaque background for the movie so that other elements in the Web page don't show through when they're behind the movie. This setting does allow your HTML to render content in front of the movie.

- ✔ **The Transparent Windowless setting** makes the Flash background color transparent so that other elements on your Web page show through (or can appear on top of) your Flash content. This setting might slow down playback.

- ✔ **The Windowless settings** embed window-related attributes in the `<object>` and `<embed>` tags. The code for Windowless has an effect only in more recent browsers running on Windows or Mac OS X — Internet Explorer version 5 and later, Netscape version 7 and later, Mozilla 1 and later, and Opera 6 and later.

## HTML Alignment

The HTML Alignment setting specifies the ALIGN attribute and specifies how the Flash Player movie is aligned within the browser window. You have five options:

- **Default** theoretically centers the Flash movie. If the browser window is smaller than the movie, this option theoretically crops the edges of the movie. But in our tests, the default is always left even though it should be center.

- **Left** aligns the movie along the left side of the browser window. If the browser window is too small, this option crops the other sides of the movie.

- **Right** aligns the movie along the right side of the browser window. If the browser window is too small, this option crops the other sides of the movie.

- **Top** aligns the movie along the top of the browser window. If the browser window is too small, this option crops the other sides of the movie.

- **Bottom** aligns the movie along the bottom of the browser window. If the browser window is too small, this option crops the other sides of the movie.

## Scale

The Scale setting defines how the movie is placed within the boundaries when (and only when) you set a width and height different from the movie's original size, using the Pixels or Percent options in the Dimensions section of the Publish Settings dialog box. You have four options:

- **Default (Show All)** displays the entire movie without distortion but might create borders on two sides of the movie.

- **No Border** scales the movie to fill the dimensions without distortion but might crop portions of the movie.

- **Exact Fit** fits the movie to the dimensions, distorting the movie if necessary.

- **No Scale** stops the movie from changing its scale if the viewer resizes the Flash Player window.

## Flash Alignment

Flash Alignment determines how the movie fits within the movie window (as opposed to the browser window). It works together with the Scale and Dimensions settings. In other words, it determines how the Flash movie fits within the dimensions that you specify. For the Horizontal setting, you can choose Left, Center, or Right. For the Vertical setting, you can choose Top, Center, or Bottom.

At the bottom of the Publish Settings dialog box is the Show Warning Messages check box. When it's enabled, you see warning messages during the publishing process. Nevertheless, the publishing process continues, but you know that you might have made an error. For example, if you've chosen a template that requires a GIF or JPEG image but you haven't selected either format on the Formats tab, you see a warning message.

After you choose your settings, click OK to return to your movie or click Publish to publish it.

# Publishing to Other Formats

You can use Flash's Publish Settings to generate files in a variety of other formats besides HTML pages and Flash Player movies, These other formats include GIF images, animated GIFs, JPEG images, PNG images, QuickTime movies, and self-playing Windows and Mac projectors.

Even if you use Flash all day every day, you might never need to generate GIF images, JPEG images, or QuickTime images from your Flash movies, so we won't clog up your life by describing the Publish Settings for those formats here.

## Creating PNG graphic files

PNG files can display millions more colors than GIF files and support transparency. They offer some of the advantages of both GIFs and JPEGs.

To create a PNG image, choose PNG Image on the Formats tab of the Publish Settings dialog box (refer to Figure 13-2). Flash creates a PNG tab in the dialog box, as shown in Figure 13-6.

Flash publishes the first frame of your movie unless you label a different frame with the label #Static. (To create a label, click the frame and choose Window➪Properties➪Properties to open the Property inspector. If necessary, click the collapse arrow on the Property inspector title bar to expand it. Type a label name in the Frame text box on the left side of the Property inspector.)

**Figure 13-6:**
Use the
PNG tab to
create PNG
images.

You have the following options:

- ✔ **Dimensions:** By default, Flash matches the dimensions of the movie. Clear the Match Movie check box to specify your own Width and Height settings.

- ✔ **Bit Depth:** Controls the number of bits per pixel, which in turn means how many colors the image contains. You can select 8-bit for 256 colors (like a GIF), 24-bit for 16.7 million colors, or 24-bit with Alpha, which allows for transparency. When you choose 24-bit with Alpha, the image's background becomes transparent. This is one of the things that designers love about PNG files.

- ✔ **Options:** See the Options settings for GIF images that we explain earlier in this chapter.

- ✔ **Dither:** See the Dither settings for GIF images that we explain earlier in this chapter. *Note:* This option applies only if you choose an 8-bit depth.

- ✔ **Palette Type:** See the Palette Type settings for GIF images that we explain earlier in this chapter. *Note:* This option applies only if you select an 8-bit depth.

- ✔ **Max Colors:** See the Palette Type settings for GIF images that we explain earlier in this chapter.

✔ **Palette:** See the Palette Type settings for GIF images that we explain earlier in this chapter.

✔ **Filter Options:** The PNG format filters an image line-by-line in order to compress it. You have these options:

- **None:** Applies no filtering. The resulting file is larger than with the other options.

- **Sub:** Filters adjoining pixel bytes (working horizontally). Works best when the image has repeated horizontal information.

- **Up:** Filters in a vertical direction. Works best when the image has repeated vertical information.

- **Average:** Uses a mixture of horizontal and vertical comparison; a good first-try option.

- **Path:** Uses a more complex method that uses the three nearest pixels to predict the next one.

- **Adaptive:** Creates a unique color table for your PNG file, based on the actual colors present. You get more accurate color, although these colors might not be Web safe. The file size might also be larger. Use this option if accurate representation of colors is most important, as in a photographic bitmap image.

After you specify your settings, click OK to return to your movie or click Publish to publish your PNG image and create the other files that you've chosen.

## Creating self-playing movies

You can also create projectors in the Publish Settings dialog box. A *projector* is a self-playing Flash movie that doesn't require the Flash Player. All the interactive and animated features of your Flash movie work in a projector. You can use a projector for a Flash movie that you want to place on a CD-ROM or even on a floppy disk.

You can create a Windows or Mac version from either platform. But if you create a Mac version in Windows, you need to use a file translator, such as BinHex, so that the Mac Finder recognizes it as an application.

To create a projector, follow these steps:

1. **Choose File⇨Publish Settings.**

   The Publish Settings dialog box opens.

2. **On the Formats tab, select the Windows Projector check box or the Macintosh Projector check box, or both.**

3. **Click Publish.**

4. **Click OK or Cancel to close the Publish Settings dialog box.**

For Windows, Flash creates an EXE file. For the Mac, Flash creates a Macintosh Projector file. If you create the Macintosh Projector file in Flash while using a Windows computer, the Macintosh Projector file is stored inside a compressed BinHex file (HQX), which can then be uncompressed on a Mac.

Don't forget to test your movie after you place it on a CD-ROM or floppy disk. Try it out with a variety of processor speeds if possible.

# Using Publish Profiles

You can save all the settings that you configure in the Publish Settings dialog box as a *publish profile*. You can then duplicate, modify, export, import, and delete your publish profiles and trade them with your collaborators. This makes it easy for you to repeatedly use any collection of settings that you need. You can create standard publish profiles, which you use to make sure that all your files are published uniformly, and you can create specialized publish profiles that are specific to a single project. The following sections tell you how.

## Creating a publish profile

To create a publish profile, follow these steps:

1. **Choose File⇨Publish Settings.**

   The Publish Settings dialog box appears.

2. **Click the Create New Profile button in the upper-left part of the dialog box.**

   The Create New Profile dialog box appears.

3. **Type in a name for your profile and click OK.**

   The Create New Profile dialog box disappears, and the name of your new profile appears in the Current Profile drop-down list of the Publish Settings dialog box.

4. **Specify the publish settings for your document in the Publish Settings dialog box, as we describe in earlier sections of this chapter, and then click OK.**

## Duplicating a publish profile

You might want to duplicate a publish profile to use it as a springboard for new variations. To duplicate a publish profile, do the following steps:

1. **Choose File⇨Publish Settings.**

   The Publish Settings dialog box appears.

2. **Select the publish profile that you want to copy in the Current Profile drop-down list (near the top of the dialog box).**

3. **Click the Duplicate Profile button in the upper-right part of the dialog box.**

   The Duplicate Profile dialog box appears.

4. **Type in a name for your duplicate profile and click OK.**

   The Duplicate Profile dialog box disappears. The name of your duplicated profile appears in the Current Profile drop-down list of the Publish Settings dialog box.

## Modifying a publish profile

You might use a particular publish profile as, for example, a standard for your co-workers. As circumstances change, you might want to modify the publish profile, and that's easy to do. To modify a publish profile, follow these steps:

1. **Choose File⇨Publish Settings.**

   The Publish Settings dialog box appears.

2. **Select the publish profile that you want to modify in the Current Profile drop-down list (near the top of the dialog box).**

3. **Select the publish settings that you want for your document in the Publish Settings dialog box, as we describe in the earlier sections of this chapter, and then click OK.**

## Deleting a publish profile

To delete a publish profile, follow these steps:

1. **Choose File⇨Publish Settings.**

   The Publish Settings dialog box appears.

2. **Select the publish profile that you want to delete in the Current Profile drop-down list (near the top of the dialog box).**

3. **Click the Delete Profile button in the upper-left part of the dialog box.**

   A dialog box appears asking you to confirm that you want to delete the profile.

4. **Click OK.**

## Exporting and importing publish profiles

To use a publish profile in documents other than the document in which you created it, first you export it from the document in which you created it. Then you import it into the new document.

This makes your work easier if, for example, you're working on a Flash project with a team and you need to publish your Flash documents according to a single standard. The entire team can easily share the same publish profile.

To export a publish profile, follow these steps:

1. **Choose File⇨Publish Settings.**

   The Publish Settings dialog box appears.

2. **Select the publish profile that you want to export in the Current Profile drop-down list (near the top of the dialog box).**

3. **Click the Import/Export Profile button (in the upper-left part of the dialog box) and select Export from the drop-down list.**

   The Export Profile dialog box appears.

4. **In the dialog box, select a location where you want to save the file and Click Save.**

   The default location is a folder named Publish Profiles, which is located within the Flash 8 application folder.

To import a publish profile, follow these steps:

1. **Choose File⇨Publish Settings.**

   The Publish Settings dialog box appears.

2. **Click the Import/Export Profile button (in the upper-left part of the dialog box) and select Import from the drop-down list.**

   The Import Profile dialog box appears.

3. **In the dialog box, browse to find the publish profile that you want to import and click Open.**

   The name of the imported publish profile appears in the Current Profile drop-down list of the Publish Settings dialog box.

# Using Publish Preview

If you want to specify publish settings, see the results, and then go back to tweak your settings, you can use Publish Preview rather than Publish. Publish Preview creates the files specified in the Publish Settings dialog box, just as the Publish command does. The only difference is that Publish Preview automatically displays the requested file, usually the SWF file. The value is in simply saving the steps of manually opening your files in your browser — helpful when you're doing lots of tweaking and going back and forth between your publish settings and your browser to see what works best.

To use Publish Preview, follow these steps:

1. **Specify your settings by using the Publish Settings dialog box (as we explain earlier in this chapter) and click OK.**

2. **Choose File⇨Publish Preview.**

3. **From the Publish Preview submenu, choose the file format that you want to preview.**

4. **When you're done, close the window or browser.**

# Posting Your Movie to Your Web Site

After you finish publishing your movie, post it on your Web site or place it on a CD-R or other media.

To put your movie on a CD-R, you can make Mac and Windows projectors and copy them onto a CD-R by using CD-burner software. Then you don't need to view it through a Web browser. Or copy your published HTML and SWF files onto a CD-R along with any external scripts, image files, or text files used by your HTML and SWF files.

Refer to the section "Understanding the HTML code for a movie," earlier in this chapter, for instructions on modifying the HTML code if you want to place your SWF file on an existing page or place your SWF file in a subfolder.

To post your movie to a Web site, upload both the HTML and the SWF file. If your HTML or SWF files load data from any external scripts, image files, or text files, you need to upload those, too.

Open your browser and load the page that contains your Flash movie. Hopefully, it works perfectly and looks great! If not, check out the HTML code, check your publish settings, and make sure that the necessary files are in the proper location on your Web site's server.

# *Exporting Movies and Images*

In addition to publishing, Flash lets you export image files and QuickTime movies. Export a Flash file when you want to use it in another application. For example, you may want to export a frame as a PNG file and insert it into a word processing document. You can use Export Movie to export to a QuickTime movie or to create a still image of every frame.

After you export a movie or image, you can then import it into the desired application for further editing or display.

Note that when you choose File➪Export➪Export Movie to export a movie to a format such as GIF, JPG, or PNG, you export a sequence of individually numbered images. That might give you some interesting raw material to import into other graphics applications.

To export a movie or image, follow these steps:

1. **Open the Flash document from which you want to export. (See Chapter 1 for information about opening an existing Flash movie.)**

2. **To export to an image, select the frame that you want to export; otherwise, skip to Step 3.**

3. **Choose File➪Export➪Export Image or File➪Export➪Export Movie.**

4. **In the dialog box, navigate to the desired location and type a name for your image or movie.**

5. **Select a type of file from the Save as Type drop-down list.**

6. **Click Save.**

7. **Depending on the format that you selected, a dialog box might appear. If so, specify the settings and then click OK.**

   These settings are similar to the kind of settings that we describe, earlier in this chapter, in the section "Creating PNG graphic files."

Table 13-2 lists the types of files that you can export.

| Table 13-2 | Export File Types | | |
|---|---|---|---|
| *File Type* | *Windows* | *Mac* | *Comments* |
| Adobe Illustrator (AI) | X | X | A vector format. |
| Drawing Exchange Format (DXF) | X | X | A format that you can import into AutoCAD, although you lose fills. |
| Encapsulated PostScript (EPS) | X | X | A vector format used in Adobe Illustrator and recognized by many other applications. |
| Graphics Interchange File (GIF) | X | X | A bitmap format, limited to 256 colors. |
| Joint Photographic Experts Group (JPEG/JPG) | X | X | A bitmap format that supports 24-bit color. |
| Macromedia Flash Video (FLV) | X | X | A video format designed for use with video conferencing and other communications applications. |
| PICT (PCT) | | X | A bitmap format that can be used with most Mac and many PC applications. The PICT format supports transparency and variable bit-depths. |
| Portable Network Graphic (PNG) | X | X | A bitmap format that supports variable bit-depth and transparency. |
| QuickTime (MOV) | X | X | A QuickTime 4 format movie. |
| QuickTime Video (MOV) | | X | On Macs only, uses the Video QuickTime 3 format, bitmapping all content. |
| Video for Windows (AVI) | X | | A bitmap video format. Files can get large. |

*(continued)*

**Table 13-2 *(continued)***

| File Type | Windows | Mac | Comments |
|---|---|---|---|
| Windows Audio (WAV) | X | | Exports just the sound. |
| Windows Bitmap (BMP) | X | | A bitmap format. Many applications recognize it. Offers variable bit-depths and transparency support. File size is large. |
| Windows Metafile and Enhanced Metafile (WMF/EMF) | X | | A vector format supported by many applications. Creates smaller files than EPS. |

# Creating Printable Movies

Suppose that you want your Web site viewers to be able to print a form on your Web site that you created in Flash. Or perhaps you want them to print your contact information so that your Web page can become your business card. The Flash Player printing features enable your viewers to print receipts, information sheets, coupons, or whatever else helps you do business on the Web. You can specify certain frames in a movie — including frames in the main Timeline, a button, or a movie clip — to be printable from the Flash Player shortcut menu. Viewers right-click (Windows) or Control+click (Mac) to access the Print command.

Your viewers need instructions on how to print, so place some text somewhere telling them what to do.

Of course, viewers can use their browser's Print command to print. The result, however, isn't nearly as controllable. When we tried it, our browser printed only the first frame, which was useless in our example. The browser also added the Uniform Resource Locator (URL), the name of the movie, the date, and the page number.

By default, the Flash Player shortcut menu lets viewers print the entire movie, frame by frame. This feature is fairly useless for most purposes. But by specifying which frames are printed and the print area, you can use the Player's Print command to make specific information or forms available to your viewers.

## Preparing your movie for printing

If you want a nice, clean result, you need a nice, clean frame. The Flash Player prints all objects on all layers of the movie. If you want to create a form, for example, put it in its own frame and make sure that objects on other layers don't continue into that frame.

Alternatively, you can specify the print area so that you include only the area that you want printed, excluding other objects on the Stage in the frame. But if you specify a small area, this area becomes the entire page size when printing, so the objects in that small area are enlarged to take up the entire printed page. You can control the layout by changing the dimension, scale, and alignment HTML settings (on the HTML tab of the Publish Settings dialog box).

Make sure that everything you want to print is on the Stage. For example, if you want to print from a movie clip, it must be on the Stage and have an instance name.

You can make a movie clip invisible by setting its _visible property to false. (Use the Actions panel.) This capability enables you to instruct viewers to print a form that they don't see on the screen.

If your movie displays text instructing users how to print from the printable area, you might want to exclude this text from the printable area. They probably don't want to print the instructions on how to print, right?

## Specifying printable frames

To specify which frame or frames you want to print when your viewers choose Print from the Flash Player shortcut menu, follow these steps:

1. **With the movie open, choose Window⇨Properties⇨Properties to open the Property inspector.**

   The shortcut is Ctrl+F3 (Windows) or ⌘+F3 (Mac).

   If necessary, click the collapse arrow on the Property inspector's title bar to expand it.

2. **Select from the Timeline the frame that you want printed.**

3. **If the frame that you selected is not a keyframe, make it a keyframe by choosing Insert⇨Timeline⇨Keyframe. (Turn to Chapter 9 for the lowdown on keyframes.)**

4. **In the Property inspector, type #p in the Frame text box, as shown in Figure 13-7. Beneath the Frame text box, set the Label Type dropdown list to Name.**

**Figure 13-7:**
Use the
Property
inspector to
label frames
for printing.

For each additional keyframe that you want to specify for printing, select the frame and then in the Property Inspector Frame text box, label it #p.

## Specifying the print area

Unless you specify the print area, the Flash Player prints the entire Stage. If you have loaded other movies, the Flash Player uses their Stage size. You might, however, want to specify a different area. As we mention earlier in this chapter, you might want to include instructions on how to print, but you may not want the instructions to be printed. You can exclude other objects on the Stage as well.

Choosing a very small print area results in an output of very big objects. The Flash Player sizes your objects to take up the entire printed page.

You create an object, usually a rectangle, to specify the print area.

To specify the print area, follow these steps:

1. **Click a frame that you have labeled #p (as we describe in the preceding section).**

2. **Create a rectangle around the area that you want to be printed.**

   You might have to experiment with different sizes of rectangles. See the instructions in the section "Printing movies from the Flash Player," a little later in this chapter, to test the printing of your movie.

   Use the No Fill feature for the rectangle so that you can see the material that you want to print.

3. **Select the rectangle and choose Edit⇨Cut to cut it to the Clipboard.**

4. **Click a frame without a #p label but on the same layer.**

   Using the next frame might be a good choice in order to keep the printing area rectangle conveniently close to the frame that you've specified for printing.

You can have only one #b label in a Timeline. Also note that if you use a #b label, it must be on the same layer as the #p label.

5. **Choose Edit⇨Paste in Place.**

 You now have a rectangle of the right size, but in its own frame — a frame without a #p label.

6. **Select the frame containing the rectangle and choose Window⇨ Properties⇨Properties to open the Property inspector.**

 If necessary, click the collapse arrow on the Property inspector's title bar to expand it.

7. **In the Frame text box on the left side of the Property inspector, type #b to signify that the shape in this frame will be used as the boundary for the print area.**

## Printing movies from the Flash Player

Before uploading your printable movie to your Web site, you should test the printing function. To do so, use the Publish Settings dialog box to specify the publish settings that you want, as we explain throughout this chapter. Then choose File⇨Publish Preview⇨Default. Your browser opens, and you see your movie play.

To test-print your movie, right-click (Windows) or Control+click (Mac) in the browser. From the Flash Player shortcut menu, choose Print.

On the Mac, the Page Setup dialog box appears; choose the printer, paper size, orientation, and scale you want, and then click OK.

Then, for both Mac and Windows, the Print dialog box appears. Choose the print range to select which frames to print or choose All. In Windows, you can also choose Selection to print the current frame. If only one frame has been made printable, the Pages option appears dimmed. Any option that you choose prints the frame that you've specified for printing. Click OK (Windows) or Print (Mac) to print.

After you upload your movie onto your Web site, viewers use the same procedure to print your movie.

Place on your page some text that explains to your viewers how to print your movie. Many viewers don't even know that the shortcut menu exists.

# Part VI
# The Part of Tens

## In this part . . .

In the famous *For Dummies* Part of Tens, we answer the ten most-asked questions — or at least the ten questions we most wanted to answer. In this part, you find some cool techniques for creating drag-and-drop objects and simulating 3-D effects in Flash. In the chapter on the ten best Flash resources, we manage to give you dozens of Flash resources, such as the many Flash resource Web sites (while convincing our publisher that only ten exist). Finally, to top off the book, we give you our votes for ten great Flash designers. Surf to see the work of all ten and be amazed and inspired by the possibilities!

# Chapter 14

# Ten Frequently Asked Questions

*I*n this chapter, we answer some frequently asked questions about Flash while explaining how to create some very cool effects and streamline the process of creating Flash movies.

## How Do I Combine Two Flash Movies into One?

It's not difficult to merge two Flash movies into one. You simply copy all the frames in each scene in your first movie to new scenes that you create in your second movie. To merge two Flash movies into one, follow these steps:

1. **Choose File⇨Open, and in the Open dialog box that appears, navigate to and select the Flash movie you want to copy from.**

   The Flash movie you select appears on the Stage.

2. **Click the Edit Scene button near the top right of the Timeline, and from the drop-down list that appears, choose the scene you want to copy.**

   The scene you select appears on the Stage.

3. **Unlock all the layers in the scene.**

   See Chapter 4 for information on unlocking layers.

4. **Choose Edit⇨Timeline⇨Select All Frames.**

   This selects all keyframes and tweens in all layers in the scene.

5. **Choose Edit⇨Timeline⇨Copy Frames.**

   This copies all the keyframes and tweens in your scene.

6. **Choose File⇨Open, and in the Open dialog box that appears, navigate to and select the Flash movie you want to copy to.**

   The Flash movie you select appears on the Stage.

7. **Choose Insert⇨Scene.**

   An empty scene appears on the Stage.

8. **Click the first frame in the Timeline and choose Edit⇨Timeline⇨ Paste Frames.**

   This pastes the scene you copied from your first movie into your new scene in your second movie.

9. **Repeat Steps 1 through 8 for each scene you want to copy from your first movie.**

10. **Choose Control⇨Test Movie.**

    Your second movie now includes all the scenes you copied from your first movie.

## Why Is Motion Tweening not Working?

For motion tweening to work, you need to make sure that several pieces are in place. (Review Chapter 9 for the basic instructions on motion tweening.)

Motion tweening problems can arise from any number of sources, a few of which follow:

- **You need to tween the right stuff.** Make sure that you've created a group, some text, or an instance of a symbol. Motion tweening doesn't work reliably on anything else.

- **You need an ending keyframe.** If you have a dashed line rather than a solid line indicating your motion tween on the Timeline, you didn't properly create an ending keyframe. Undo the steps that created the tween, create an ending keyframe, and try again.

- **You need to tween a keyframe.** If you're having trouble changing the length of the tween by dragging on one of the keyframes, that keyframe wasn't included when you created the motion tween. Select the offending keyframe by itself (press Ctrl for Windows or ⌘ for Mac while you select, if necessary), and select Motion from the Tweening drop-down list of the Property inspector.

- **You need to isolate the problem.** If you can't figure out why your motion tweening isn't working, you might have some action or setting that you don't even remember. Movies can get very complex, and comprehending all the relationships and interconnections can be difficult. Try copying to the Clipboard the object that you're animating and pasting it into a new, "clean" movie. You can copy and paste frames as well. In the new movie, you should be able to analyze the situation more clearly.

- **You need to undo or revert.** If the animation worked previously, try undoing your last several actions. You can also try removing any recently created objects or ActionScript. If you can revert to the time your animation worked, you can start again from there.

✔ **You need to try choosing Control⇨Test Movie.** Only the simplest ActionScript and button behaviors work on the Stage. If you're trying to run your animation by using the Controller or pressing Enter, try choosing Control⇨Test Movie instead. If your movie has more than one scene, choose Control⇨Test Scene to try to isolate the problem to one scene.

✔ **You need to put each object on its own layer.** If you have more than one object on a layer, place each object on its own layer. (Refer to Chapter 6 for a discussion of working with layers.) Animate only one object on a layer. (This solves many tweening problems.)

## How Can I Sync Sound with Motion?

Suppose that you want certain parts of your animation synchronized with specific sounds. For example, you want a bouncing ball to synchronize with the beat of some music you imported into Flash. Without specifically synchronizing the sounds, the sound and the animation might play at different speeds. A faster computer might play the animation faster but doesn't adjust the length of the sound. (For basic information on adding sound to Flash, refer to Chapter 11.)

To synchronize animation with the sound, you need to use a stream sound. When you add the sound file to a frame, choose Stream from the Sync drop-down list in the Property inspector. Then adjust the keyframes so that the animation and the sound end at the same time.

To be more precise, you can synchronize your animation with specific parts of the sound. To accomplish this task, choose Modify⇨Timeline⇨Layer Properties and choose 200% or 300% from the Layer Height drop-down list. You can also click the little button in the upper-right corner of the Timeline and choose Medium or Large for the size of the frames from the option menu that appears. Now you can see the shape of your sound wave more clearly so that you can adjust the keyframes of your animation to match certain parts of the sound.

One way to pinpoint which frame to use for placing an animation event is to drag the playhead (the red rectangle) just above the Timeline. This technique lets you control the speed of the animation. You can drag left or right until you find the exact frame that you want to work with. You can then move a keyframe to that frame, for example, to move an animation event to a frame that contains a specific portion of your sound.

## What Is the Best Way to Import Bitmaps?

Maybe you need to put into your Flash animation your boss's photograph or a photo of the product that you sell. Or maybe you want an effect in your

Flash movie that you can create only in Photoshop. So you need to use a bitmap image. What format of bitmap do you use?

You might not have a choice of format. If your information systems department hands you a logo in JPEG format, you probably have to use it.

A trick for changing a file's format is to open an existing bitmap file in an image-editing program. Most let you save that file in another format.

At other times, you can choose your format. For example, when you scan a photo, most scanner software lets you choose from among several formats. A digital camera may also let you choose the format. Of course, if you create the bitmap in an image-editing program, you can choose from any format that the program supports. (Turn to Chapter 3 for instructions on importing bitmap images. *Hint:* Choose File⇨Import⇨Import to Stage or File⇨Import⇨ Import to Library.)

Here are some commonly used bitmap formats:

- ✔ The **GIF file** format, which generally displays well in a browser, can't have more than 256 colors. You can use the GIF format for simple drawings that have a limited color palette, but you may be better off with the PNG format, described later in this list.

- ✔ **JPEG files** can display many more colors than GIF files and therefore produce more realistic photos and other complex drawings. Although JPEG graphics can be highly compressed to reduce file size, they lose some fidelity as a result. Also, when Flash compresses the file again during export or publishing, you might end up with an unfocused mess.

- ✔ **BMP** doesn't lose quality when compressed, but the BMP format results in larger file sizes than GIF or JPEG.

- ✔ **PNG** is a nice compromise between file size and image quality. The PNG format doesn't lose quality when compressed and allows many more colors than the GIF format. And it provides the capability for transparency. Formerly, the PNG format wasn't supported in all Web browsers, but now it is supported in almost all current browsers. If you want the smallest file size but don't want to compromise quality, the PNG format is a good choice. The Flash image compressor works best and most efficiently with images that have not been compressed using techniques that may lose some image quality.

Your final result is the .swf file that you publish. Flash compresses bitmaps (as well as the entire movie) when the movie is exported to an .swf Flash Player file. Therefore, you need to think about the entire round-trip journey that your bitmap will make. You might have to test varying bitmap formats and publish the movie for each one to see the exact results.

When you export, you can set the JPEG quality on the SWF tab of the Publish Settings dialog box. You also set the overall quality on the HTML tab. For that quality setting, only the High and Best settings *smooth* (anti-alias) the bitmaps in the movie. (Refer to Chapter 13 for more information about publishing your Flash movie.)

When you import a bitmap image into Flash, you can take the following steps to ensure good-looking results:

✔ **Save your graphics in the highest quality possible.** If you have a photograph, don't import it as a GIF file.

✔ **Don't overcompress your original bitmaps, but don't import 100K files, either.** Find a happy medium. Try saving an image in several formats to see the difference in quality and size.

✔ **Set the compression type and quality in the Bitmap Properties dialog box.** After you import the image, open the Library (choose Window➪ Library) and right-click (Windows) or Control+click (Mac) the image and choose Properties to open the Bitmap Properties dialog box, as shown in Figure 14-1.

**Figure 14-1:** Use the Bitmap Properties dialog box to fiddle with your bitmaps.

Bitmap Properties

skateboarder.BMP

.\skateboarder.BMP

Wednesday, December 22, 1999  12:41 PM
400 x 400 pixels at 32 bits per pixel

☑ Allow smoothing

Compression: Photo (JPEG)

☑ Use document default quality

Will use JPEG setting from Export Movie

OK
Cancel
Update
Import...
Test
Advanced

# How Do I Rescale My Movie's Size?

You create a beautiful Flash movie that takes up the entire page. But then your boss says that you need to fit it into an existing HTML page, which translates into reducing the size of the whole thing by 25 percent. What do you do? Get a new boss, if possible.

Barring that, you can rescale the size of the movie by following these steps:

1. **Decide the amount of the reduction you need to achieve, such as 25 percent.**

2. **If you have any hidden layers, right-click (Windows) or Control+click (Mac) any layer and choose Show All from the contextual menu that appears.**

   This step ensures that all layers are considered in the reduction.

3. **Click the Edit Multiple Frames button (just below the Timeline).**

4. **Drag the onion skin markers to the beginning and ending frames of your animation.**

   See Chapter 9 if you need more information on how to use the onion skin markers.

5. **Choose Edit⇨Select All.**

6. **Choose Window⇨Info to open the Info panel.**

   You see the Width (W) and Height (H), and X and Y coordinates.

7. **Multiply all the numbers in the Info panel by the reduction percentage.**

   Write down the results of your calculations, just to be safe.

8. **Click in the W (Width) text box and type the new number for the reduction percentage; then press Tab to move to the next box.**

9. **Repeat Step 8 for the H (Height), X, and Y text boxes.**

You're done! Flash scales your entire movie by the percentage you specified. You may have to drag everything so that it fits appropriately within your smaller-sized movie.

Size requirements are key pieces of information that you need to nail down before building a Flash movie so that you can (you hope!) avoid any need to rescale your movie's size.

## What Are the Best Movie-Creating Tips?

Every Flash user collects a number of techniques that make creating a Flash movie easier. The following items are a few ideas to help you get started.

✔ Save multiple versions of your movie by choosing File⇨Save As. If a problem arises, you can always go back to a previous version and start again.

✔ As soon as you have an overall structure, test your movie in a variety of browsers (for example, Internet Explorer, Mozilla Firefox, and Apple's Safari) at various resolutions, if possible. You can more easily fix problems early, before your project becomes too complex. Choose Control⇨

Test Movie as soon as you develop your animation and continue to test it in this way for each new significant change.

✔ Add comments (see Chapter 10) to your ActionScript so that you can figure out what you did when you go back to your movie after your vacation.

✔ Use consistent names for symbols. Many Flash users add the type of symbol after the name, so a button could be called *Contact_btn,* and a movie clip could be called *Intro_mc.* When you start creating movie clips inside buttons, you might get confused if you don't name your symbols intelligently.

✔ Use meaningful names for your instances. If you have three instances of a button symbol, you need to be able to distinguish which is which. You can name them by their purpose, such as Email, Services, and Clients.

✔ When you complete work on a layer, lock the layer to avoid making unwanted changes.

You're sure to discover other techniques as you become more experienced in Flash.

## Can Flash Do 3-D?

You can't really create 3-D in Flash. Flash is decidedly a 2-D program. But, not to be deterred, Flash users have created many tricks to make you think you're seeing 3-D.

One simple approach is to rotate a 2-D object in what appears to be 3-D space. For example, you can draw a circle and scale it in one dimension so that it becomes progressively more of an oval until all you see is a straight line. Continue to expand it from the line through fatter and fatter ovals until you have a circle again. You've just apparently rotated the circle 180 degrees. Continue until you're finished. You can select a group of frames and copy them or reverse them. (Turn to Chapter 9 for more details.) You can see a simple example in Figure 14-2.

You can use shape tweening to create this 3-D effect. You can shape tween a circle into a line and back again to make it look like it's rotating.

For fancier results, you can use software packages, such as Swift 3D, that are designed for creating 3-D animation for Flash. Also, some high-end 3-D animation packages, such as Maya, have Flash export capabilities built in.

Another technique for simulating 3-D is to import an object from a 3-D program, such as 3D Studio Max, AutoCAD, or Maya.

**Figure 14-2:**
The circle is
2-D, but it
looks like it's
rotating in
3-D; here,
you see the
first quarter
revolution.

In the following steps, we use AutoCAD as an example. To import an object from AutoCAD, follow these steps:

1. **Within AutoCAD, create the 3-D object, display the view that you want to start with, and then choose File⇨Export.**

   The Export Data dialog box opens. The Files of Type drop-down list should read `Metafile (*.wmf)`.

2. **In the File Name text box, enter a name for the file. Add a 1 after the filename. Click Save and select the object when prompted.**

3. **Rotate the 3-D model slightly.**

   In AutoCAD 2000 and later, you can use the 3D Orbit command for this step.

4. **Save this new view as a `.wmf` file as we explain in Step 2, consecutively numbered from the first file.**

   For example, if the first file is `3d1.wmf`, name the second file `3d2.wmf`.

5. **Repeat Steps 2 through 4 until you've rotated the model 360 degrees.**

6. **In Flash, choose File⇨Import⇨Import to Stage.**

7. **Select Windows Metafile (*.wmf) from the Files of Type drop-down list, select the first WMF file that you created, and then click Open.**

8. **When Flash asks whether you want to import all the files in the sequence, click Yes.**

    Flash imports all the files, placing them in consecutive keyframes. The WMF file may be imported with a border as well as the lines that make up the object.

9. **For each keyframe, do the following:**

    a. *If your graphic has a border:* Click anywhere outside the objects, select just the border, and press Delete.

    b. *If your graphic is imported as one object:* Select all the objects and then choose Modify⇨Break Apart.

    c. Select the objects and then choose Modify⇨Convert to Symbol.

You can now play your animation. Note that you lose any shading or materials that you created in AutoCAD, so your model has a wire-frame look. You can use fills to modify your 3-D object in Flash to create the appearance of solidity.

For an example of creating a simple 3-D animation using this technique, look in the Ch14 folder of the companion Web site for 3d rotation.fla. (The companion site is at www.dummies.com/go/flash8.) You can also use ActionScript to scale, layer, and move 2-D objects interactively according to the movement of the mouse, and this can give the effect of moving in 3-D space. For a cool example of this, see basic_3d.fla in the Ch14 folder of the companion Web site. *(Thanks again to Keith Peters of The BIT-101 Lab, at www.bit-101.com, for this file.)*

What if you don't have a 3-D program? Well, do you have Microsoft Word? Yes, folks, you can create 3-D objects in your lowly word processing program.

To create a 3-D object by using Microsoft Word, follow these steps:

1. **Open Microsoft Word and, in a new document, open the Drawing toolbar if it isn't already open by choosing View⇨Toolbars⇨Drawing.**

2. **On the Drawing toolbar, click the AutoShapes drop-down arrow and select any shape that you want.**

    You can even draw your own shape by using the Scribble tool (one of the options on the Lines submenu, under AutoShapes).

3. **Click in your blank document to place the shape.**

    If you want, use the Fill Color tool to change the fill. Select the shape and then, from the Fill Color drop-down list, select Fill Effects and create a cool gradient on the Gradient tab.

4. **Click the 3-D button at the right end of the Drawing toolbar and select from the box that opens a 3-D perspective that you like.**

    You might need to try out a few choices until you get the best effect.

5. **Click the 3-D button again and choose the 3-D Settings button at the bottom of the box to open the 3-D Settings toolbar.**

   Use the Tilt Left, Right, Up, or Down button to tilt the object until it looks perfectly flat so that you don't see any of the 3-D effect. Keep the 3-D Settings toolbar open.

6. **Choose Edit⇨Copy to copy the shape to the Clipboard.**

7. **Return to Flash and choose Insert⇨New Symbol; specify a movie clip behavior for the symbol and then name it.**

8. **Click OK.**

9. **Choose Edit⇨Paste to paste the shape into the first frame.**

10. **Go back to Word and decide which way you want your shape to rotate.**

    You can choose up, down, left, or right.

11. **Select your 3-D shape in the Word document and click twice on Tilt Left (or Right, Up, or Down) on the 3-D Settings toolbar.**

12. **Copy the shape to the Clipboard.**

13. **Go to Flash and create a keyframe in the next frame.**

14. **Paste the shape from the Clipboard.**

15. **Repeat Steps 11 through 14 until you're looking at your shape on edge.**

16. **Select all the frames except the first and the last, and then choose Edit⇨Timeline⇨Copy Frames.**

17. **Click the first empty frame (the one after your last frame) and then choose Edit⇨Timeline⇨Paste Frames.**

    You now have the quarter revolution twice, and you need to modify the second set so that it becomes the second quarter revolution.

18. **Select all the frames that you've pasted and choose Modify⇨Timeline⇨ Reverse Frames.**

    If you play the animation now, it looks as though the shape is revolving one quarter and then back again.

19. **Select the first of the frames that you pasted and choose Modify⇨ Transform⇨Flip Horizontal (if you used Tilt Left or Right in Word) or Flip Vertical (if you chose Tilt Up or Down in Word).**

20. **Repeat Step 19 with the remaining frames that you've pasted.**

    You now have a half revolution.

21. **Select all but the first and last frames and then choose Edit⇨Timeline⇨ Copy Frames.**

22. **Click the first empty frame after the last frame and choose Edit⇨ Timeline⇨Paste Frames.**

23. **Select all the frames that you've pasted and choose Modify⇨Timeline⇨ Reverse Frames.**

You're done! Play your animation and watch your shape roll.

This method does have some disadvantages. First, all your images from Word are imported as bitmaps, not vector images. Second, you're animating frame by frame. As a result, your file is larger and downloads slower. If you use this method for just a small animation, however, it beats learning how to use a fancy 3-D program (and paying for it, too). Test the results and see whether it works for you.

Look in the Ch14 folder on our companion Web site (www.dummies.com/go/ flash8) for rotating star.fla, which is an example of using Word to create 3-D objects. The animation is in a movie clip, so choose Control⇨Test Movie to see the results (or open the .swf file directly).

## How Do I Center a Flash Movie in a Web Page?

As we discuss in Chapter 13, you can make your Flash movie appear in a Web page by choosing both the Flash and HTML formats in your Publish Settings and then publishing your movie. Flash then generates the HTML code (like the code in Figure 13-4) for a Web page. This Web page appears to contain your Flash movie when you view the Web page in a browser. To make the Flash movie centered in that Web page, you just need to add a little bit of extra code to the HTML page, which you can do with a text editor.

To add the HTML code for centering your Flash movie in the Web page, follow these steps:

1. **After choosing the Publish Settings for Flash and HTML (as we describe in Chapter 13), choose File⇨Publish.**

   Flash creates a Flash Player (.swf) file and a Web page (HTML) file.

2. **Start a text editor or an HTML editor, and open the HTML page within the editor.**

   You can use an HTML editor such as Macromedia Dreamweaver or a text editor such as Notepad (Windows) or TextEdit (Mac). (In TextEdit, choose TextEdit⇨Preferences, and when the Preferences window appears, in the New Document Attributes section, select Plain Text rather than Rich Text.)

3. **Find `<object` in the file and insert** `<div align="center">` **before it.**

4. **Find `</object>` in the file and insert** `</div>` **after it.**

   In HTML lingo, the word `<div>` and `<object>` and any other words starting with a bracket (`<`) are called *tags*. The `<div>` tag defines the beginning of a division or section of a Web page, and the `</div>` tag defines the end of it.

   Figure 14-3 shows an example of an HTML file with the `<div>` and `</div>` tags added.

5. **In the editor, save the file with the changes you made.**

   Now when you view the HTML page in a Web browser, your Flash movie appears centered in the Web page.

**Figure 14-3:** Here's the code previously shown in Figure 13-4, revised with `<div>` and `</div>` tags, which center the movie in the Web page.

```
<html xmlns="http://www.w3.org/1999/xhtml" xml:lang="en" lang="en">
<head>
<meta http-equiv="Content-Type" content="text/html; charset=iso-8859-1" />
<title>movie of the year</title>
</head>
<body bgcolor="#ffffff">
<!--url's used in the movie-->
<!--text used in the movie-->
<!-- saved from url=(0013)about:internet -->
<div align="center">
<object classid="clsid:d27cdb6e-ae6d-11cf-96b8-444553540000" codebase="http:/
/fpdownload.macromedia.com/pub/shockwave/cabs/flash/
swflash.cab#version=8,0,0,0" width="550" height="400" id="movie of the year"
align="middle">
<param name="allowScriptAccess" value="sameDomain" />
<param name="movie" value="movie of the year.swf" />
<param name="loop" value="false" />
<param name="quality" value="high" />
<param name="bgcolor" value="#ffffff" />
<embed src="movie of the year.swf" loop="false" quality="high"
bgcolor="#ffffff" width="550" height="400" name="movie of the year"
align="middle" allowScriptAccess="sameDomain" type="application/x-shockwave-
flash" pluginspage="http://www.macromedia.com/go/getflashplayer" />
</object>
</div>
</body>
</html>
```

## What Are the Size Limits for a Flash Movie?

Usually you won't be too concerned about how big a movie you can create with Flash because one of the reasons to use Flash is that it employs vector graphics and tweening to create small files which download quickly over the Web. So if you're using Flash to create gigantic projects, that can be great fun and even very workable in some cases, but it's good to keep in mind that that isn't what Flash is primarily designed to do. On the other hand, more and more studios are using Flash for production animation (including broadcast TV shows), and video is now an important feature of Flash.

In any case, it's interesting to know that, in addition to limits imposed by your computer's RAM, CPU, hard drive, video card, browser, and operating system, there are a few hard limits to the size of a Flash movie. For example, your Flash movie can have a maximum of 16,000 frames.

If you need longer Flash movies, you can create them in pieces by using fewer than 16,000 frames in each piece, and then play them in sequence with `loadMovie`. (See Chapter 11 for more information on `loadMovie`.)

By coincidence or a strange twist of fate, 16,000 is also the maximum number of layers, the maximum number of loaded movies, and the maximum number of symbol instances you might have in your Flash movie.

## *How Do I Dynamically Load Music from the Web?*

You can use an ActionScript to load music into your movie live from the Web by using the ActionScript `loadsound` method. (Turn to Chapter 10 to find out more about ActionScript.)

To load an MP3 file on the Web into your movie while your movie is playing, follow these steps:

1. **Create a new layer.**

   Chapter 6 explains how to add a new layer.

2. **Click a keyframe.**

   If the frame that you want to use is not a keyframe, right-click it (Windows) or Control+click it (Mac) and choose Insert Keyframe.

3. **Choose Window⇨Actions to open the Actions panel.**

   If necessary, click the Actions panel title bar to expand the panel.

4. **In the left pane of the Actions panel, choose ActionScript 2.0 Classes⇨ Media⇨Sound and then double-click new Sound.**

   new Sound() should appear in the Expression text field at the top of the Actions panel.

5. **Decide on an instance name, such as `mySound`, and type this name and an equal sign in the Expression text box at the top of the Actions panel.**

   The text in the Expression text box should be

   ```
   mySound = new Sound();
   ```

   This step creates an instance of a new sound object with the name mySound.

6. **Click in the Script pane of the Actions panel on the line below the line you just created (in our example, `mySound = new Sound`) to start a new line of code.**

7. **In the left pane of the Actions panel, click the ActionScript 2.0 Classes category, then the Media category, then the Sound category, then the Methods category, and then double-click `loadSound`.**

   The text in the Script pane should now be

   ```
   mySound = new Sound();
   not_yet_set.loadSound();
   ```

8. **Enter the sound's instance name (such as `mySound`) in the Object text box at the top of the Actions panel. Enter the URL (enclosed in quotation marks) of an MP3 file in the URL text box. In the `isStreaming` text field, enter the word** true.

   This step signifies that it's true you want to stream the sound. (You hear *streaming audio* as it's being sent over the Web to you. You don't have to download the entire audio file before you can start hearing it.)

   Now your code in the lower-right pane of the Actions panel should look like this (except with your own URL):

   ```
   mySound = new Sound();
   mySound.loadSound("http://www.example.com/fun-sound.mp3",
         true);
   ```

9. **Choose Control⇨Test Movie and enjoy the music.**

# Chapter 15

# The Ten Best Flash Resources

*F*lash is such a flexible program that you never stop discovering what it can do. And just when you think you've got it, out comes a new version! In this chapter, we point you to the many resources that you can turn to when you want to increase your knowledge about Flash.

Of course, we think that this book is a great resource on Flash. But you're already using this book, and much more about Flash is out there, readily available to help you become a truly great Flash designer and animator.

## Play Around with the Samples

Flash comes with a set of sample files that showcase many capabilities. You can find information on each of these samples by choosing Help➪Flash Help, and then, in the Help window that appears, navigating to the Flash Samples "book" in the list on the left pane, and clicking the chapter that you want. Each chapter tells you where to find the sample file on your hard drive. A great way to find out more about Flash is to play with, take apart, and analyze each sample that interests you.

If your computer is connected to the Internet, you can get the latest updated version of Help from Macromedia by clicking the green arrow labeled Update in the upper-right area of the Help window.

## Visit Our Site

Check out the *Macromedia Flash 8 For Dummies* page on the Wiley Web site. You can find the site by surfing to `www.dummies.com/go/flash8`. It contains sample files from the book, tips, and updates. We hope that you find the site helpful!

## Take a Course

Many colleges and universities offer courses in Flash. Sometimes these courses are part of a Web design or graphic arts course, or they might stand alone. To find these courses, call local educational institutions and ask.

The advantage of a course led by a teacher is that you have a chance to ask questions — and receive answers. A teacher also guides the learning process and possibly even gives you lots of tips and hints!

You might also consider taking courses from Macromedia University, which offers both self-paced and instructor-led courses in the use of Flash and other Macromedia products. Choose Help⇨Macromedia Training for more information, including free sample lessons.

## Look on the Flash Web Page

Macromedia maintains a large resource on its Web site. Point your browser to `www.macromedia.com/go/flash_support`, where you can find tips, tutorials, support, technical notes, news, and updates.

## Join a Flash Discussion Group

Macromedia maintains several Flash newsgroups where anyone can ask questions and get expert answers. The two main newsgroups are

- ✔ **Flash:** For technical issues relating to Flash and Flash Player.
- ✔ **Flash Site Design:** For discussing techniques as well as technical issues.

To read messages from and send messages to these groups, just point your Web browser to `http://webforums.macromedia.com/flash`.

If you have software for reading newsgroups on your computer, you can alternatively go to `news://forums.macromedia.com/macromedia.flash` and `news://forums.macromedia.com/macromedia.flash.sitedesign` to read messages from and send messages to the two main groups.

Several other excellent active discussion groups reside on Web sites. The best way to tell whether a discussion group is active is to see how many messages have been posted in the past one or two days. You can also check out how many different people are participating. See the following section in this chapter.

You can also subscribe to electronic mailing lists for ongoing discussions sent by e-mail. With more than 3,000 members, the Yahoo! FLASHmacromedia list is one of the largest lists specifically for users who want to discuss Flash techniques. You can ask questions and get answers from the community of Flash users. To sign up or to view the Web archive of messages, go to `http://groups.yahoo.com/group/FLASHmacromedia`. You can also subscribe by sending a blank e-mail to `FLASHmacromedia-subscribe@yahoogroups.com`.

You can find more than 100 other Macromedia Flash e-mail discussion groups at Yahoo! alone. Find them by surfing the Web to `http://groups.yahoo.com` and typing **Macromedia Flash** into the Search box.

## Check Out the Flash Resource Sites

A huge Flash community is on the Internet . . . so vast, in fact, that you'll probably never be able to participate in all its offerings. These Web sites offer news, tutorials, discussion groups, tips, and links to other Flash resources.

Some of these sites are more up to date, lively, and complete than others. The quality of the tips and tutorials varies widely. Some specialize in tips for beginners; others are geared toward advanced users. The following list briefly reviews the ones that we find most useful, in alphabetical order:

- `www.actionscript.org`: This site is a well-designed, comprehensive resource on ActionScript. It includes extremely active discussion forums (with tens of thousands of messages); more than 200 tutorials on ActionScript at beginning, intermediate, and advanced levels; a library with more than 600 ActionScripts, more than 900 Flash movies, and more than 40 components; links; an employment section; and a Flash bookstore.

- `www.bestflashanimationsite.com`: This site showcases Flash sites that have been voted the best by viewers. This is a good place to find top-notch examples of Flash in a variety of categories, including Applications, Corporate, Experimental, Technical Merit, Video, and more.

- `www.canfieldstudios.com`: Here you can find dozens of example `.fla` files to download and study. You can use these to learn everything from creating embossed text to adding animated fog to a background photo.

- `www.d-art.ch`: This is another site with a few dozen cool Flash files you can preview, download, and study. Many of the experiments shown here are striking, including text rotating in 3-D, graphics that wobble when you click them, and interactive elastic lines that you can create.

✔ www.flashkit.com: Flash Kit is probably the largest Flash site, and it's up to date. (We define *up to date* as having Flash 8 material within days after it has shipped.) You can find thousands of .fla files to download and study, hundreds of tutorials, dozens of active discussion forums (some with hundreds of thousands of posts), links, thousands of sounds, more than a thousand downloadable fonts — if you can think of it, you can find it here.

✔ www.flashgoddess.com: Flashgoddess is an informative site showcasing women who do brilliant work with Flash. It includes profiles of and articles on terrific Flash designers, a gallery of work by featured artists, and more.

✔ www.flashmagazine.com: This site includes news and reviews of Flash and Flash-related products. You also find links, articles, and a list of hundreds of applications that can output Flash Player files.

✔ www.kirupa.com: This is MIT student Karupa Chinnathamei's site all about Flash, with interviews, reviews, dozens of tutorials, and discussion forums with thousands of posts.

✔ www.moock.org/webdesign/flash: Colin Moock is a master Flash designer, and his Web site contains tons of advanced technical information, Flash industry news, his blog, annotated links, and more. You can generally find lots to chew on here.

✔ www.peterjoel.com/Samples: Peter Joel Hall's site includes about two dozen sample .fla files that you may preview, download, and study. You can discover how to use Flash to make text follow a path, how to create interactive color fills, and how to perform other interesting Flash tricks.

✔ www.flashcomponents.net: Flash components hosts a collection of more than 200 pre-built components you can download and use in your Flash documents. Here you can find components for video effects, user interface widgets, mouse trailers, pan and zoomers, and more.

✔ www.ultrashock.com: Ultrashock is a multifaceted site that includes tutorials, downloads of .fla files, and discussion forums with more than half a million posts.

✔ www.were-here.com: At We're Here Forums, you find a wealth of resources: discussion forums with almost a million posts, daily news about Flash, Flash games, dozens of tutorials, and more than 100 .fla file downloads.

## Check Out Sites That Use Flash

You can get ideas by looking at what others do. (It's interesting, for instance, that simple Flash sites are sometimes the most beautiful and practical.) In Chapter 16, we list sites by ten great designers that use Flash. And many resource sites have galleries of great sites, as does Macromedia.

## Attend a Flash Conference

Attending a conference on Flash is an exciting way to find out much more about Flash from an array of experts, see award-winning Flash movies, participate in workshops and seminars, hear the latest news from Macromedia, make contacts with others interested in Flash, and generally immerse yourself in the world of Flash. Even just visiting the Web sites of some of these conferences can be quite instructive. Conferences you might consider attending include:

- ✔ **Flashforward (including the Flash Film Festival):** A three-day conference held in the spring in San Francisco and in the summer in New York City. For information, visit www.flashforwardconference.com.

- ✔ **Flash in the Can Conference:** A three-day conference in the spring in Toronto, Ontario, Canada. For information, visit www.fitc.ca.

- ✔ **Powered by Detroit Conference:** A two-day conference on Flash and Cold Fusion, sponsored by Macromedia in Detroit in the spring. For information, visit www.poweredbydetroit.org.

- ✔ **FlashBelt Conference:** A two-day conference in Minneapolis in June. For information, visit www.flashbelt.com.

## Collect Flash Movies

Many Flash resource Web sites let you download .fla files. You can also trade .fla files with others who you know use Flash. Analyzing .fla files is a great way to see how effects are created. In Chapter 14, we explain how to use the Movie Explorer to ferret out all the hidden details of an .fla file.

Be sure to check out the Library of an .fla file — many of the secrets lie there. And you can use the Movie Explorer to find and study all the actions in an .fla file. You'll soon be on your way to adapting the techniques that you see to your own projects.

## Reuse Your Best Stuff

After you've created some great Flash movies, you can reuse your best stuff. *Fadeouts* (changing transparency), *glows* (soft edges), and masks are simple effects that you can use again and again. You can also reuse ActionScript on new objects. After you get a technique down, you don't need to re-create the wheel. If you've created an animated logo, you might be able to use it over and over. Certain simple animations can be created in new colors, using the same original symbols.

You can import items from the Library of any movie into your current movie. Choose File➪Import➪Open External Library and choose the Flash file that contains the Library that you want to use. Then drag the items that you want from the imported movie Library onto the Stage or into the Library of your current movie. This is a really nifty Flash feature.

# Chapter 16

# Ten Flash Designers to Watch

・・・・・・・・・・・・・・・・・・・・・・・・・・・・・・・・・・・・・・

*T*rying to choose ten of the best designers that use Flash is almost absurd — so many brilliant designers are out there. Nevertheless, we give you a shortcut to finding some of the most innovative and skilled Flash designers so that you can check out their work, get ideas, and see the possibilities.

Note that some of the sites they've designed can take a really long time to load if you don't have a broadband connection to the Web.

## Ola Berger

Swedish animator Ola Berger took more than a year to create his acclaimed Gooberstory animation, which you may view along with many other treats at www.goober.nu. The tranquil quality and reflective pace of his work are an interesting contrast to the animated energy of Ben Hantoot (whom we discuss later in this chapter).

## Hillman Curtis

Hillman Curtis' studio is one of the most well-known Flash design firms in the world. His clients include MTV, Apple Computer, OgilvyOne Worldwide, British Airways, and many more. His studio has won dozens of design awards. His motto is "making the invisible visible," and his work combines simplicity, freshness, and sophistication. You can check out the work of Hillman and his crew at www.hillmancurtis.com.

## Joshua Davis

Joshua Davis is one of the most relentless explorers of Flash's capabilities. His legendary "praystation" site, an archive that you may see at `http://ps3.praystation.com/pound/v2`, originally went online in 1997 as a spoof of PlayStation graphics, but soon morphed into one of the most aggressively experimental Flash sites on the Web. He then moved on to create Once Upon A Forest (which you may see at `www.once-upon-a-forest.com`), a visually poetic series of computer-generated imagery that is easier to experience than describe. (He likes to bury his links, so you may have to search to find anything clickable.) You may see his current work at `www.joshuadavis.com`. Benek Lisefski's essay on Joshua Davis, at `www.pixelinspectors.com/reviews/joshua-davis.html`, can help you understand his mysterious work a little more clearly. (Incidentally, Alek Lisefski's Web site, located at `www.pixelinspectors.com`, features meaty reviews and interviews with other top Flash designers that you might find of interest.)

## Anthony Eden

Australian designer Anthony Eden showcases a fascinating group of Flash experiments at his site, `www.arseiam.com`.

## Ben Hantoot

Young Ben Hantoot is already one of the most, as he says, "over-the-top" animators on the planet. Other Flash sites look positively motionless compared to the site of his studio, `www.webfeatsdesign.com`. The incessant inventiveness of his work is outrageously delightful.

## Shane Mielke

Shane Mielke is the art director of 2Advanced Studios. Shane's Web site, at `www.2advanced.com`, features impressive and sophisticated use of Flash. Shane's clients include Lexus, Sony, Toshiba, Toyota, Elektra Records, Ford Motor Company, and many more. You can view his outstanding personal portfolio at `www.pixelranger.com`.

Shane supplied us with a beautiful Flash animation that we use as an example of animated mask layers at the end of Chapter 6. You can download the animation (`fffd_reveal.fla`) from the Ch06 folder of our companion Web site at `www.dummies.com/go/flash8`.

## Keith Peters

The BIT-101 Lab at Keith Peters' Web site www.bit-101.com is his personal online laboratory, where you can find the results of more than 500 of his explorations with Flash in which he uses various principles of math and physics to take Flash into interesting new artistic realms. He says, "It was my original intention, possibly now achieved, to have the largest repository of single-author experimental Flash files on the Web." We think you'll agree it's an outstanding achievement. At www.bit-101.com/dev, you can also see his portfolio links to other cutting-edge projects he's worked on.

Keith provided us with two Flash movies that are great examples of drag-and-drop objects and 3-D effects in Flash, which we discuss in Chapter 14. You can download them (drag_and_drop.fla and basic_3d.fla) from the Ch14 folder of our companion Web site www.dummies.com/go/flash8.

## Ellen Pronk

Ellen Pronk is a Dutch artist whose personal Web site, www.lfs.nl/preview. php, is her visual diary and sketchbook in which she records her doodles, photos, and mostly abstract Flash animations. Each animation does one thing simply but well. *Lfs* is a kind of shorthand for *liefs,* which translates to *with love.*

## Micaël Reynaud

The young French award-winning Flash designer Micaël Reynaud has created in www.dunun.com a site full of surprises that, like several of the sites in this chapter, is difficult to describe but charming to experience. The site combines music, imagery, and unusual user-interface techniques to showcase a panoramic view of this artist's multiple skills.

## Craig Swann

Craig Swann is a member of CRASH!MEDIA, an award-winning and prolific studio that has been doing cutting-edge Flash work for years, for clients such as Chevrolet, Pontiac, Honda, Cadillac, Mercedes-Benz, and many others. You can view the work of Craig and his team at www.crashmedia.com.

# Part VII
# Appendixes

The 5th Wave                    By Rich Tennant

"Evidently he died of natural causes following a marathon session animating everything on his personal Web site. And no, Morganstern – the irony isn't lost on me!"

## In this part . . .

*I*n the appendixes, we dump everything that we couldn't fit elsewhere but thought too useful to forget. We explain how to install Flash (it's a snap), customize your preferences, and create your own keyboard shortcuts. One appendix shows you all the Flash 8 panels, and labels them carefully so that you know what they do. We also tell you what's on the companion Web site (lots of stuff!).

# Appendix A

# Installing Flash and Setting Your Preferences

*Installing* Flash is simple. Nevertheless, sometimes a few pointers can help. After you're up and running, you might want to customize how Flash works. You can set quite a number of preferences. You can also create your own keyboard shortcuts.

Now, time to stop stalling and start installing.

## *Installing Flash*

Installing Flash is a cinch, although you have a couple of options. Here's the lowdown on getting started.

You can install Flash in four different ways:

- ✔ Install it from a CD (onto a PC).
- ✔ Download it to a PC.
- ✔ Install it from a CD (onto a Mac).
- ✔ Download it to a Mac.

We discuss these methods separately in the next four sections.

# Installing Flash onto a PC from a CD

So you went out and bought Flash in the box, and you have a CD-ROM drive on your PC. To install Flash from the box, follow these steps:

1. **Exit all Windows programs.**

2. **Insert the CD-ROM.**

   In most cases, the setup program starts automatically. If not, choose Start⇨Run and click Browse. Then find and double-click `Setup.exe` on your CD-ROM drive. Click Run.

3. **Follow the instructions on the various screens that appear.**

   Unless you want to save space by not installing the lessons and samples, choose the typical installation. Other than that, the most significant choice that you have is where you install Flash. You can browse to change the location or accept the default, which is `C:\Program Files\ Macromedia\Flash 8`.

4. **After you follow the on-screen instructions, the setup program starts copying files; when it is completed, click Finish.**

5. **Read the ReadMe file offered on the last screen.**

   Although we guarantee that most of the stuff in the file is irrelevant to you, sometimes this file has just the weird detail that applies to your situation, so take the two minutes to read it.

# Installing Flash by downloading it to your PC

If you like, you can download the Flash trial directly from the Macromedia Web site. You can then pay for it within 30 days or it stops working. Follow these steps:

1. **Go to `www.macromedia.com/software/downloads`.**

2. **From the list of Macromedia products, choose Flash Basic 8 or Flash Professional 8.**

   You need to choose a location and answer a few questions.

3. **Follow the instructions on the screen for downloading the installation file.**

   When you download the file, you select a location on your hard drive. If you have a Downloads folder, you can use that. Another good option is the Desktop. Remember this location.

4. **When the download is complete, double-click the installation file.**

   Here's where you need to remember where you saved it. The installation program guides you through the process of installing Flash.

5. **Choose the typical installation, unless you want to save space by not installing the lessons and samples.**

   The only other significant choice that you have is where you install Flash. You can browse to change the location or accept the default, which is `C:\Program Files\Macromedia\Flash 8`.

After you install Flash, you can play with it! You can buy it at any time by clicking Buy Now on the first screen when you open Flash.

# Installing Flash onto a Mac from a CD

If you bought Flash in a box, you have a CD-ROM drive that you can use to install Flash.

To install Flash on your Mac from a CD, follow these steps:

1. **Insert the CD-ROM.**

   An installer icon appears on your desktop.

2. **Double-click the Flash 8 Installer icon.**

3. **When a window appears, displaying a software license agreement, click the Accept button so that you can continue the installation.**

   Of course, being the responsible people we are, we recommend reading the license agreement.

4. **Unless you want to save space by not installing the lessons and samples, choose the Easy Install option, which is the default.**

   Other than that, the most significant choice that you have is where you install Flash. You can browse to change the location or accept the default location, which is in the Applications folder on the startup disk drive.

5. **Click Install.**

   The installer program starts copying files. When it's done, you see the Macromedia Flash 8 folder displayed on your computer screen, containing the Flash 8 program, a few documents, and a bunch of other folders. One of the documents is the `ReadMe.html` file. You can view the contents of this file by simply double-clicking it. Although most of the stuff in the file is irrelevant to you, sometimes this file has a detail that applies to your situation, so reading it can be worthwhile.

## Installing Flash by downloading it to your Mac

In this ultramodern day and age, you can install Flash on your computer without ever leaving your Web browser. To download Flash, follow these steps (or something like them, assuming that the Macromedia Web site doesn't change too much):

1. **Go to www.macromedia.com/software/downloads.**

2. **From the list of Macromedia products, choose Flash Basic 8 or Flash Professional 8.**

   You need to choose a geographic location, complete or create a password, and answer a few questions.

3. **Follow the instructions on the screen for downloading the installation file.**

4. **When the download is complete, find and double-click the installation file.**

   The installation program guides you through the process of installing Flash.

   The most significant choice that you have is where you install Flash. You can browse to change the location or accept the default, which is the Applications folder on the startup disk drive.

After you install Flash, you can play with it for 30 days before it stops working. If you download the trial version, you can buy it at any time by clicking Buy Now on the first screen when you open Flash.

## Setting Your Preferences

Flash offers numerous ways to customize how you work. Why not make Flash suit you?

The main location for setting preferences is the Preferences dialog box, as shown in Figure A-1, with the General tab on top. To open the Preferences dialog box, choose Edit➪Preferences (Windows) or Flash➪Preferences (Mac).

**Figure A-1:**
Use the
Preferences
dialog box
to bend
Flash to
your will.

The following sections describe how to use this dialog box.

## General category

Click the General category to set the following options:

- **On Launch:** When Flash opens, it can show a start page that gives you options of opening an existing document or starting a new one. This is the default, but if you find the start page useless, you can choose to always start a new document, open the documents that you were using the last time you used Flash, or start with no document and decide where to go from there.

- **Undo:** Here you choose whether you want to use object-level or document-level undo (as we explain in Chapter 4). Then choose the number of actions you want to keep. The text box is set to 100 by default; you can enter any value from 2 to 300. The higher the value, the more memory Flash takes to remember all those steps. You might be surprised by how many commands you give in a short period of time, so

100 is probably a good setting. However, if you want to save commands from the History panel that you executed, set the number of actions higher.

✔ **Printing — Disable PostScript:** (For Windows only.) Selecting this check box disables PostScript output when you print to a PostScript printer. Mark this check box only if you have trouble printing to a PostScript printer. This option is deselected by default.

✔ **Document — Open Documents in Tabs:** (For Mac only.) This option is marked by default so that new documents open in a single window with tabs. Deselect this check box if you want each new document to open in a separate window.

✔ **Test Movie — Open Test Movie in Tabs:** By default, Flash opens a new window to play your movie when you test it. Select this check box to instead open a new document tab (like the ones Flash creates for each open document).

✔ **Selection — Shift Select:** This option is enabled by default. It means that you have to press Shift to select more than one object (by clicking). If you don't press Shift, the first object is deselected. Clearing this option means that you can click as many objects as you want to select them. This method is an efficient way to work, but most people aren't familiar with it. If you select something by accident, press Shift and click the object to deselect it.

✔ **Selection — Show Tooltips:** By default, this option shows short explanations of Flash interface features (such as toolbars and buttons) when you hover your cursor over them. You can make the ToolTips go away by clearing this check box.

✔ **Selection — Contact-Sensitive Selection and Lasso Tools:** By default, you need to completely surround objects with the selection or lasso tools to select them. Mark this check box so that you can select any object that is just partly within the selection or lasso selection border.

✔ **Timeline — Span Based Selection:** Lets you click between two keyframes to select the entire section between them, à la Flash 5.

✔ **Timeline — Named Anchor on Scene:** Automatically creates a named anchor at the beginning of each scene.

✔ **Highlight Color:** Lets you specify the color of the box around selected symbols and groups. Click the color swatch to display all the available colors and pick a different color. Or you can select Use Layer Color to use the layer's outline color.

Flash 8 Professional has a couple options that apply to projects, which are available in the Professional version only.

# *ActionScript category*

The ActionScript category offers settings relating to the ActionScript Editor so that you can customize how ActionScript looks and functions on the Action panel:

- **Editing:** By default, any ActionScript that you type is automatically indented. The tab size (amount of indentation) is four spaces. You can remove the automatic indentation or change the tab size. Code hints provide pop-up text in the Actions panel that helps you complete your code based on what you're typing. You can remove these hints and set a time delay for the display of the hints.

- **Font:** You can set the font type and size in the ActionScript Editor. For Windows only: Select the Use Dynamic Font Mapping check box to have Flash substitute a font if the selected font family doesn't have the required glyphs (character shapes). Dynamic font mapping is generally useful if you're working with multilingual text.

- **Open/Import:** This specifies the encoding used for fonts when opening or importing. The default, UTF-8, provides Unicode encoding that supports multiple languages.

- **Save/Export:** This specifies the encoding used for fonts when saving or exporting. The default, UTF-8, provides Unicode encoding that supports multiple languages.

- **Reload Modified Files:** You can have Flash prompt you to reload modified files or choose Never or Always options. Reloading files keeps your ActionScript up to date.

- **Syntax Coloring:** By default, ActionScript is colored based on the syntax of your code. For example, comments are highlighted in gray. You can remove coloring completely or change the colors for each syntax type.

- **Language:** You can put ActionScript in frames, buttons, movie clips, and multiple separate ActionScript text files. If you click the ActionScript 2.0 Settings button here, you can modify the places that Flash searches when your ActionScript in one place references certain kinds of ActionScript (called *classes*), which might be elsewhere. If you're just starting out with Flash, you almost certainly are not defining new class definition files in ActionScript, in which case you definitely don't have to worry about this.

Click the Reset to Defaults button to return all the settings in this category to their defaults.

## Auto Format category

This category offers specific options for formatting ActionScript. Programmers are picky about how their code looks, and this category lets you format your code the way you like. Select the various check boxes; the preview pane shows the result.

## Clipboard category

The Clipboard category enables you to set preferences for displaying, exporting, and importing certain objects. Here are your choices:

- ✔ **Bitmaps — Color Depth:** (For Windows only.) Specifies the color depth for bitmaps copied to the Clipboard. You can choose to match the screen or set a color depth from 4-bit to 32-bit with Alpha. You can use this setting to reduce the size of bitmaps that you paste into Flash from the Windows Clipboard.

- ✔ **Bitmaps — Resolution:** (For Windows only.) Sets the resolution of bitmaps copied to the Clipboard. Select Screen to match your screen resolution or select 72, 150, or 300. You can use this setting to reduce the size of bitmaps you paste into Flash from the Windows Clipboard.

- ✔ **Bitmaps — Size Limit:** (For Windows only.) Lets you specify a size limit in kilobytes for the amount of RAM (memory) that is used for a bitmap on the Windows Clipboard. If you have large images, you might need to increase this number, which is set to 250K by default.

- ✔ **Bitmaps — Smooth:** (For Windows only.) This box, marked by default, applies anti-aliasing to bitmaps. *Anti-aliasing* smoothes the appearance of bitmaps so that they don't appear so jagged. You can affect the smoothing of bitmaps during publishing by choosing the quality of the output, which we explain in the discussion of the HTML tab in Chapter 13.

- ✔ **Gradient Quality:** (For Windows only.) Lets you specify the quality of gradients that you copy to the Clipboard for use in other applications. Your options range from None to Best.

- ✔ **PICT Settings:** (For Mac only.) Lets you specify the method and resolution used to copy art to the Clipboard. From the Type menu, select Objects to copy art as vector graphics, or select one of the bitmap settings to copy it as a bitmap. In the Resolution input box, type in the resolution that you desire in dots per inch. If you want to include PostScript data, select the Include PostScript check box. In the Gradients menu, select the Gradient quality you want when you paste the Clipboard into a document outside of Flash. (When pasting within Flash, this setting is ignored, and you always get the full gradient quality.)

- ✔ **FreeHand Text:** By default, the Maintain Text as Blocks check box is marked so that text pasted from FreeHand can be edited in Flash.

# Drawing category

Click the Drawing category to set the following items:

- ✔ **Pen Tool — Show Pen Preview:** Displays a preview of the line or curve segment before you click the next point. Recommended!

- ✔ **Pen Tool — Show Solid Points:** When marked, shows filled points at vertices.

- ✔ **Pen Tool — Show Precise Cursors:** Displays a small crosshair rather than the pen-shaped cursor, for more precise placement of points.

We cover the rest of the drawing settings in this category in Chapter 3.

# Text category

The text category allows you to specify your text preferences, as follows:

- ✔ **Font Mapping Default:** This is the default that Flash uses when you open a movie that contains a font that you don't have on your computer. Select an option from the drop-down list.

- ✔ **Vertical Text — Default Text Orientation:** Sets vertical text as the default. Use this option for some Asian fonts.

- ✔ **Right to Left Text Flow:** Sets text lines to flow from right to left by default. This option is usually used for Arabic and Hebrew.

- ✔ **No Kerning:** Removes kerning from vertical text.

- ✔ **Input Method:** If you're working in Japanese, Chinese, or Korean, select the appropriate language.

# Warnings category

The Warnings category lists 13 (Windows) or 12 (Mac) situations in which Flash displays a warning message. All are enabled by default, so you're safe. If you find these warnings annoying or unnecessary, you can clear the appropriate check box.

# Customizing Keyboard Shortcuts

You can create a shortcut for any menu item and change existing shortcuts. (See the Cheat Sheet at the front of this book for commonly used keyboard shortcuts.) Besides the standard set of shortcuts, Flash 8 comes with some built-in shortcuts based on other programs, such as FreeHand, Illustrator, and Photoshop, so that you can use those same familiar shortcuts in Flash 8.

To create shortcuts, choose Edit➪Keyboard Shortcuts (Windows) or Flash 8➪ Keyboard Shortcuts (Mac) to open the Keyboard Shortcuts dialog box, as shown in Figure A-2 with the Drawing Menu Commands option displayed from the Commands drop-down list.

**Figure A-2:**
The
Keyboard
Shortcuts
dialog box
enables you
to use your
fingers the
way *you*
want.

You can't change the original set of shortcuts. Instead, create a duplicate set of shortcuts and modify the duplicate. Give the duplicate a new name, such as *MyWay,* and then use these shortcuts:

 **To duplicate a shortcut set,** click the Duplicate Set button at the top of the Keyboard Shortcuts dialog box.

 **To rename a set of shortcuts,** click the Rename Set button at the top of the Keyboard Shortcuts dialog box. (This option is not available until you duplicate a shortcut set.)

 **To delete a set of shortcuts,** click the Delete Set button at the top of the Keyboard Shortcuts dialog box.

When you have a new set of shortcuts, select from the Commands drop-down list the types of commands that you want to change. You can change all six (Windows) or eight (Mac) types of commands, but only one at a time:

✔ **Drawing Menu Commands:** Changes shortcuts for commands from the menu.

✔ **Tools Panel:** Changes shortcuts for the tools in the Tools panel.

✔ **Test Movie Menu Commands:** Changes shortcuts for commands from the menu that appears when you choose Control⇨Test Movie.

✔ **Script Edit Commands:** (Mac only.) Changes shortcuts for commands from the menu that appears when you are using the Script window. This is the editor window that appears when you choose File⇨New (or File⇨ Open) and then choose a script file to edit, such as an ActionScript (.as) file or a Flash JavaScript (.jsfl) file.

✔ **Timeline Commands:** Changes shortcuts for commands that move and selects frames on the Timeline.

✔ **Workspace Accessibility Commands:** Changes shortcuts for commands that change the focus to the Stage or the Timeline, selects panels, and selects objects within a panel.

✔ **Mobile Menu Commands:** (Flash Professional 8 only.) Changes shortcuts for the menu that appears when you choose Control⇨Test Movie for a Flash Lite movie. (In Flash Professional 8, you can create a Flash Lite movie, designed to run on certain PDAs, cell phones, or other mobile devices, by choosing File⇨Publish Settings, choosing the Flash tab in the Publish Settings window, and selecting a Flash Lite player in the Version drop-down list.)

✔ **Actions Panel Commands:** Changes shortcuts for working in the Actions panel.

For each type of command set, click the plus sign (+) (in Windows) or the right-pointing arrow (on the Mac) on the list to display all the commands and their current shortcuts. Here's how to create a new shortcut:

1. **Select the command that you want to customize.**

2. **Click the Add Shortcut button.**

   Flash adds a new shortcut, named empty.

3. **Press the keyboard combination that you want to use.**

   You must include Ctrl (Windows)/⌘ (Mac), Alt (Windows)/Option (Mac), or Shift before the second key. Flash tells you whether that combination is already assigned to another shortcut.

   • If you want to use that shortcut, click Change. Flash alerts you if the shortcut is already taken and lets you reassign the shortcut.

- If you don't want to use that shortcut, select the `empty` shortcut from the Shortcuts list and click the Remove Shortcut button.

4. **Repeat Steps 2 and 3 to change as many shortcuts as you want.**

5. **Click OK when you finish changing shortcuts.**

Until you get used to your new shortcuts, create a list and tape it to the side of your monitor or place it nearby for easy reference.

# Appendix B

# The Property Inspector and the Panels

● ● ● ● ● ● ● ● ● ● ● ● ● ● ● ● ● ● ● ● ● ● ● ● ● ● ● ● ● ● ● ● ● ● ● ● ● ● ● ● ● ● ● ● ● ● ● ● ●

**S**everal panels have been changed in Flash 8. In this appendix, we help you discover these features in more detail. The panels often have unlabeled buttons and menus that hold hidden treasures — or at least hidden features — if you know where to look.

## The Tools Panel

The Tools panel contains all the drawing tools as well as many editing tools. You'll use this panel a lot!

Most drawing tools have their own *modifiers* that control how the drawing tool works. In this figure, you see only one set of modifiers — for the Brush tool. However, other tools offer different modifiers, so the options section of the Tools panel looks different, depending on the tool you're using.

If you're upgrading from an earlier version of Flash, you might notice that the order of some of the tools is different. The Free Transform and Fill Transform buttons are now near the top, instead of tucked away somewhere in the middle of the panel. That's probably because they're so useful. Check out Chapter 3 for the full scoop on the Tools panel and all its helpful tools.

Selection — Subselection
Free Transform — Fill Transform
Line — Lasso
Pen — Text
Oval — Rectangle
Pencil — Brush
Ink Bottle — Paint Bucket
Eyedropper — Eraser
Hand (pan) — Zoom
Stroke color
No color — Fill color
Black and white — Swap colors
Object Drawing mode — Lock fill
Brush mode
Brush size
Brush shape
Use Pressure — Use Tilt

# The Property Inspector Gadget

The Property inspector is *context sensitive,* which means that it displays information that's useful to what you're doing at the time. In this section, you see some variations on this theme.

## Property inspector with no selection

When no object is selected and the cursor is on the Stage, you see the document properties, as shown here.

Background color

Document properties        Frame rate

## *Property inspector with a shape selected*

When you select a shape, the Property inspector displays properties of the shape so that you can edit them, as you see here.

Stroke color    Stroke height    Custom stroke style    Cap type

Fill color    Stroke style    Join type

## *Property inspector with keyframe selected*

When you click a keyframe on the Timeline, the Property inspector displays properties of the frame, as you see here.

Tween type    Sound name

Frame label    Sync sound    Number of times to loop

## *Property inspector with a symbol instance selected*

When you select an instance of a symbol, the Property inspector displays properties of the instance so that you can edit them, as in the variation shown here.

Instance behavior        Color style

Instance name        Swap symbol

# The Align Panel

The Align Panel gets your objects in line, where they ought to be. For more information, flip to Chapter 4.

Distribute objects evenly

Align objects horizontally

Align objects vertically

Align/distribute relative to entire stage

Match size by width, height, or both        Space objects evenly horizontally/vertically

# The Color Mixer Panel

The Color Mixer panel is similar to an artist's palette. You can create your own colors for both strokes (lines) and fills.

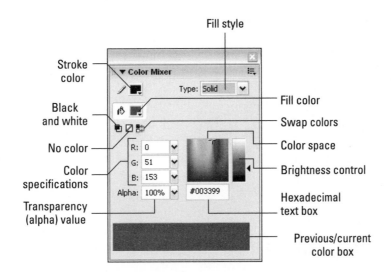

# The Color Swatches Panel

You can use the Color Swatches panel to manage your colors. New colors and fills that you create appear on this panel for easy access. (See Chapter 3 for more information.)

# The Info Panel

The Info panel lets you control the precise size and location of objects. (Check out Chapter 4 for more information on using this panel.) The X and Y measurements are relative to the upper-left corner of the Stage.

Width                    X location

Height                    Y location

# The Scene Panel

The Scene panel is quite simple. You can use it to move from one scene to another, change the order of scenes, and rename, add, and delete scenes.

Duplicate scene    Delete scene

Add scene

# The Transform Panel

Use the Transform panel to scale, rotate, and skew objects with precision. You scale by percentage, and you rotate and skew by degrees (increasing degrees going clockwise). To use the Copy and Apply Transform button, select an object and specify any transform settings that you want. Then click Copy and Apply Transform. Flash creates a new object with the new settings on top of the old object. You can leave the new object there to create a composite object or immediately move it to a new location. Use the Reset button to return a transformed object to its original properties. Chapter 4 gives you more information about this panel.

Width   Height

Rotations

Reset

Skew horizontally    Copy and Apply Transform

Skew vertically

# The Actions Panel

The Actions panel is where all the action is — the ActionScript, that is. On this panel, you write or insert code that makes your movies interactive. Chapter 10 offers more information on this panel.

Insert a target path    AutoFormat    Script Assist

Add a new item to the script    Debug options

Actions toolbox    Find    Check    Show code hint    Script pane
syntax

# The Debugger Panel

The Debugger panel contains features to help you debug your ActionScript code. You can set *breakpoints,* which are points where the ActionScript stops, to help you find out where the bugs are. You can also step through your code bit by bit to find those elusive bugs. You use the Debugger panel while movies are playing in the Flash Player, on your hard drive, or even on a Web server. To use the Debugger panel with an .fla movie on your hard drive, choose Control⇨Debug Movie.

Toggle breakpoint   Step out

Continue   Step over

Stop debugging   Step in

Remove all breakpoints

# The Movie Explorer Panel

Explore the depths of your movie with the Movie Explorer. Refer to Chapter 12 for details.

Show ActionScript

Show
text

Show
frames and layers

Show buttons,
movie clips,
and graphics

Customize
which items
to show

Show video, sounds, and bitmaps

# The Output Tab of the Property Inspector

Use the Output tab as a way to test your movie. Choose Control➪Test Movie
and then choose Window➪Output. Some errors are displayed automatically,
and you can also choose List Objects or List Variables from the Debug menu
in the Player window to view a list of objects and variables.

On the Mac, you have a standalone Output panel.

```
Level #0: Frame=1
  Movie Clip: Frame=1 Target="_level0.target"
    Shape:
  Movie Clip: Frame=1 Target="_level0.ball"
    Shape:
  Edit Text: Target="_level0.instance1" Variable= Visible=true
Text = drag\rme\r"
```

# The Accessibility Panel

Accessibility features make your movies more accessible to people with certain disabilities or limitations — for example, limited or no sight. You can display or hide objects, depending on the needs of your viewers. These features make some of the nongraphical objects in your movie available to screen readers, which read parts of the screen out loud. Choose Window➪Other Panels➪Accessibility.

# The Components Panel

*Components* are prebuilt movie clips that come with predefined parameters that you can set to alter their appearance and behavior. They allow you to build complex Flash applications even if you don't have an advanced understanding of ActionScript. Some components are nonvisual and allow you to do such things as manipulate information from data sources (for a Flash movie with a news ticker, for instance). Other components are interface elements, such as check boxes, radio buttons, and drop-down lists (combo boxes), which you can add to your movies to create interactivity. For more information, see Chapter 12.

***Note:*** Flash 8 Basic does not offer as many components as Flash 8 Professional.

# The Component Inspector

Use this panel to assign labels and parameters to components, such as check boxes, lists, and other interface elements.

# The History Panel

The History panel stores all your commands. You can review them, repeat them, or save them to use again later. See Chapter 4 for details.

# The Strings Panel

Use the Strings panel to create strings of text in various languages. These can be used for Web sites in multiple languages.

# The Behaviors Panel

Use the Behaviors panel to choose ActionScript from a dialog box.

# Appendix C

# What's on the Companion Web Site

. . . . . . . . . . . . . . . . . . . . . . . . . . . . . . . . . . . . . . . . .

**H**ere's some of the cool stuff that you find on the *Macromedia Flash 8 For Dummies* companion Web site, at www.dummies.com/go/flash8:

- ✔ A library of geometric, whimsical, and artistic vector graphics ready to be instantly opened in any Flash movie
- ✔ Flash movies that you can dissect and learn from

## Your Own Personal Library of Vector Graphics

We've created more than 50 vector graphics that you can use in your Flash movies. Some are geometric shapes that are hard to create in Flash. We added some fun shapes . . . some practical and others whimsical, such as our thought bubble and explosion. Finally, we included some artistic drawings of everyday objects. We hope you like them! (Please keep in mind that these files are provided for your personal use and are not to be sold or redistributed.)

To download the library of graphics, point your Web browser to www.dummies.com/go/flash8 and choose the file named Flash 8 For Dummies Library.fla.

All that you see when you open the Flash file is a blank screen. To see the graphics, choose Window⇨Library. To use these shapes in another Flash file, choose File⇨Import to Library and choose the file named Flash 8 For Dummies Library.fla, which you downloaded from the companion Web site to your computer.

An even better idea is to copy the `.fla` file from wherever it is on your computer to the Libraries subfolder of your Flash 8 folder. (In Windows, you find this at `Program Files\Macromedia\Flash 8\en\Configuration\Libraries` on your hard drive. On the Mac, you find it at `Applications/Macromedia Flash 8/Configuration/Libraries` on your hard drive.) Then you can access this file at any time by choosing Window⇨Other Panels⇨ Common Libraries.

# Flash Movies Galore

Throughout this book, we refer you to the companion Web site to look at Flash movies as examples of the features that we are explaining. These movies are organized by chapter. They help you understand some of the more complex capabilities of Flash that are hard to explain or show in a figure. Some of these movies are real-world Flash movies that come from active Web sites. Others are examples that we created for you to isolate the Flash feature. Either way, we hope that you can use them to further your understanding of Flash.

To examine and use these movie files, you need to first download them to your hard drive. Point your Web browser to `www.dummies.com/go/flash8` and select the file you want. Then the file downloads to your hard drive. When it's finished downloading, double-click the file to open it.

Here are a few troubleshooting tips to keep in mind when you use the Flash movie files provided on the Web site:

- ✔ **The Flash movie doesn't play.** Sometimes when you open a Flash movie, nothing happens when you try to play the animation. Choose Control⇨ Test Movie to see the animation.
- ✔ **The fonts look different.** If some of the fonts required by the Flash files aren't available on your system, you might see less-than-satisfactory substitutions when you play the Flash Player files.

# Bonus Chapter

Also on the Web site, you'll find a bonus chapter entitled "What Those Obscure Terms Really Mean." It's a glossary of need-to-know terms for flash Designers. Be sure to check it out.

# Index